STUDIA POHL: SERIES MAIOR

DISSERTATIONES SCIENTIFICAE DE REBUS ORIENTIS ANTIQUI

12

E PONTIFICIO INSTITUTO BIBLICO
ROMAE

JEREMY A. BLACK

SUMERIAN GRAMMAR IN BABYLONIAN THEORY

Second, revised edition

First reprint

EDITRICE PONTIFICIO ISTITUTO BIBLICO

ROMA 2004

The Pontifical Biblical Institute dedicates this series to the memory of P. Alfred Pohl, founder of its Faculty of Ancient Near Eastern Studies. *Studia Pohl* reproduces in offset studies on Ancient Near Eastern history and philology, and is intended particularly to benefit younger scholars who wish to present the results of their doctoral studies to a wider public.

This work was originally submitted in fulfilment of the requirements for the degree of Doctor of Philosophy in the University of Oxford, in 1980.

ISBN 88-7653-442-3

Editrice Pontificio Istituto Biblico
Piazza della Pilotta 35 - 00187 Roma, Italia

Preface to the second edition

All the works studied in this volume have been published before, with the exception of a few new fragmentary texts in the revised appendices 5.3 and 5.4. The present detailed investigation takes as its excuse that while these works are often called as witnesses in support of various philological arguments, no unified attempt to evaluate them in their context as the products of an ancient scholarly discipline has so far appeared. Yet they form a distinct genus of treatise with its own rules of interpretation and its own practical aims; and the contentions which are argued from them (whether justifiably or not) have a wider general bearing on how we translate Sumerian texts, or at least, on how we describe the Sumerian language. As, quite simply, by far the earliest recorded attempts to write grammar, these Babylonian works are of the greatest interest to linguists, as well as to students of Mesopotamian culture. There is room for considerable work still to be done evaluating the Mesopotamian grammatical achievement: in particular, comparing grammatical theory with the praxis of translation both in Old Babylonian texts (as has been done by Krispijn) and in later bilingual literature; estimating just how idiomatic the words and phrases in the grammatical texts really were within their own languages as preserved in contemporary texts; and refining our assessment of the (already hypothesized) adaptation of the content of the grammatical analysis texts, or their epitomes, in the light of the changing grammar of 'post-Sumerian' Sumerian during the latter course of their transmission. One may still feel inclined to predict that the results of such research would be to emphasise the idiosyncrasy of grammatical theory.

The argument in the last part of this study centres on the verbal system. I have tried to show that current analyses of the Sumerian forms into tenses or 'aspects' are based on a misunderstanding of the way the Babylonians set some of *their* tenses (or aspects or whatever they are) against Sumerian forms in these grammatical texts. Then I have attempted to describe the various ways in which the choice of forms may operate in Sumerian, and finally made a suggestion as to how these might have developed. Since the first edition appeared, some reviewers have taken issue with aspects of this; these contributions have been noted in the bibliography. I now regret that I did not employ originally what has since become a more widespread terminology among students of Sumerian, 'ergative' and 'absolutive', to describe the principal nominal rections. In preparing this second edition, it has not been feasible to undertake major rewriting. I have added some new items to the bibliography, corrected some errors (following p. xi), and added some new information. Appendices 5.3 and 5.4 have been completely revised, incorporating a study of the (now essentially complete) Nippur paradigm N3513+N3592.

It is a pleasure to record here my gratitude and obligation to a number of teachers, colleagues and friends: principally to O. R. Gurney, to the late E. Sollberger and to D. O. Edzard, from whom I received every encouragement and the inestimable benefit of their experienced advice. M. Civil generously communicated transliterations of a number of previously unpublished grammatical texts; and has specially collated these tablets, resulting in numerous improvements, for the second edition. T. Jacobsen read through the whole manuscript and made numerous suggestions from all of which I have profited. Å. Sjöberg made it possible for me to collate some tablets in the University Museum, Philadelphia, and the late D. A. Kennedy allowed me, in advance of publication, to use his transliterations of the Ras Shamra grammatical texts. G. J. P. McEwan made the copy of the Toronto verbal paradigm which is published here. Other kindnesses are acknowledged below in the appropriate places.

The more technical aspects of publication also necessitate the co-operation of several agencies. My thanks go especially to the late M. Dahood and to W. Mayer, of the Pontifical Biblical Institute, for extending to this volume the hospitality of Studia Pohl, *series maior*, and now for undertaking to produce a second impression of the work. The British Academy, the British School of Archaeology in Iraq and the Pontifical Biblical Institute all made liberal subventions towards the expenses of publication. O. R. Gurney made the index and T. F. Potts rendered much invaluable assistance. Special credit is due to R. Glynn, who helped to set parts of a difficult manuscript using the Lasercomp phototypesetter at the Oxford University Computing Service. Finally I am grateful to the administrators of that department for their helpfulness.

Oxford, 1991 *J. A. Black*

CONTENTS

Bibliography

Items added to the bibliography in the second edition are marked thus **

Ali, F. A., *Sumerian Letters...* , Pennsylvania dissertation (1964) (University Microfilms, Ann Arbor).

The Assyrian Dictionary of the Oriental Institute of the University of Chicago (Chicago and Glückstadt, 1956–).

Balkan, K., *Kassitenstudien*, I. Die Sprache der Kassiten (New Haven, 1954).

** Black, J. A., review of M. Civil *et al.*, *Materials for the Sumerian Lexicon. Supplementary Series*, I (Rome, 1986), in *WZKM* 78 (1988), pp. 271–4.

** — 'The Babylonian grammatical tradition: the first grammars of Sumerian', in *Transactions of the Philological Society* 87/1 (1989), pp. 75–99.

Bezold, C., *Babylonisch-Assyrisches Glossar* (Heidelberg, 1926).

Cavigneaux, A., *Die sumerisch-akkadischen Zeichenlisten: Überlieferungsprobleme* (Munich, 1976).

Civil, M., 'Les limites de l'information textuelle', in *L'archéologie de l'Iraq du début de l'époque néolithique à 333 avant notre ère: perspectives et limites de l'interprétation anthropologique des documents*, Colloques internationaux du Centre National de la Recherche Scientifique, no. 580 (Paris 1978), pp. 225–232.

** Civil, M., O. R. Gurney and D. A. Kennedy, *The Sag-Tablet, Lexical Texts in the Ashmolean Museum, Middle Babylonian Grammatical Texts, Miscellaneous Texts.* Materials for the Sumerian Lexicon. Supplementary Series, I (Rome, 1986).

Comrie, B., *Aspect* (Cambridge, 1976).

** D'Agostino, F., *Il sistema verbale sumerico nei testi lessicali di Ebla*, Studi semitici, nuova serie 7 (Rome, 1990).

** — 'The study of Sumerian grammar at Ebla, part I', in *ASJ* 13 (1991 [in press]).

Deimel, A., *Šumerische Grammatik der archaistischen Texte* (Rome, 1924).

— *Das Šumerische Verbum* (Rome, 1935).

Delitzsch, F., *Assyrische Lesestücke*, 2nd edn. (Leipzig, 1914).

— *Grundzüge der sumerischen Grammatik* (Leipzig, 1914).

— *Kleine sumerische Sprachlehre für Nichtassyriologen* (Leipzig, 1914).

— *Sumerisches Glossar (Leipzig, 1914).*

Denz, A., *Die Verbalsyntax des neuarabischen Dialektes von Kwayriš (Irak)* (Wiesbaden, 1971).

Edzard, D. O., *Sumerische Rechtsurkunden des III. Jahrtausends...* (Munich, 1968).

— 'Fragen der sumerischen Syntax', in *ZDMG* 109 (1959), pp. 234–252.

— 'Grammatik', in *RlA* III (Berlin, 1957–), pp. 610–16.

— 'Das sumerische Verbalmorphem /ed/ in den alt- und neusumerischen Texten', in Edzard, ed., *Heidelberger Studien zum alten Orient* (Wiesbaden, 1967).

— '*Hamṭu, marû* und freie Reduplikation beim sumerischen Verbum', in *ZA* 61 (1971), pp. 208–232; 61 (1972), pp. 1–34 and 66 (1976), pp. 45–61.

— '"Du hast mir gegeben", "ich habe dir gegeben". Über das sumerische Verbum sum', in *WdO* 8 (1975–6), pp. 159–77.

Falkenstein, A., *Archaische Texte aus Uruk* (Berlin, 1936).

— *Grammatik der Sprache Gudeas von Lagaš*, 2 vols., *AnOr* 28 & 29 (Rome, 1949–50).

— *Das Sumerische*, Handbuch der Orientalistik (Leiden, 1959).

— 'Untersuchungen zur sumerischen Grammatik, 4. Das affirmative Präformativ *ši-/ša-*', in *ZA* 48 (1944), pp. 69–118.

Finkel, I. L., with M. Civil, edd., *MSL*, XVI. The Series SIG$_7$.ALAN = *nabnītu* (Rome, 1982).
Fish, T., *Catalogue of Sumerian tablets in the John Rylands Library* (Manchester, 1932).
Foxvog, D. A., *The Sumerian Ventive* (University of California at Berkeley dissertation, 1974).
— 'The Sumerian Ergative Construction', in *OrNS* 44 (1975), pp. 395–425.
Gadd, C. J., *A Sumerian Reading-Book* (Oxford, 1924).
— *Teachers and Students in the Oldest Schools* (London, 1956).
** Geller, M., review of *SGBT*, in *BSOAS* 49/2 (1986), pp. 563–5.
** Gragg, G., review of *SGBT*, in *AulaOr* 6 (1988), pp. 108–9.
Gurney, O. R., *Ur Excavations Texts* VII (London, 1974).
Haupt, P., *Die akkadische Sprache* (Berlin, 1883).
Jacobsen, Th., 'Introduction to the Chicago Grammatical Texts', in *MSL* IV (1956), pp. 1*–50*.
— *'Ittallak niāti'*, in *JNES* 19 (1960), pp. 101–116; subsequently in *Toward the Image of Tammuz* (Harvard, 1970), pp. 271–292.
— 'The Akkadian Ablative Accusative', in *JNES* 22 (1963), pp. 18–29; subsequently in *Toward the Image of Tammuz*, pp. 245–270.
— 'Very Ancient Linguistics: Babylonian Grammatical Texts', in Dell Hymes, ed., *Studies in the History of Linguistics: Traditions and Paradigms* (Bloomington and London, 1974), pp. 41–62 (writen in 1968).
Jestin, R., *Le verbe sumérien*, 2 vols. (Paris, 1943 and 1946; complément, 1954).
— *Abrégé de grammaire sumérienne* (Paris, 1951).
Kaneva, I. T., 'Participles in Sumerian', *MIO* 16 (1970), pp. 541–565.
Kienast, B., 'Probleme der sumerischen Grammatik. 4–6', in *ZA* 70 (1981), pp. 1–35.
Kramer, S. N., M. Çığ and H. Kızılyay, *Istanbul Arkeoloji Müzelerinde Bulunan Sumer Edebî Tablet ve Parçaları* I (Ankara, 1969)
** Komoróczy, G., 'Holt nyelvészet [Dead linguistics]', in *Nyelvpedagógiai irások* 2 (1979), pp. 24–34 (in Hungarian).
Kraus, F. R., *Text zur babylonischen Physiognomatik*, *AfO* Beiheft 3 (Berlin, 1939).
** Krebernik, M., review of *SGBT*, in *WZKM* 78 (1988), pp. 282–5.
** Krispijn, Th. J. H., 'Das Verb in den zweisprachigen Inschriften der Hammurabi-Dynastie', in G. van Driel *et al.*, edd., *Zikir šumim. Assyriological studies presented to F. R. Kraus...* (Brill, 1982), pp. 145–62.
** Lambert, W. F., review of *SGBT*, in *JRAS* (1986), pp. 95–6.
Landsberger, B., *et al.*, edd., *Materialien zum sumerischen Lexikon. Vokabulare und Formbücher*, I. *ana ittišu* (Rome 1937); IV (Rome 1956); V (Rome 1957).
— and O. R. Gurney, 'igi-duh-a = *tāmartu*, short version', in *AfO* 18 (1957–8), pp. 81–86.
Langdon, S., *A Sumerian Grammar and Chrestomathy* (Paris, 1911).
— 'Assyrian Grammatical Texts' in *RA* 13 (1916), pp. 91–97.
Lyons, J., *Language and Linguistics: an Introduction* (Cambridge, 1981).
Leichty, E., 'Two late commentaries', in *AfO* 24 (1973), pp. 79–82.
** Malbran-Labat, F., review of *SGBT*, in *Bulletin de la Société de Linguistique de Paris* 81/2 (1986), pp. 316–22.
Marr, N., and M. Brière, *La langue géorgienne* (Paris, 1931).
Michalowski, P., 'Sumerian as an ergative language. I', in *JCS* 32 (1980), pp. 86–103.
Muss-Arnolt, W., *A Concise Dictionary of the Assyrian Language* (Berlin, 1899–1905).
Palmer, L. R., *Descriptive and Comparative Linguistics: a Critical Introduction* (London, 1972).
Peiser, F. E., 'Die assyrische Zeichenordnung auf Grund von S^a und VR 45', in *ZA* 1 (1886), pp. 95–125.
— 'Das Prinzip der assyrischen Zeichenordnung', in *ZA* 2 (1887), pp. 316–320.
Poebel, A., *Grundzüge der sumerischen Grammatik* (Rostock, 1923).
— 'The verb uzuzzu, "to stand"', in *Studies in Akkadian Grammar*, *AS* 9 (Chicago, 1939), pp. 75–196.
Postgate, N., 'Two points of grammar in Gudea', in *JCS* 26 (1974), pp. 16–54.

Powell, M. A., 'Ukubi to Mother... The Situation is Desperate: A Plaidoyer for Methodological Rigor in Editing and Interpreting Sumerian Texts with an Excursus on the Verb taka: da_x-da_x(TAG$_4$)', in *ZA* 68 (1978), pp. 163–195.

** Reiner, E., ed., *La linguistica del Vicino e Medio Oriente* (=vol. I of G. C. Lepschy, ed., *Storia della linguistica*), ch. 3 with sections on Sumerian (by M. Civil) and Akkadian (by E. Reiner) (n.p.: Il Mulino, 1990), pp. 95–118.

Renou, L., *La grammaire de Pāṇini* (Paris, 1966).

Rössler, O. 'Die Präfixkonjugation Qal der Verba I[ae] Nun im Althebräischen und das Problem der sogenannten Tempora', in *Zeitschrift für die alttestamentliche Wissenschaft* 74 (1962), pp. 123–141.

Rowton, M. B., 'The use of the permansive in Classic Babylonian', in *JNES* 21 (1962), pp. 233–303.

Schuster, H., 'Die nach Zeichen geordneten sumerisch-akkadischen Vokabulare', in *ZA* 44 (1938), pp. 217–270.

Shaffer, A., 'TA *ša kīma* A *ītenerrubu*: a study in native Babylonian philology', in *OrNs* 38 (1969), pp. 433–446.

Siedl, S. H., *Gedanken zum Tempussystem im Hebräischen und Akkadischen* (Wiesbaden, 1971).

Sjöberg, Å., 'Der Examenstext A', in *ZA* 64 (1975), pp. 138–176.

— 'The Old Babylonian Eduba', in *AS* 20 (Chicago, 1975), pp. 159–179.

Soden, W. von, *Grundriss der akkadischen Grammatik* (Rome, 1952; Ergänzungsheft, 1969).

— *Zweisprachigkeit in der geistigen Kultur Babyloniens* (Vienna, 1960).

— *Akkadisches Handwörterbuch* (Wiesbaden, 1965–81).

— 'Das akkadische t-Perfekt in Haupt- und Nebensätzen und sumerische Verbalformen mit den Präfixen ba-, imma-, und u-', in *AS* 16 (Chicago, 1965), pp. 103–110.

Sollberger, E., *Le système verbal dans les inscriptions "royales" présargoniques de Lagaš* (Geneva, 1952).

Steiner, G., 'The vocalisation of the Sumerian verbal morpheme /-ED/ and its significance', in *JNES* 40 (1981), pp. 21–41.

— '*Hamṭu* und *marû* als verbale Kategorien im Sumerischen und im Akkadischen', in *RA* 75 (1981), pp. 1–14.

Steinkeller, P., 'Notes on Sumerian Plural Verbs', in *OrNS* 484 (1979), pp. 54–67.

** Thomsen, M.-L., review of *SGBT*, in *BiOr* 43 (1986), pp. 720–2.

Thureau-Dangin, F., 'Formes grammaticales sumériennes d'après une tablette inédite du Louvre', in *RA* 32 (1935), pp. 89–114.

van Dijk, J. J. A., 'La "confusion de langues"', in *OrNS* 39 (1970), pp. 302–310.

Vanstiphout, H. J. L., 'How did they learn Sumerian?', in *JCS* 31 (1979), pp. 118–126.

Wilcke, C., *Das Lugalbandaepos* (Wiesbaden, 1969).

Yoshikawa, M., 'Neo-babylonian Grammatical Texts ni okeru bunpō-jutsugo ni tsuite [On grammatical terms in neo-Babylonian grammatical texts *marû/hamṭu*]', in *Hiroshima University Studies, Faculty of Letters*, 1 (26/2, Dec. 1966), pp. 1–28; 4 (29/2, March 1970), pp. 207–233; 6 (31/2, March 1972), pp. 151–188; 7 (32/2, March 1973), pp. 212–231 (in Japanese).

— 'On the grammatical function of -e- of the Sumerian verbal suffix -e-dè/-e-da(m)', in *JNES* 27 (1968), pp. 251–261.

— 'The *marû* and *hamṭu* aspects in the Sumerian verbal system', in *OrNS* 37 (1968), pp. 401–417.

— 'The *marû* conjugation in the Sumerian verbal system', in *OrNS* 43 (1974), pp. 17–39.

— 'Neo-Babylonian Grammatical Texts ni okeru bunpō-jutsugo *šushurtum* to *riātum* no kenkyū [A Study of the Grammatical Terms *šushurtum* and *riātum* in neo-Babylonian Grammatical Texts]', *Hiroshima University Studies, Faculty of Letters*, vol. 33, Special Publication 3 (Hiroshima, 1974; in Japanese).

— 'Sumerian Ventive and Ientive', in *OrNS* 47 (1978), pp. 461–482.

— 'The Sumerian Verbal Prefixes mu-, i- and Topicality', in *OrNS* 48 (1979), pp. 54–67.

Zimmern, H. *Babylonische Busspsalmen* (Leipzig, 1885).

Addenda and corrigenda

p. 14 after line 5 add: Unusually the tablet has double rulings between every entry.

p. 19 OBGT VI 163: the tablet has ⌜it⌝-ta-aš-ka-an-⌜šum⌝ (break on edge of tablet).

OBGT VII 190: the tablet probably has ta-at-tál-ka-šum (difficult to tell because of glue on surface).

p. 20 lines 11f.: the verbs are *qu''ûm* in line 3 and *waqûm* in line 9.

p. 30 line 3: collated, as copied.

p. 55 line 4: for 'the fragments OBGT 1a and 1b' read 'the text represented by OBGT 1a and other fragments (see p. 57 under N1761)'.

at end of first paragraph add: The Middle Babylonian grammatical texts are now published in full in *MSL SS* 1, pp. 71–91.

line 8 f.b.: for '18 out of the 102' read '18 out of the approximately 900 lines preserved'.

p. 57 the entry for N1761 should read: *N1761* is another fragment joining the tablet UM 29-16-30 (OBGT 1a) + CBS 6568 (OBGT Ib; not N6568) + CBS 6563 (unpubl.).

p. 58 line 2: *wašābu hamṭu ša ištēn*, see p. 100.

p. 100 after line 7: add, in the third column, *ša* DIŠ (in the colophon of NBGT I), perhaps to be read *ša ištiat*.

line 7 f.b.: for *ištiāt* read *ištiat*.

p. 105 The reference to fn. 158 should be added at the end of the third paragraph ('elucidation of these terms.').

p. 111 line 14: for -e-dé read -e-dè.

p. 114 fn. 183: for p. 217 read p. 129.

p. 126 line 4 f.b.: for -e-en read -e-ne.

p. 134 line 5: for 'word of the immediate' read 'word or the immediate'.

0 *Introduction: Babylonian Grammatical Texts*

0. Introduction: Babylonian Grammatical Texts

Lists of one sort or another are an important feature of the surviving cuneiform literature. Already at the very earliest periods there were single-column lists of the signs of the cuneiform writing system, intended no doubt for instructive purposes. As Sumerian died out as an everyday spoken language (however lively it may have remained in literate circles), and scribal training was increasingly directed at Babylonian pupils who were native speakers of Akkadian, parallel, second and sometimes third columns were added. The Babylonian scribes, conscious that Sumerian provided the key to the religious and intellectual culture of which they were the heirs, began to codify vast amounts of information in the form of lists of words and phrases, meticulously detailing the countables and nameables of their world. These subsequently formed a basis of instruction in the é-dub-ba-a, scribal 'colleges' or workshops. The old lists of cuneiform signs were collected together and filled out, in the parallel second column, with phonetically indicated pronunciations, and, in a third, possible renderings into Akkadian of the words denoted by the signs or of the grammatical elements which could be written with them.[1] Sometimes the names of the signs were added. These could then be used as a sort of (memorised) dictionary, to teach not only writing but Sumerian as well. Many of these lexical vocabularies, grouped into series, were immensely long, and from them shorter epitomes were made, as for example from the series called from its first entry igi-du$_8$-a = *tāmartu*, and from that called a:A = *nâqu*.[2]

Grammatical texts, which are always lists of two columns,[3] are clearly closely related to lexical vocabularies, although it is not possible to show that one is derived from the other[4]. In some lexical lists, attempts are made in the case of those signs which, in addition to their 'logographic' function of writing whole words, may also be used for their phonetic value (and of those which are used only for their phonetic value) in writing grammatical affixes, to give some indication of Akkadian words corresponding to the Sumerian grammatical elements written with them.[5] In certain cases, technical grammatical terms are also added. However, a

1. Single-column lists from as early as the third millennium include repetition of signs, suggesting perhaps that already various Akkadian equivalents were included in the oral interpretation of the texts. The series a: A = *nâqum*, izi = *išātum* and ká-gal = *abullum* had all acquired their Akkadian columns by the Old Babylonian period. Other series, such as ur$_5$-ra = *hubullu* and lú = *ša* are not attested with Akkadian columns until Bogh. or RS.
2. *V.* Landsberger and Gurney, 'igi-duh-a = *tāmartu*, short version', in *AfO* 18 (1967-8), pp. 81-86; and H. Schuster, 'Die nach Zeichen geordneten sumerisch-akkadischen Vokabulare', in *ZA* 44 (1938), pp. 244-6.,
3. With the apparent exception of the little OB paradigm from Nippur, N3513, which lists Sumerian only (see appendix 5.4.2 below).
4. Passages of monoglot Sumerian verbal paradigms occur in Eblan texts, see for example G. Pettinato, *Testi lessicali monolingui della biblioteca L.2769*, Materiali epigraphici di Ebla, 3 (Naples, 1983), text 53, v 12-19. This would push back the evidence for the separate existence of grammatical texts and grammatical study by at least five hundred years. Strictly, however, their being 'monoglot' is irrelevant since their very existence implies a culture in which Sumerian was *not* the everyday idiom. Ebla is parallel to eighteenth-century Babylonia in this respect.
5. E.g. in Old Babylonian Proto-Aa (*MSL* XIV, Rome, 1979), lines 2:1f., 8:1ff. (p. 89), 71:6 (p.91), 146:3' (p. 94). 167:3f., 168:2 (p. 96), 450:1 (p. 99), 462:2 (p. 100) etc.

grammatical text differs from a lexical text in one important respect: the words or phrases in the latter are listed for their own sake, so that the user may learn them and their meaning. For convenience of reference they may be organised by subject matter. Thus the vocabulary ki-ulutin-bi-šè = *ana ittišu* contains legal words and phrases,[6] and lú = *ša* lists occupations;[7] while ur$_5$-ra = *hubullu* is largely organised, at least in its earlier portions, according to the material from which objects are made.[8] But the entries in a grammatical text are there not only for their own sake, but because they are paradigmatic, i.e. from them the behaviour of other comparable elements of speech may be predicted. In these works the arrangement is not merely convenient but crucial, since at least part of the 'message' of the text consists in the order in which the entries are listed. This arrangement is sometimes highly complex.

Three species of grammatical text may be distinguished, one of which does not survive in its original form. Texts may also be of mixed type, i.e. contain separate sections characteristic of more than one type of grammatical text. (Some lexical vocabularies such as *ana ittišu* also contain sections typical of grammatical texts, and works such as SIG$_7$.ALAN = *nabnītu* contain grammatical entries;[9] but these will be used only as subsidiary evidence, because the grammatical material is not systematically arranged and therefore gives no insights into the grammatical theory; rather, these sections must be interpreted *from* the grammatical texts.) The three species are:

1) the verbal paradigm, a list of various forms of a given verb arranged according to various grammatically determined patterns,

2) the grammatical vocabulary, a list usually of pronominal, prepositional and adverbial expressions arranged in paradigmatic groups in which one or more elements are systematically varied, and

3) the grammatical analysis, a presentation in analytic form of the grammatical elements which appear in the verbal paradigms and grammatical vocabularies.

No original, complete texts of this third form survive but their existence is readily hypothesized from the survival of epitomes. Because in this species of text grammatical affixes were quoted out of the context of whole grammatical forms, technical terms (which we assume were already used in the oral exposition of grammar) were written in as a form of explanation.[10] Shortened epitomes were made of these analysis texts, and two survive in corrupt, late copies. It will be suggested below that some of the corruption may be due to incompetent epitomization in which elements were listed under the wrong headings, or, less probably, to the possibility that grammatical terms were added at a later date than that of the compilation of the texts.

However, the basic distinction between Old Babylonian and neo-Babylonian grammatical texts made by the editors of *MSL* IV[11] is here abandoned (although the initials OBGT and NBGT are retained for purposes of identification). The "bold and radical step"[12] required to reduce the paradigms and vocabularies to analytic form may be hypothesized already for the Old Babylonian period on the basis of the entries in lexicographical works referred to (see n. 5 above). I see no reason to suppose that the grammatical analyses are any later in origin than the other sorts of grammatical text, although we cannot fix with certainty at what date the epitomes were made. Passages of grammatical analysis are also to be found in a grammatical text of mixed content found at Ugarit and dating from about 1200 BC, and in the probably

---

6. Landsberger et al., edd., *MSL* I (Rome, 1937).
7. M. Civil et al., edd., *MSL* XII (Rome, 1969).
8. Landsberger et al., edd., *MSL* V - XI (Rome, 1957-74).
9. e.g. Nabnītu I 99ff., III 291f., 295f., in I.L. Finkel, ed., *MSL* XVI (Rome, 1982).
10. Without these grammatical labels, homographous affixes might be confounded with one another. Thus e can be an infix of the second person or a suffix of the third person. A technical term identifying its function or behaviour is required to clarify which of the two possibilities is intended in the given context.
11. Landsberger et al., edd., *MSL* IV (Rome, 1956). Almost all the grammatical texts are published in transliteration in this volume.
12. Jacobsen in 'Very Ancient Linguistics: Babylonian Grammatical Texts', in Dell Hymes, ed., *Studies in the History of Linguistics: Traditions and Paradigms* (Bloomington and London, 1974) (written 1968), pp. 41-62, esp. p. 54 (but misleadingly summarised by the editor on p. 5).

Middle Babylonian text NBGT III (see below p. 56, section 2.1). In an article dedicated to Jacobsen on the curriculum of 'The Old Babylonian Eduba' (scribal college), Å. Sjöberg distinguished four principal faculties of study: language, mathematics with surveying, music and literature.[13] Earlier C.J. Gadd, in an inaugural lecture on *Teachers and Students in the Earliest Schools*,[14] had assumed that all instruction was given in Sumerian, although as Sjöberg points out, there is ample evidence that the native tongue of the scribes was Babylonian.[15] The most likely conclusion seems to be that they learned Sumerian on entering the college, and that the instruction in the later stages may have been entirely in that language. Of the aspects of language studied, Sjöberg lists the following: copying and studying of sign-lists and lexical vocabularies; legal phraseology and study of a famous trial and codes of laws, as training to be a 'judge's clerk'; letter-writing, in Akkadian as well; drafting of business documents and writing stelae; and learning the professional jargon of various priestly offices and other occupations. (This last is evidenced only by a dialogue between two scribes, edited under the title of Examination Text A, of which the oldest surviving mss. date from no earlier than 1000 BC, see section 2.6 below.[16]) But two brief, passing references on p. 164, n. 20 and p. 170 are the only mention made by Sjöberg of the study of grammar. This omission ignores about a dozen extant grammatical vocabularies and verbal paradigms dating from the Old Babylonian period. The *ductus* and orthography of these texts suggest that they were written in the 18th or 17th century BC.[17] It is misleading not to make a clear distinction between these and the 'lexical' vocabularies referred to above.

Now the clearest evidence for the study of grammar is the existence of a technical grammatical terminology. Some eighteen terms altogether are known: most of these occur in the grammatical epitomes, and some also in Examination Text A. The remainder of the content of Examination Text A, if we omit for a moment the grammatical section and that referring to professional jargon, fits perfectly with what Sjöberg describes as the curriculum of study in Old Babylonian times. Given that the type of institution in question seems to have died out after the end of the Old Babylonian period, this seems to me to argue in favour of dating the grammatical terms *and hence* grammatical theory back to that date. Alternatively we would have to conclude that Examination Text A contains anachronistic features. However, it will be argued that the grammatical theory underlying the terminology is also evident from the very structure of the paradigm texts, which are indisputably Old Babylonian. Thus the opposition between basic and causative themes of the verb (to the virtual exclusion of D (factitive or intensive) and N (passive)), referred to in the epitome NBGT II as *šuāti* and *šuāti šuāti* respectively, is central to the arrangement of OBGT VI, VII, VIII and IX. If our interpretation is correct, the term *šushurtum* occurring in the grammatical epitomes and in the sign-list Aa refers to an opposition evident in the arrangement of OBGT VI, VII, VIII and IX. The spelling of a term such as *riātum* may suggest a frozen Old Babylonian writing. Finally, if, as Sjöberg assumes, scribal training after the Old Babylonian period was largely private, it is difficult to see how a complex theory of interpretation could have been formulated and found its way to Ur, Nippur, Babylon, Borsippa, Ashur, Nineveh, and as far afield as Ugarit and Boğazköy. This wide spread of the texts, taken with the other evidence, argues convincingly for the dating of grammatical theory in its fully developed form to the Old Babylonian period.

It seems highly probable that texts of this nature were largely committed to memory by the pupils.[18] The purpose of an epitome will then have been largely that of an *aide-mémoire* and it will be seen that some sections appear to have been epitomized by quoting merely the first and last lines. The oral explanation is of course lost to us but can to some extent be deduced from

13. In *AS* 20 (Chicago, 1975), pp. 159-179.
14. (London, 1956).
15. i.e. Akkadian, *ibid.*, pp. 161f.
16. *V*. Sjöberg, 'Der Examenstext A', in *ZA* 64 (1975), pp. 138-176.
17. Thus Edzard in 'Grammatik', in *RlA* 3 (Berlin, 1957-), p. 611.
18. H.L.J. Vanstiphout in 'How did they learn Sumerian ?', in *JCS* 31 (1979), pp. 118-126, esp. pp. 119f., ingeniously hypothesizes the existence of a work along the lines 'First Steps in Sumerian'. I suspect Babylonian language teaching methods were less enlightened.

the structure of the texts themselves. It is this that is here presented as 'grammatical theory'. The list is a form of literature that is neither prose nor verse and it has, in effect, its own syntax. One needs to know how to 'read' it. In particular, the precise implication of the fact that two words or entries stand opposite each other in parallel columns is far less constant than is often supposed. The point has been very clearly made in an excellent study by A. Cavigneaux that the list literature was intended for use by highly qualified scribes.[19] Without their special knowledge there is considerable danger of misunderstanding. In most lexical lists the entries are not repeated, where repetition is required, for each line of the opposite column, nor are dittos marked regularly. A Sumerian entry is assumed to be 'carried down', i.e. to apply successively to each entry in the Akkadian column, until cancelled by a new entry. Sometimes the converse is true. Verbal paradigms, however, generally repeat the entry in full, where repetition is required, although they may instead leave blanks which are to be filled in with the corresponding forms of the other persons. Thus an entry *iškun* 'he put', followed by two blanks, must be completed *aškun* 'I put', *taškun* 'you put'. Sometimes one needs to know more about the arrangement of the paradigms in order to complete the blanks. For instance, the two blanks following OBGT VIII 31 (Akkadian *lusmam ana ṣēriya*, 'run hither to me') must be filled in *lulsimakkum* 'let me run hither to you' and *lilsimakkum* 'let him run hither to you' (see p. 18 below). The epitome of the lexical list a: A = *nâqu* is exceptional in that throughout both reading and sign are either actually repeated or marked by a ditto.[20] With grammatical vocabularies and epitomes, the general principle of the sign-lists is followed, viz. when an entry appears in *either* column, it is understood to apply to all subsequent entries in the opposite column until cancelled by another sign. However, this is not always true of the grammatical terms appended to the entries, a fact which will be of some importance in our attempts to elucidate the significance of these terms.

The u-a-i-e principle of vowel order, familiar from sign-lists, is preserved where possible in the grammatical epitomes.[21] To some extent the analysis is hampered by the inability of the cuneiform writing system to deal with elements which are shorter than one syllable, i.e. morphemes consisting only of one consonant (-b-, -n-, -m-; in certain circumstances -t-, -š-, -d-, -ng-, -r-). Thus to isolate the morpheme -n- it is necessary to list the syllable-signs -un-, -an-, -in- and -en-, i.e. the morpheme preceded by any of the vowels which may accompany it. The texts should be viewed as an analysis of written Sumerian.

Occasional instances of phonetic spelling occur, i.e. spelling which departs from the conventional orthography, here apparently in order to indicate the pronunciation more clearly. This feature is normally associated with Sumerian texts written outside Babylonia,[22] but it will be readily appreciated that this need not apply to grammatical texts.

From the frequency with which both Sumerian elements and Akkadian forms are repeated in different places, it is clear that no absolute equations were envisaged. For instance, in the text NBGT I, ta is in two places set against *ištu* and elsewhere also against *itti*, *ana* and *eli*; while *eli* is elsewhere set against da, and so on. It is not the universal 'wherever ta occurs in Sumerian, it may be rendered as *ištu*' but the existential 'there are contexts where ta may be rendered *ištu*'. The principle of inclusion is encyclopaedic, not systematic.

This leads us to consider the purpose of the grammatical texts. It cannot be stressed too much that this was practical, to instruct pupils in Sumerian grammar, and not speculative. It is only when viewed in this way that the texts make sense. To impute the modern sort of speculatively descriptive analysis of grammar to the Babylonians is an anachronism, and this is relevant to our attempt to interpret the texts, as will be seen in the section concerning *hamṭu* and *marû*. Because it is purely practical, Babylonian grammatical theory is also, by modern

19. A. Cavigneaux, *Die sumerisch-akkadischen Zeichenlisten: Überlieferungsprobleme* (Munich, 1976).
20. *V.* Schuster, *loc. cit.*, p. 244.
21. On principles of arrangement generally, *v.* H. Ehelolf and B. Meissner in *ZA* 34 (1922), p. 31; M. Čığ and H. Kızılyay, *Zwei altbabylonische Schulbücher aus Nippur* (Ankara, 1959), pp. 59ff; J. Nougayrol in *AS* 16 (Chicago, 1965), pp. 29-31.
22. *V.* Krecher in *ZA* 58 (1967), pp. 16-65, and remarks by Civil in *JNES* 26 (1967), pp. 200-211, esp. p. 209. Clearly "phonetic" spelling is employed in literary texts for a variety of reasons.

standards, incomplete. The Babylonians made only such divisions and labelled only such features as were necessary for their purposes.

It is interesting in this context to compare the circumstances that gave rise to the study of grammar in ancient Mesopotamia with those which prompted Pāṇini and other Indian scholars before and after him to codify the grammar and pronunciation of classical Vedic Sanskrit in India more than a thousand years later, and with the beginnings of European grammar in the works of Aristotle at about the same time. As Jacobsen observed in 'Very Ancient Linguistics: Babylonian Grammatical Texts' (p. 41), the comparison with Pāṇini is indeed apt: the only difference being that the subject of his work is an earlier form, fast becoming archaic, of the same tongue that he himself spoke (although this point precisely is debated), while for the Mesopotamian grammarians Sumerian was a dying or dead language utterly alien in structure to their native Akkadian. But in both cases they sought continued access to a medium of religious and intellectual culture (not forgetting the humbler everyday needs of scribe-craft).[23] The Babylonian origins of Indian mathematics and astronomy, transmitted to north-west India during the 5th, 4th and 3rd centuries BC along the cultural corridor of the Achaemenid Empire, are now assured.[24] The traditions about the man Pāṇini are uncertain, but it is reported that he was born (some time in the period 5th to 2nd centuries BC) in Śalātura in Gāndhāra (at one time within the Achaemenid Empire). The possibility should certainly be considered that elements of Babylonian grammatical theory, in particular perhaps the use of actual linguistic forms as metalinguistic indicators, and the extreme reliance on structural arrangement to convey the principles of analysis, were transferred to India and absorbed into the Sanskrit grammatical tradition.

The situation of Aristotle is altogether different, and more akin to some aims of modern linguistics: Aristotle was speculatively interested in language as a medium of communication, and wrote in and about his native Greek. Finally, of his successors, the Alexandrian grammarians, it may be said that their principal motive was to preserve what they saw as declining Classical standards, and in this they were typical of their age. It is doubtful if any such normative tendencies can be detected in the Babylonian texts.

The study here presented, then, is an analysis of the system of Sumerian grammar that the Babylonians had devised, a system more complex than is generally recognised, developed at an earlier date than has generally been allowed. It is likely that this system in its fully developed form was an important element in the curriculum of scribal training in the Old Babylonian period. It will further be maintained that, as a subsidiary result of a study of this system, some insights can be gained into the grammatical structure of Sumerian: but with reservations. Material from the grammatical texts must be used only very circumspectly. Many false conclusions have been drawn from evidence indiscriminately cited from them. Essentially the Babylonians, as good teachers, had developed a 'method' for teaching Sumerian, but it was inevitably oriented from the point of view of a native speaker of the quite different Akkadian, so that confusion resulted in certain areas, e.g. in regard to the tense system and causative system of the Akkadian verb. In some cases it seems that we know Sumerian better than the compilers, or copyists, of our texts. By starting from what we already know both of Sumerian and Akkadian grammar from our reading of texts, and proceeding to the study of Babylonian grammatical works (and not *vice versa*), we may be encouraged to review our analysis in certain respects in the light of distinctions made by the ancient grammarians.

As examples of this, the following points may be made:

1) The text OBGT V observes throughout a unique and deliberate distinction in spelling between the suffix of the 2nd person singular (spelt -e-en) and that of the 1st person (spelt -en). This distinction is not generally maintained in literary texts, but it may confirm the suspicion that a difference of pronunciation existed.

---

23. It is doubtful whether the same motive can be ascribed to later Babylonian attempts to study the Kassite language, *v.* K. Balkan, *Kassitenstudien*, I. Die Sprache der Kassiten (New Haven, 1954).

24. *V.* D. Pingree, 'History of Mathematical Astronomy in India', in *Dictionary of Scientific Biography*, vol. 15 (1978), pp. 536-8.

2) The texts reveal the unmistakeable existence of a verbal element -m- with by-forms (-)ma- and (-)mu-, and this (-)mu- is clearly distinct from the conjugation prefix mu-/mi-.

3) Two separate functions of the prefix ba- are acknowledged against one of which are set the tenses of the -t- infix themes, and against the other the stative of the Š and N themes.

4) Forms such as im-ma-, am-ma- are treated as derived from i+m+ba, a+m+ba etc.

5) Against a prefix a-, of which al- and Ø are by-forms, are set different Akkadian forms depending on the type of construction used in the Sumerian.

6) Most important, the use by modern scholars of the terms *hamṭu* and *marû* (which, meaning literally 'quick' and 'slow', are terms of Akkadian grammar, i.e. terms referring to grammatical features of Akkadian) to mean forms of the Sumerian verb, and the equation of them with tenses, 'aspects' or *Aktionsarten*, is quite clearly misleading, and should be abandoned in translation of Sumerian texts. Choice of tense in translation must be determined by context alone (which in practice it often is).

Finally, a note on terminology. In speaking of Sumerian grammar, I have used the words 'cause' and 'inert' to refer to nouns standing respectively in the agentive -e case and the unmarked case (Falkenstein's accusative)[25] or to pronominal elements in the verb which might incorporate such nouns, and have avoided subject/object, transitive/intransitive and active/passive altogether.[26] For the Sumerian verbal forms with prefixes ì, a-, mu-, ma-, bí-, or ba-, and, respectively, for those with ga- or hé- or the 2nd person imperative construction, which are opposed, as if two moods, in the texts, I have used for convenience' sake 'indicative' and 'non-indicative'. Rather than speak of the 'author' of a grammatical text, I have used 'compiler(s)', and have on the whole preferred the neutral 'set against' in reference to the relationship between entries in parallel columns to the tendentious 'translate', 'render' or 'correspond to'. It has not been found necessary to use the term 'ergative' which has been fashionably employed of Sumerian because it is supposed to resemble Basque or Georgian or Dyirbal in certain respects. It is important to remember that nothing can be predicted on the basis of such a comparison, as 'ergativity' is not an inherent property of such languages, but a way of describing some features of them. The use of the word adds nothing to the discussion. However, one or two comparisons are made with Classical Georgian.

Abbreviations follow the usage of the *Chicago Assyrian Dictionary*. Sumerian is set in Roman, Akkadian (except when in transliteration) in italic. A transliteration of the paradigms from Ur is appended. I have assumed throughout that the reader will have beside him a copy of *MSL* IV (with corrections and additions, *MSL* V (ed. Landsberger, Rome, 1957), pp. 195-9) and the new MBGTs (*MSL Supplementary Studies* I (forthcoming)). (Some collations to the texts published in *MSL* IV are given as appendix 5.6 below.) Some parts of the book, for example sections 1.1, 2.1 and 4, are designed to be read straight through, as a connected introduction to the grammatical texts. Other sections will be consulted more for reference, by using the index of texts and passages cited (appendix 5.6).

---

25. *V.* Falkenstein, *Das Sumerische*, Handbuch der Orientalistik (Leiden, 1959), pp. 38, 55.
26. In an attempt to universalize the concept of transitivity to all languages, P.J. Hopper and S.A. Thompson in 'Transitivity in Grammar and Discourse', in *Language* 56 (1980), pp. 251-299, have proposed a definition involving a continuum of degrees of transitivity and intransitivity, to the extent that some sentences involving only one participant can be regarded as more "transitive" than some with two participants. This work is drawn on, with reference to Sumerian, by P. Michalowski, in *JCS* 32 (1980), pp. 86-103, esp. pp. 101f.; but I prefer myself not to use the words transitive and intransitive in this wider sense.

1 *Verbal Paradigms*

1.1 Description of the texts

1.2 Rationale of the verbal paradigms

1.2.1 verbal suffixes

1.2.1.1 pronoun complements

1.2.1.2 the ventive suffix

1.2.2 themes

1.2.3 moods

1.2.4 tenses

1.3 The paradigms from Ur

1.1 Description of the texts

The first class of grammatical text is best represented by OBGT VII, of which UET VII 97, 98, 100 and 101 are another version. Other texts of this class, listed in decreasing order of length and complexity, are OBGT VIII, IX, VI, IV, X, V and NBGT VI. (The paradigms from Ur, *UET* VII, 102 and 99, are described in Section 1.3 below.) Most of these are Old Babylonian tablets from Nippur; the texts from Ur are also Old Babylonian, while NBGT VI is from the library of Ashurbanipal. OBGT VI, VII, VIII, IX and X are (in contrast to the shorter 'excerpt' paradigms) beautifully and minutely written tablets. These are all what we may term *verbal paradigms*, that is, they are lists of verbal forms arranged according to various grammatically defined patterns. A number of other texts containing sections of verbal paradigms among other material is also described below. The features susceptible of analysis in a two-column, i.e. two-dimensional list, are:

1) the arrangement of entries,
2) the selection of forms from either language, and
3) the juxtaposition of particular Sumerian forms and Akkadian forms.

OBGT VII; UET VII 97, 98, 100 and 101

These mss. represent two traditions of the same text, which lists forms of the Sumerian verbs gen, du, re,[27] and sub, Akkadian *alākum*, 'to go'. Not only is this text the longest and most complex of the surviving Old Babylonian verbal paradigms, it is also the only one to be extant in more than one exemplar. The Nippur ms., OBGT VII, is the most complete. The considerably shorter version from Ur, of which the text is presented as Appendix 5.1.1 below, is also analyzed by D.A. Foxvog.[28] It omits all but three sections of the forms with plural personal pronoun complements, and also sections 11, 14, 15, 44, 47 and 48 of the Nippur text. The arrangement of the sections is also rather different. The first eleven lines are missing from the Nippur tablet, but can be restored with some certainty from lines 96 ff. of that version, as follows:

1	gá-nu-um	al-kam
2	ga-am-gen	lu-ul-li-kam
3	hé-em-du	li-il-li-kam
4	gá-a-mu-un-še	al-kaš-šum
5	ga-am-ši-gen	lu-ul-li-kaš-šum
6	hé-em-ši-du	li-il-li-kaš-šum
7	gá-a-mu-še	al-kam a-na ṣe-ri-ya
8	ga-mu-e-ši-gen	lu-ul-li-ka-ak-kum
9	ḫé-mu-e-ši-du	li-il-li-ka-ak-kum
10	gá-nam-ma	at-la-kam
11	ga-àm-ma-gen	lu-ut-tal-kam

27. Reading following Edzard in *ZA* 61 (1971), p. 224, after Krecher in *WdO* 4 (1967/8), pp. 1-7.
28. In *The Sumerian Ventive*, unpublished dissertation, University of California at Berkeley (1974).

These restorations differ from those of Landsberger in *MSL* IV, p. 88.
The forms are preserved in the Ur version, with slight variations as follows:

1	gen-àm
4	gen-àm-še
7	gen-àm-mu-še
10	gen-àm-ma

The Ur version does not use gá-a as a spelling of gen before mu/m, and spells certain other forms slightly differently.

The structure of this marvellously complex text is analyzed in the table opposite, which may be compared with Jacobsen's analysis in his 'Introduction to the Chicago Grammatical Texts' in *MSL* IV, pp. 3*-10*. The Sumerian 2nd person, together with forms with the preformatives ga- and hé-, set against the Akkadian 2nd person imperative, 1st person volitive (with *lu-*) and 3rd person optative (with *li-*) respectively, are treated as the three persons of one mood (hereinafter referred to as non-indicative forms), always listed in that order, and contrasted in the arrangement with the three persons of the Akkadian indicative (Sumerian with prefixes ì-, ba-, ma-, a-) which are always listed in the reverse order, 3rd, 1st and 2nd persons. Note that this order is maintained even in the four-line sections lines 191-246 (sections 67-80). The four-line sections of indicative forms are to be regarded as double two-line sections, preserving the order of persons but omitting impossible combinations, the first of each pair dealing with 1st person plural pronoun complements, the 2nd with 2nd person complements, rather than as a four-line section with the order of persons 3rd, 2nd, 3rd, 1st, which would infringe the principle. (But this observation applies to the indicative four-line sections only, not to the non-indicative.) In the non-indicative section, both mss. A and C of the Ur version preserve a deviant order at lines 180-1 and 184-5 (sections 67 and 68).

OBGT VIII
lists forms of kas_4...du_{11}/e (Akkadian *lasāmum*, 'to run'). It is analyzed by Jacobsen in *MSL* IV, pp. 10*-17*. 1-36 give non-indicative forms in the order 2nd, 1st, 3rd person, all singular, of the G and Š themes. 37-65 gives indicatives in the order 3rd, 1st, 2nd person, all singular, of the G, Gt, Š and Št preterite, with G present, with a variety of suffixes including *-akkum*. The remainder of the tablet (66-91) is taken up with forms of kú, Akkadian *akālum*, 'to eat', with non-indicative in the usual order, and indicative of the 3rd person only.

OBGT IX
is very similar to OBGT VIII, listing forms of sá...du_{11}/e, Akkadian *kašādum*, 'to reach', non-indicative forms of G and Š. It is analyzed by Jacobsen in *MSL* IV, pp.17*-32*. These texts are not as systematically organized as OBGT VII. In particular, Akkadian present tense forms are not listed with any regularity. The remainder of the tablet OBGT IX is filled out with a list of the 2nd, 1st and 3rd person singular non-indicative forms of tuš (*wašābum*, 'to sit'), zi (*tebûm*, 'to get up'), be_5 (*teṣûm*, 'to excrete'), dúr-dúr (*ṣarātum*, 'to break wind'), ul_4 (*hamāṭum*, 'to hasten'), ku-nu (*qerēbum*, 'to approach'), kú (*akālum*, 'to eat'), nag (*šatûm*, 'to drink') and gub (*uzuzzum*, 'to stand). It is impossible not to feel that the selection of verbs used here, especially be_5 and dúr-dúr, reflects a schoolboyish humour on the part of the compiler.

OBGT VI
is somewhat more diffuse. It is analyzed by Jacobsen in *MSL* IV, pp. 33*-50*. It lists singular forms of gar (Akkadian *šakānum*, 'to put'), beginning with non-indicatives of G and Š, then N and Gt themes (1-78). Note that the secondary, reduplicated, base gá-gá is not used at all. There follow G and Š statives (79-99), G and Š preterites (100-141), Gt, Št and Nt preterites (142-207) without (142-165) and with (166-207) ventive endings. After a further section of statives (208-210), preterites with the suffix *-kum* are listed (211-220), and finally a short series of present tense forms (221-227).

OBGT IV
gives on one side some forms of zi (*tebûm*, 'to get up'), and on the reverse, forms of sá...du_{11} (*kašādum*, 'to reach'), including negative forms.

Structure of the paradigm gen etc, = *alākum*, according to the Akkadian forms (Nippur version)

Non-indicative (Ni) is used here as a convenient shorthand for 1st person volitive/cohortative, 2nd person imperative and 3rd person optative. Ps = present; Pt = preterite; V = with ventive suffix; 1,2,3 = with pronoun complements of 1st, 2nd, 3rd person. Plural forms are in italics. Figures in brackets are line numbers, other figures are section numbers. Note the chiastic arrangement of forms with and without ventive in the indicative sections 85-92 (259-282) and 97-104 (295-318). This follows the essentially chiastic arrangement of forms with and without ventive in the indicative sections 11-33 (31-95) and 44-66 (126-190), viz. G without ventive, G with ventive, Gt with ventive, Gt without ventive, where the pattern is, however, broken up by the intrusion of G theme forms with V 2 suffixes (starred in the diagram). The Ur version follows the same pattern for the non-indicative forms as the Nippur version; but for the groups of sections 11-23, 24-33, 44-56 and 57-66, it has a straightforward rather than a chiastic arrangement, omitting the duplicating sections 11, 14, 15, 44, 47 and 48 (which use different prefixes in the Sumerian) and treating the material in the following order: G with ventive, e.g. 16, 17, 21, Gt with ventive, e.g. 18, 19, 20, G without ventive, e.g. 12, 13, Gt without ventive, e.g. 22, 23.

(1-30)

1	G	Ni	V	
2		Ni	V	3
3		Ni	V	1/2
4	Gt	Ni	V	
5		Ni	V	3
6		Ni	V	1/2
7	G	Ni		
8		Ni		3
9	Gt	Ni		
10		Ni		3

(31-67)

11	G	Ps		
12		Ps		
13		Ps		3
14		Ps		3
15		Ps		3
16		Ps	V	
17		Ps	V	3
18	Gt	Ps	V	
19		Ps	V	3
20		Ps	V	2
21	G	Ps	V	2*
22	Gt	Ps		
23		Ps		3

(68-95)

24	G	Pt		
25		Pt		3
26		Pt	V	
27		Pt	V	3
28	Gt	Pt	V	
29		Pt	V	
30		Pt	V	2
31	G	Pt	V	2*
32	Gt	Pt		
33		Pt		3

(96-125)

34	G	*Ni*	V	
35		*Ni*	V	3
36		*Ni*	V	1/2
37	Gt	*Ni*	V	
38		*Ni*	V	3
39		*Ni*	V	1/2
40	G	*Ni*		
41		*Ni*		3
42	Gt	*Ni*		
43		*Ni*		3

(126-162)

44	G	*Ps*		
45		*Ps*		
46		*Ps*		3
47		*Ps*		3
48		*Ps*		3
49		*Ps*	V	
50		*Ps*	V	3
51	Gt	*Ps*	V	
52		*Ps*	V	3
53		*Ps*	V	2
54	G	*Ps*	V	2*
55	Gt	*Ps*		
56		*Ps*		3

(163-190)

57	G	*Pt*		
58		*Pt*		3
59		*Pt*	V	
60		*Pt*	V	3
61	Gt	*Pt*	V	
62		*Pt*	V	3
63		*Pt*	V	2
64	G	*Pt*	V	2*
65	Gt	*Pt*		
66		*Pt*		3

(191-222)

67	G	Ni	V	*1/2*
68	Gt	Ni	V	*1/2*
69	G	Ps	V	*1/2*
70	Gt	Ps	V	*1/2*
71	Gt	Ps		*1/2*
72	G	Pt	V	*1/2*
73	Gt	Pt	V	*1/2*
74	Gt	Pt		*1/2*

(223-244)

75	G	*Ni*	V	*1/2*
76	Gt	*Ni*	V	*1/2*
77	G	*Ps*	V	*1/2*
78	Gt	*Ps*	V	*1/2*
79	G	*Pt*	V	*1/2*
80	Gt	*Pt*	V	*1/2*

(247-282)

81	G	Ni	V	*3*
82	Gt	Ni	V	*3*
83	G	Ni		*3*
84	Gt	Ni		*3*
85	G	Ps		*3*
86	G	Ps	V	*3*
87	Gt	Ps	V	*3*
88	Gt	Ps		*3*
89	G	Pt		*3*
90	G	Pt	V	*3*
91	Gt	Pt	V	*3*
92	Gt	Pt		*3*

(283-318)

93	G	*Ni*	V	*3*
94	Gt	*Ni*	V	*3*
95	G	*Ni*		*3*
96	Gt	*Ni*		*3*
97	G	*Ps*		*3*
98	G	*Ps*	V	*3*
99	Gt	*Ps*	V	*3*
100	Gt	*Ps*		*3*
101	G	*Pt*		*3*
102	G	*Pt*	V	*3*
103	Gt	*Pt*	V	*3*
104	Gt	*Pt*		*3*

OBGT X
is a diffuse list of forms of gub (*uzuzzum*, 'to stand'), in which 2nd person imperatives and some 1st person volitives (Sumerian with ga-) (1-19) are followed by statives (20-25) and preterites of G and Š (26-39), Gt and Št (40-51), other forms including some with the suffix *-kum* (52-65) and some presents (66-74). All the indicatives are only given in the 3rd person singular.
OBGT V
also gives a few forms of gub (*uzuzzum*) on its reverse, and on the obverse forms of te (*ṭehûm*, 'to approach'), including negatives and prohibitives (Sumerian with na-). This text, although brief, is interesting in that

a) it demonstrates the use of an extended form of the verbal base in the Sumerian forms corresponding to those constructed with a present tense in Akkadian (*lā tetehhišum*, *lā taṭehhiam* and *ūla eṭehhiakkum*), viz. te-ge$_x$-d[29], and

b) it makes a unique attempt to separate the Sumerian 1st and 2nd person suffixes (both normally written -en) by spelling: the 1st person is always spelt -en, the 2nd -e-en.
NBGT VI
is also a verbal paradigm, although surviving only in a neo-Babylonian fragment. Whether this is a copy of a lost Old Babylonian text or not it is impossible to say. Unfortunately the Akkadian is destroyed, but the Sumerian forms show the verb gub, 'to stand', with and without the suffix -ed-.

To the paradigms already described and analyzed may be added certain other texts which contain sections of verbal paradigms amongst various lexical material.
OBGT II
The reverse of OBGT II includes at least 17 entries of forms of sum (Akkadian *nadānum*, 'to give'), as follows (collated):

4'	sum$_6$-ma]-ab	*idin*
5'	sum$_6$-ma-na]-ab	*idinšum*
6'	sum$_6$-ma]-ab	*idnam*
7'	sum$_6$-ma-ni]-ib	*šuddinam*
8'	ga-ab]-sum$_6$	*luddin*
9'	ga-na-ab]-sum$_6$	*luddinšum*
10'	ga-ra-ab]-sum$_6$	*luddinkum*
11'	ga-mu-ra-ab]-sum$_6$	*luddinakkum*
12'	ga-ab-su]m$_6$?-sum$_6$	lu-u[t-ta]-ad-di-in (*luttaddin*)
13'	]-sum$_6$	]-*in*
14'	-na]-ab?-s[um$_6$	]-*inšum*
15'	-mu-na]-ab-[	]-*naššum*
16'		]-*šum*
17'		]-*šum* etc.

This text prefers phonetic spellings, hence sum$_6$ (=ŠUM) for sum. The restorations after line 12' are difficult and there is little evidence for the completion of the lacunae. The passage is restored from OBGT VI, which lists comparable forms. The chief feature of interest is in line 12' where it appears from the printed edition that the doubling of the Sumerian verb could be rendered in Akkadian by the Gtn theme, which denotes iteration. However, examination of the tablet shows that all that remains of the first sum$_6$ is part of a vertical slightly below the ruling, suggesting that the sign was in fact ab. In line 14' it is unlikely that sum$_6$ could have been written twice in the space available; in any case the traces of -ab-sum$_6$ are very faint. Again in line 15' the position of ab makes it unlikely that there was more than one sum$_6$ after it. Of the signs on the edge, the first sign in the Akkadian column is *not* lu. It looks like ú. Two horizontals only, above the line, and two, perhaps three, verticals are visible.

29. Reading following Edzard in *ZA* 66 (1976), p. 51, n. 203.

This cannot be used as evidence of the equation, in grammatical texts, of the reduplicated base with the Akkadian Gtn theme, although the equation is found in bilingual literary texts. The Gtn theme appears in no other extant grammatical text: reduplication of the base is associated instead with the D theme.

OBGT III

'OBGT III', which we separate into two texts, OBGT III(A) and OBGT III(B), is put together from two exemplars which overlap at lines 104-108 and 232-247 only. At these passages the following may be reconstructed:

	A		B	
104	ab-tum$_x$-tum$_x$-me-en	a-na-ku ú-ṣa-ap	a-ab-tum$_x$-tum$_x$-en	ú-ṣa-ap
105	ab-tum$_x$-tum$_x$e	šu-ú ú-ṣa-ap	ab-tum$_x$-tum$_x$-e	ú-ṣa-ap
106	[x x]-i	pi-qa-a-tim pu-ut-ti	kad-kad-ì	pu-u[t-ti]
107	[ ]x	lu-pe-ti	ga-ab-kad-kad	lu-pe-[et-ti]
108	[	l]i-pe-[ti]	ga-kad-kad-e	li-pe-et-[ti]
109	[	]	[	]pa-[ ]
232	mu-ti-ti	ú-re-še-an-ni	mu-un-ti-ti	[ ]
233	nu-mu-ti-ti	ú-la ú-re-[še-an-ni]	nu-mu-un-ti-ti	ú-ul [ ]
234	an-ni-ib-ti-ti	ú-re-še-[ ]	an-ni-ib-ti-ti	ú-re- [ ]
235	nu-un-ni-ib-ti-ti	ú-la[ ]	nu-un-ni-ib-ti-ti	ú-ul [ ]
236	hé-ni-ib-ti-ti	li-[ ]	hé-ni-ib-ti-ti	li-re-eš-ši-šu
237	[ ]	[la] ú-re-še-šu	na-an-ni-ib-ti-ti	la ú-re-eš-ši-šu
238	[ ]	ru-uš-ši-šu	ti-ti-a	ru-uš-ši
239	[ ]	ú-re-še-a-ni	ti-ti-⌜a-mu-ub⌝	ru-uš-ši-a-an-ni
240	[ ]x	ú-ki-da-an-ni	ti-ti-mu-un-ak	ú-ki-id-da-an-ni
241	[x]DU			
242	[ ]sa$_6$ an-tuku	sú-ur-ra-am i-šu	KA-zu sa$_6$ an-tuku	ri-dam i-šu
243	[z]u-sa$_6$ a-tuku	sú-ur-ra-am		
244		a-na-ku i-šu	KA-zu sa$_6$ a-tuku	a-na-ku i-šu
245			KA-zu sa$_6$ e-tuku	ri-dam ti-šu
246	[ ]	[sú-ur-r]a-am ú-la		
247		[i-š]u	[s]a$_6$ nu-tuku	ú-ul i-šu

The rest of the text is made up as follows:

	A	B
1-17		verbal phrase with *ele'e* etc., 2 forms of *sanāqum* (i)
16a-36	phrases with še, Akk. broken (r. i)	
54-67		gi-dub-ba-zu e-da-gál verbal drill (ii)
82-109	paradigms with *epēšum*; *ṣâpum*; *petûm* (r. ii)	*ṣâpum*, *petûm* (overlap) (iii)
151-180	*ubbuṭum*, *nuppuhum*, *nuṭṭupum* etc. (r. iii)	
186-193		*baṭālum* (r. i)
221-247	short paradigms contd.: *sukkukum*, *šêrum*, *ruššûm*, *surram išu* (r. iv)	*ruššûm*, *rīdam išu* (overlap) (r. ii)
281-288		mixed vocabulary (comm.?)(r. iii)
291-299	[broken] (r. v)	
	A is a 10-col. tablet, reverse only is preserved	B is a 6-col. tablet

B ends with line 288. Obviously A contained slightly more than twice as much material as B. Apart from lines 16a-36 (A col. vi), which is concerned with phrases using the word še (mainly, but not all, verbal) and lines 281-288 (B col. r. iii = vi), which is mixed vocabulary, possibly of commentary type, both tablets are made up of short sections of verbal paradigms arranged in a non-rigorous way. The longest sections are dím = *epēšum* (18 lines), *ruššûm*, *ubbuṭum*, gi-dub-ba (8 lines) and *le'ûm* (7 lines). A fair variety of verb types (including verbal phrases) is included.

Thus although B certainly more or less duplicates A for two passages totalling 18 out of the 102 preserved lines (of A's estimated total of 700 lines), more cannot be said. If A contained a whole 'work' clearly B contained only excerpts of it. Both are grammatical texts of 'mixed' species.

There are a number of rather confused paradigm sections in these texts:
58-64: here Sumerian forms literally translatable as 'your stylus is with you/me/him' or 'is held by you/me/him' are rendered by Akkadian forms of the stative in its active sense: 'you are/I am/he is holding'. These sentences are an early equivalent of 'La plume de ma tante...' Note the incorrect negation nu-an-da-gál, mechanically formed by prefixing nu- to an-da-gál, at 64.[30]
84-101: the chief feature of interest here is the alternation between the forms dím and dím-e.
151-159: note the alternation between húl-húl (after nu-, al- and ga-) and ha-ha (after hé- and na-). In literary texts húl-húl appears as a freely reduplicated form of húl 'to rejoice, be glad', but in this text it is treated as a grammatical pair of the verb ha-ha 'to quake, burst (out laughing?)'; that is, ha-ha is here treated as if it were the suppletive base to be used after the preformatives hé- and na-, much as du alternates with gen. In 158-9 the Sumerian should read nam-mu-un-ha-ha-en. (Poebel's copy in *PBS* V 142 is correct.)
160-176: lines 166-7 are a conflation of

al-zi-in-zi-im-me-en	*nuṭṭupāku*
nu-zi-in-zi-im-me-en	*ūla nuṭṭupāku*

191-193: see §1.2.3 below.
224-247a: do.

OBGT XI

Of the preserved parts of OBGT XI, certain passages evidently contain verbal paradigm sections.

NBGT VIII

The practice tablet NBGT VIII gives part of a paradigm of *nenzuhu*, 'to gird oneself'.

N3321, N3513 and N5475

(Old Babylonian, all unpublished; for transliteration see appendix 5.4 below). The transliterations of these texts were generously communicated to me by M. Civil. N3321 and N3513 contain parts of paradigms of the ever-popular verbs gen etc. = ***alākum***, and N5475 seems to have the same but possibly something else as well. N3513, interestingly, appears to be written out entirely in Sumerian, and has some forms with prefix na- (and base du). The forms are in general followed by their corresponding negatives (with nu-). However, not enough of these texts is preserved to analyse closely the arrangement of forms.

1.2 Rationale of the verbal paradigms

Even a casual glance at the verbal paradigms shows that these texts exhibit a high degree of organization and consistency both in terms of arrangement and in terms of the regularity with which certain Sumerian forms are set against certain Akkadian forms. Our present task, then, will be to lay bare as many as possible of the assumptions on which the equivalences listed in the texts are based. This will be particularly helpful in our further study of the grammatical terms. For the purpose of this exercise we shall confine our attention principally to OBGT VI, VII, VIII 1-65, IX 1-136 and X,

30. Recorded by Edzard in *RlA* 3, p. 611.

i.e. to the paradigms of the verbs appearing in Akkadian as *šakānum*, *alākum*, *lasāmum*, *kašādum* and *uzuzzum*. This is a corpus of 820 verbal forms, of which a certain number are duplicated. It will be noticed in the course of this investigation that the consistency which is maintained in the setting of certain Sumerian elements against certain Akkadian features occasionally produces forms which cannot have had much naturalness in either language, and which resemble the sort of strictly ungrammatical but none the less comprehensible forms that are to be found in grammatical paradigms of any other language. In particular (so far as I am aware) forms like *ittallak niāti* (VII 207), *šulsimaššum* (VIII 25) and *innanziz* (X 73) are concoctions which are unique: so is the Nt theme. These are all discussed below in the relevant places. For convenience, the analysis follows the Akkadian forms.

1.2.1 Verbal suffixes

The Akkadian verbal forms with suffixed elements will be studied under two heads, those with accusative or dative pronoun complements, and those with the ventive suffix. Note that the normal assimilations are not observed in these theoretically 'pure' forms, e.g. *littalkam niāši* not *littalkanniāši*. The form taken by the verbal suffixes (including the ventive) depends on whether the verbal form itself carries a suffixed subject marker (2nd and 3rd person plural) or not (singular forms and 1st person plural). Singular and 1st person plural forms are found bearing the following verbal suffixes:

singular	1st person	2nd person	3rd person
	-anni (ventive + accus.)	*-ka* (accusative)	*-šu* (accusative)
		-akka (ventive + accus.)	*-aššu* (ventive + accus.)
		-kum (dative)	*-šum* (dative)
	-am ana ṣērīya	*-akkum* (ventive + dat.)	*-aššum* (ventive + dat.)
		(1 × *-akku* OBGT IX 122)	

The first person accusative suffix can occur only when preceded by the ventive. As the first person dative suffix formally coincides in Akkadian with the ventive suffix, the phrase *-am ana ṣērīya* (where *ana ṣērīya* lit. = 'on(to) my back', idiomatically 'on(to)', 'to') is concocted to bring out the fact that in the Sumerian there are two distinct elements, one corresponding to the ventive, the other to the dative.

plural	1st person	2nd person	3rd person
	-niāti	*-kunūti*	*-šunūši*
	-am niāši	*-am kunūši*	*-am šunūši*

The plural suffixes are confined to OBGT VII. All the forms are dative, or ventive with dative, with the exception of the accusatives *-niāti* and *-kunūti* which occur only at 207 ff. and 219 ff. and form the subject of two papers by Jacobsen.[31] They are unique forms, in that in the corresponding forms (both by reason of arrangement and according to the Sumerian elements used) in all persons, both singular and plural, as well as in the directly corresponding forms with ventive, *dative* suffixes are used. I still find it difficult, despite Jacobsen's suggestions, to understand what could be meant by an accusative personal pronominal suffix for the verb 'to go'. His argument, I think, does not take account of cases where the separative -t- themes (Sumerian ba-/-ma-) are used together with directional dative suffixes such as *-šum* (Sumerian -na-) obviously meaning 'towards'. Separative ('away') and ventive ('hither') are not mutually exclusive. Many forms have neither while yet having directional dative suffixes ('towards'). In view of the otherwise exemplary regularity of this text, it seems highly likely that these forms are to be regarded as the errors of a careless scribe. This particular conclusion does not, it seems to me, impugn Jacobsen's wider conclusions about the functions of the accusative case.

31. '*Ittallak niāti*', in *Toward the Image of Tammuz* (Harvard, 1970), pp. 271-292, and 'The Akkadian Ablative Accusative', *ibid.*, pp. 293-311.

In addition, the following suffixes occur after 2nd and 3rd person plural forms only (also confined to OBGT VII):

-nim ventive

singular	1st person	2nd person	3rd person
	-nim ana ṣērīya (vent. +dat.)	*-nikkum* (vent. + dat.)	*-niššum* (vent. + dat.)
plural	1st person	2nd person	3rd person
	-nim niāši (vent. + dat.)	*-nim kunūši* (vent. + dat.)	*-nim šunūši* (vent. + dat.)

For the first person singular dative with ventive here, a suffixed phrase is again used.

Thus the possibilities are ventive or non-ventive, accusative or dative, and any combination of those, with the exceptions that first person accusative and dative forms can only occur with the ventive, and that plural suffixes occur only in the dative, not accusative (with the exception of *-niāti* and *-kunūti*, mentioned above).

Where blanks are left in the Akkadian columns of the texts, it is, generally speaking, simple to fill them in by merely varying the prefix, e.g. after *iškun* one fills in *aškun* and *taškun* and so on; but in the case of the suffixes for 1st and 2nd persons, the procedure is not quite so simple. In OBGT VI 19, *šuknam*, the *-am* functions merely as the ventive; but in 37, also *šuknam*, it is the ending for 1st person singular dative; that is clear from the arrangement of the forms. Consequently 38, where the verb is 1st person singular, cannot be filled in with the same ending but must read *luškukkum*, 1st person singular with 2nd person singular dative suffix.

Similarly

OBGT VI	39	should read	*liškukkum*
	47		*luškukka*
	48		*liškukka*
	52		*lušaškikka*
	53		*lišaškikka*
VIII	29		*lušalsimakka*
	30		*lišalsimakka*
	32		*lulsimakkum*
	33		*lilsimakkum*
	35		*lušalsimakkum*
	36		*lišalsimakkum*
	50		*alassumakkum* (and delete line 51)
IX	56		*lukšudka*
	57		*likšudka*
	59		*luštakšidka*
	60		*lišakšidka*
	62		*lukšudakkum*
	63		*likšudakkum*
	65		*lušakšidakkum*
	66		*lišakšidakkum*

There are, finally, a number of improbable forms in the texts as they stand. Many can be improved simply by inspection. I am not here proposing emendations to the printed texts, carefully copied by the editors of *MSL* IV. Rather some of these improbable forms are ancient copyists' errors; others may actually be contractions due to pronunciation. In either case it is helpful for our purposes to restore the theoretically complete forms, based on the otherwise rigorous structure of the paradigms. Thus

OBGT VI	37	gar-ma-ra	should be read as	gar-ma-ab
	163	⸢it⸣-ta-aš-ka-an		⸢it⸣-ta-aš-ka-an <-šum>
VII	108	gá-nam-an-še-en-zé-en		gá-nam <-ma> -an-še-en-zé-en
	162	ta-at-tál-la-ak-šum		ta-at-tál-la-ka-šum
	187	[ta-a]t-ta-lak		[ta-a]t-ta-al-ka
	190	ta-at-tál-ka-aš-šum		ta-at-tál-ka-šum
	193	hé-me-du		hé <-em> -me-du
	195	gá-nam-me-a		gá-nam- <ma> -me-a
	196	ga-⸢a-na-mu⸣-e-ne-du		ga-àm (i.e. a-an)-mu-e-ne-gen
	197	⸢hé⸣-em-me-du		⸢hé⸣-em <-ma> -me-du
	225	[hé-me]-su$_{8}$-bé-eš		[hé-em-me]-su$_{8}$-bé-eš
	229	[hé]-em-me-⸢su$_{8}$-bé-eš⸣		[hé]-em <-ma> -me-⸢su$_{8}$-bé-eš⸣
	230	[h]é-e[m-e-ne]-⸢su$_{8}$⸣-bé-eš		[h]é-e[m-mu-e-ne]-⸢su$_{8}$⸣-bé-eš
	243/4	[i]m-me-		[i]m <-ma> -me-
	286	gá-nam-ne-a-en-zé!-en		gá-nam <-ma> -ne-a-en-zé!-en
VIII	84	im-⸢ma⸣-an-ni(!)-íb-kú		im-⸢ma⸣-di-ni!-íb-kú
IX	28	⸢šu⸣-ta-ak-ši-da-aš-šum		šu-uk-ši-da-aš-šum
	31	sá ⸢du$_{11}$⸣-ga-ab-ta		sá ⸢du$_{11}$⸣-ga-ba-ab
	58	šu-ta-ak-ši-da-ni		šu-uk-ši-da-an-ni
	73	⸢sá⸣ ba-an-na-du$_{11}$		⸢sá⸣ ba-na-an-du$_{11}$(already Jacobsen, *MSL* IV, p. 40*)
	77	⸢sá ba-na-ni⸣-íb-du$_{11}$		⸢sá ba-na-ni⸣-du$_{11}$
	103	ik-ta-aš-da-ak-ka		ik-ta-aš <-ša> -da-ak-ka

1.2.1.1 Pronoun complements

The pronoun complements occurring after singular or 1st person plural verbs may be analyzed as follows.

Suffixes of the 3rd person singular

These are *-šu -aššu -šum* and *-aššum*. They are set against forms of the Sumerian infixes -ši- -na- -ni- and -da- as shown in the table below. Forms set against an Akkadian N theme are marked by a superscript N; a superscript Š indicates a Š theme; otherwise the elements listed occur in forms set against the Akkadian G theme.

	VI	VII	VIII	IX	X
-šu, -aššu	da nda da^{Š} di^{Š} ndi^{Š} še^{N}			ni ni^{Š}	da nda da^{Š} da^{Š} ndi^{Š} ni^{Š}
-šum, *-aššum*	na nna na^{Š} nna^{Š} na^{N} nna^{N} ši ši^{Š} še^{N}	ši nši nše	na na^{Š} ši še ši^{Š}	na na^{Š}	na nna na^{Š} nna^{Š} nna^{N} ši ši^{Š}

There are certain irregularities here. -še- for *aššu* with an N theme form at VI 70ff. is probably misleading, as *-aššu* almost certainly stands for *-aššum* here: the accusative pronoun complement after the N imperative of *šakānum* would make no sense. It must be *naškinaššum* 'be placed here for him'. -ni- for *-šu* with Š theme at X 4 and 10 is also misleading. The Sumerian forms here properly lack any feature which is directly translatable by *-šu*, since -ni- strictly indicates the Š theme (which is treated in detail below). -ni- for *-šu* with both G and Š themes in IX is a special case, since the Sumerian verb set against *kašādum* is a compound verbal phrase. A literal rendering of e.g. sá ga-mu-ni-íb-du$_{11}$ (=(*lušakšidaššu*)23) would perhaps be 'I will cause (so-and-so) to effect a reaching at him here', where -ni- is represented by 'at him'.

Apart from these unusual usages, the regular pattern seems to be:

a) that with the verbs *šakānum* 'to put' and *uzuzzum* 'to stand', forms of the infix -da- (-di, -nda-, -ndi-) are rendered by *-šu* (*v. infra* p. 38). This sometimes produces unexpected forms in Akkadian, as when the forms of the (usually intransitive) *uzuzzum* have an accusative suffix tacked on: *izzussu* (30, 36), *izzassu* (68). In fact *uzuzzum* does occur with pronominal suffixes in more or less this sense, for example *4R* 17:18 *izzazku* (rendering 17 ša-mu-ra-da-an-gub), *ibid.* 16:22 *izzazzūka* (ša-mu-ra-da-ab-súg-ge-eš), both meaning 'wait upon you, stand by you'; and *YOS* 2 38:22 *mahar dayyānī i-zi-is-sú-ma*, cf. 16 *i-zi-is-sú* (OB letter). Indeed *uzuzzum* is treated in the paradigm rather as if it were a transitive verb, with an N theme (*innanziz*, 73). In a study of this verb, Poebel compared the phrase *maṣṣartam uzuzzum*, 'to stand guard' and drew attention to the suppletive use in OBGT X of the verb *waqûm* 'to guard, watch over', at lines 3 and 9.[32] This may explain the use of -da-: gub-an-da 'stand *with* him, guard him'.[33]

b) that with *alākum* 'to go', forms of -ši- (-nši-, -nše-) are rendered by *-šum*. This almost certainly (in view of the meaning of the verb) indicates direction and not benefaction, unidiomatic as this may seem in Akkadian, and is thus an alternative for *ana šuāšum* or *ana ṣērīšu*.

c) that with *kašādum* 'to reach', -na- is rendered by *-šum*. The sense of this is probably the 'person reached', not the ethic or benefactive dative, 'to him, for him'.

With the remaining verbs (*šakānum*, 'put', *lasāmum* 'run' and *uzuzzum* 'stand'), -ši- (-še-, -nši-, -nše-) and -na- (-nna-) both occur opposite *-šum*. With *lasāmum* this probably indicates direction; with *šakānum* and *uzuzzum* the benefactive usage is more likely. What factors govern the choice of -ši- or -na-? The only forms in which -ši- occurs are the following (when a group of three non-indicative forms occurs, only the form with ga- is listed, for conciseness' sake):

ga-àm-ma-še-éb-gar
ga-am-ma-še-gar
ma-ši-(in-)gar
ma-ši-ni-(in-)gar

kas$_4$ ga-àm-ši-du$_{11}$
kas$_4$ ga-àm-ma-ši-íb-du$_{11}$
kas$_4$ mu-ši-íb-bé(-en)

kas$_4$ àm-ši-ìb-bé(-en)
ma-ši-in-gub
ma-ši-ni-(in-)gub

In other words, -ši- is only permitted when preceded by some form of the element -m-/ma-/mu-; if that element is absent, the use of -na- instead seems imperative. The forms kas$_4$ mu-ši-íb -bé(-en) (= *ilassumsum* etc., VII 40ff.) appear to be exceptions to this principle, since the mu- here is the conjugation prefix mu- and not the element elsewhere set against the Akkadian ventive. (These -m- elements are discussed below in § 1.2.1.2.) The exception is probably due to confusion between the two similar elements.

-na- occurs in the following sets of forms which *are* set against ventive forms:

ga-mu-un-na-ab-gar
ga-mu-na-ni-íb-gar
im-ma-na-(an-)gar

gub-mu-un-na-ab
gub-mu-na-ni-íb
im-ma-na-an-gub
im-ma-na-ni-in-gub

} X 11-12 but cf. X 5-6, where mu is the conjugational prefix.

We may conclude then, that -na- is regular; and that -ši- may be used instead of it, but only if the element -m-/ma-/mu- is present, i.e. if it is accompanied by some other direction-marking element.

Suffixes of the 2nd person singular

These are *-ka -kum -akka* and *-akkum* (appearing once as *-akku*). They are set against -eda-, -eši-, -e-, -ra- and -ri- as follows:

---

32. 'The verb *uzuzzu*, "to stand" ', in *AS* 9 (Chicago, 1939), pp. 75-196, esp. pp. 192-6.

33. VI 112 and 130 show the apparent incompatibility of -nda- and -n-. In 131-2 the scribe has erroneously written -da- for the fuller -nda-, apparently by confusing the -n- of -nda- with the cause marker -n-, which he omitted in 130 (and 112). In 112 and 130 we should in theory have expected in-da-an-gar, mu-un-da-an-gar.

	VI	VII	VIII	IX	X
-ka, *-akka*	eda ri^{š}		ri^{š}	ra^{š} ri ra^{š} ri^{š} e	ri^{š}
-kum, *-akkum*	ra ra^{š} ri^{š} ra^{N} eda	eši	eši ri ri^{š}	ra ri ri^{š}	ra ra

Thus, in general, -ri- is represented by the accusative suffix and -ra- by the dative. In the paradigms of *alākum* and *lasāmum*, the verbs of motion, -eši- is used to indicate motion 'towards you', but with *lasāmum*, of which the Sumerian equivalent is the verbal phrase kas$_4$...du$_{11}$, *-kum* is also set against -ri- which marks the 'goal' of the action ('he effects running "at you" or "to you"'). Curiously -ri- is confined to the base du$_{11}$ (Akkadian preterite), while -eši- is used with the base e (Akkadian present). This is presumably idiomatic. The passage OBGT VI 46-55 is rather confusing as it stands:

46	gar-mu-um	*šuknanni*
	ga-e-da-gar	(*luškukka*)
	hé-e-da-gar	(*liškukka*)
	ga-mu-e-da-gar	*luškunakkum*
50	hé-mu-e-da-gar	(*liškunakkum*)
	gar-mu-ub	*šuškinanni*
	ga-ri-ib-gar	(*lušaškikka*)
	hé-ri-ib-gar	(*lišaškikka*)
	ga-mu-ri-íb-gar	*lušaškinakkum*
	hu-mu-ri-ib-gar	(*lišaškinakkum*)

Here -eda- is represented in 47-8, as we should expect, by the accusative suffix *-ka*. In 49-50, however, it is apparently rendered by *-kum*. Similarly, in 52-3, -ri- is set against the accusative *-ka* (by implication from the accusative *-anni* in 51), while in 54-5 it is apparently set against *-kum*. But if we restore *-ka* for *-kum* in 49 and 54, the forms listed will conform exactly to the principles so far uncovered. This emendation is supported by the fact that the Akkadian entries as they stand duplicate those in 42 and 44. They seem to have been erroneously repeated by the scribe.

In the paradigm of *kašādum*, a couple of forms require comment. These are OBGT IX 103f.:

sá im-mu-e-a	ik-ta-aš-<ša>-da-ak-ka
sá im-mu-e-a-en	(*aktaššadakka*)

They represent i+m+ba+e+e and i+m+ba+e+en, i.e. an infix -e- for second person goal, the so-called *marû* verb e, and, in 104, the suffix -en for first person. (For discussion of the terms *hamṭu* and *marû*, see section 3.6.1 below.) The derivation of im-mu- from i+m+ba is discussed below in § 1.2.1.2.

Finally mention may be made of the apparently indifferent alternation between -ri- and -ra-, *-ka* and *-kum* in some other forms of *kašādum*:

i-ra-an-du$_{11}$	= *ikšudka*	ga-ra-ab-du$_{11}$	= *lukšudka*
i-ri-íb-du$_{11}$	= *ušakšidka*	ga-ri-íb-du$_{11}$	= *luštakšidka*
mu-ri-in-du$_{11}$	= *ikšudakka*	ma-ra-an-du$_{11}$	= *ikšudakka*
mu-ri-íb-du$_{11}$	= *ušakšidakka*	ma-ra-ni-íb-du$_{11}$	= *ušakšidakka*
im-ma-ri-in-du$_{11}$	= *iktašdakkum*	ga-mu-ra-ab- du$_{11}$	= *lukšudakkum*
im-ma-ri-íb-du$_{11}$	= *uštakšidakku(m)*	ga-mu-ri-ib-du$_{11}$	= *lušakšidakkum*

The alternation becomes slightly less confusing when we consider the meanings of these forms. *kašādum* is to reach, and the suffix of the 2nd person singular can only indicate the goal of the action, surely, the person reached (unless, much less likely, it could indicate an ethic dative). So presumably it is of little consequence in Akkadian whether the dative or accusative form of the suffix is used. We should expect to find -ri- in those Sumerian forms set against Š themes (for -ri- is the corresponding 2nd person infix to 3rd person -ni-, which is the standard infix for marking the 'instrumental agent' of an action when the real cause is someone else), and this is in fact the case. The unexplained alternation between -ri- and -ra- is then confined to forms set against G themes, and it is probably of no significance in this verb, owing to its meaning.

Suffixes of the 1st person singular

These are *-anni* and *-am ana ṣērīya*, the latter more properly a suffixed phrase. They are set against Sumerian forms of the infixes -mu- and -muše- as follows:

	VI	VII	VIII	IX	X
-anni	-mu-un -mu-ub$^{\check{S}}$		(-ga)-mu-ub$^{\check{S}}$	(-ga)-mu-un (-ga)-mu-ub$^{\check{S}}$	-mu-ub$^{\check{S}}$
-am ana ṣērīya		(-n)am-mu-še	(-ga)-mu-še (-ga)-ám-mu-še$^{\check{S}}$	(-ga)-mu-še (-ga)-mu-še-éb$^{\check{S}}$	

As can be seen, these forms occur only in 2nd person imperatives (and this explains the final -n or -b in some cases). They are all also combined with the element -m-/ma-/mu-, which is regularly set against the Akkadian ventive, as will be shown. What the 1st person infix in Sumerian is which is rendered by the accusative *-anni* in Akkadian we cannot say; only that it combines with -m-/ma-/mu- to give mu-. Similarly (while 3rd and 2nd person infixes produce the combinations -mši-/maši- and -muеši- respectively) for the 1st person -še- combines with -m- to produce -mu-še-.

Plural suffixes

These are briefly dealt with. They are confined to OBGT VII. The Sumerian forms, indifferently of whether the Akkadian shows dative or accusative, are:

1st person	(*-am niāši, -niāti, -nim niāši*)	-me-
2nd person	(*-am kunūsi, -kunūti, -nim kunūši*)	-ene-
3rd person	(*-am šunūši, -šunūši, -nim šunūši*)	-ne-

An element corresponding to the Akkadian ventive appears in the appropriate place. The likelihood that the apparently accusative forms were scribal errors was discussed above, p. 17.

The above are the pronoun complements occurring after singular or 1st person plural verb forms. There remain those which occur after 2nd and 3rd person plural forms. These are the dative-with-ventive suffixes:

Singular suffixes

1st person	*-nim ana ṣērīya*
2nd person	*-nikkum*
3rd person	*-niššum*

In the Sumerian forms against which these are set, the plurality of subject is marked by a suffix and so the infixes (corresponding to these Akkadian suffixes) are not affected. Accordingly they are:

1st person	*-muše-*
2nd person	*(-)muеši-*
3rd person	*-nši-, -ši-.*

Plural suffixes

1st person	*-nim niāši*
2nd person	*-nim kunūši*
3rd person	*-nim šunūši*

Again the behaviour of the Sumerian infixes is absolutely predictable and is not affected by the plurality of the subject. The infixes are:

1st person	-me-
2nd person	-ene-
3rd person	-ne-.

1.2.1.2 The ventive suffix

That completes our account of the behaviour of the suffixed Akkadian pronoun complements occurring in the paradigms. We shall look next at the suffix *-am/-nim*, known as the ventive from one of its functions, that of marking movement towards the speaker with verbs of motion. The question may be asked whether there is any such comparable form in Sumerian, or at least whether the compilers of our texts regarded any single Sumerian element or group of elements as sufficiently similar to to be plausibly and regularly set against the Akkadian ventive. To talk of the 'Sumerian ventive', as is done by Yoshikawa and Foxvog, is merely to beg this extremely interesting question.[34] Our purpose here will be to investigate the exact form of the elements set against the Akkadian ventive, and to this end a list has been made of the prefix chains occurring in the paradigms OBGT VI-X (indicative forms only) which are set against such forms. This is as follows:

i-im
i-im-ši
i-im-me
i-im-ne

àm
àm-ši
àm-ši-íb
àm-me
àm-ne

im-ma
im-ma-an
im-ma-ni
im-ma-ni-in
im-ma-ni-íb
im-mu-e-ši
im-mu-e-ne

im-mu-e
im-ma-ra
im-ma-ra-an
im-ma-ra-ni-in
im-ma-ri
im-ma-ri-in
im-ma-ri-íb
im-ma-ši
im-ma-na
im-ma-na-an
im-ma-na-ni
im-ma-na-ni-in
im-ma-na-ni-íb
im-ma-da
im-ma-da-an
im-ma-di-ni
im-ma-ne
im-<ma->me

àm-ma
àm-mu-e-ne
àm-mu-e-ši
àm-mu-e-ši-íb
àm-ma-ši
àm-ma-me
àm-ma-ne

ma
ma-an
ma-ni
ma-ni-in
ma-ni-íb
ma-ra
ma-ra-an
ma-ra-ni
ma-ra-ni-in

ma-ra-ni-íb
ma-ši
ma-ši-in
ma-ši-ni
ma-ši-ni-in
ma-da
ma-da-an
ma-di-ni
ma-di-ni-in
ma-di-ni-íb
mu-e
mu-e-ne
mu-e-ši
mu-ri
mu-ri-in
mu-ri-íb

and also	kas$_4$ mu-un-du$_{11}$	=	*ilsumam*
	kas$_4$ mu-du$_{11}$	=	(*alsumam*) (OBGT VIII 55-56)

34. Yoshikawa, most recently, in 'Sumerian Ventive and Ientive' in *OrNS* 47 (1978), pp. 461-482, and Foxvog in *The Sumerian Ventive* (University of Berkeley, California, dissertation, 1974).

Discarding the elements known to be associated with other Akkadian features (e.g. the various personal elements), we are left with the following:

i-im
àm
im-ma (im-mu before e)
àm-ma (àm-mu before e)
ma (mu before e and ri)
+ two exceptional cases where mu- is used for ma-, probably owing to vocalic assimilation.

If we wished to isolate a single morpheme from these, the most obvious candidate would be -m-, with morphologically conditioned variants ma- and mu-. -m- is regarded by Falkenstein[35] as a phonologically conditioned variant of the personal elements -n- and -b-. It is isolated as a separate morpheme by Jacobsen, although he regards ma and mu as equally separate and distinct features.[36] Foxvog also isolates -m-, and regards mu and ma as by-forms of it.[37] Let us then assume that -m- is the feature set against the Akkadian ventive. i-im- and àm- will then be that feature preceded by the conjugation prefixes i- and a- (which, as will be shown below, appears as al- in the absence of any infixes). ma- may be thought of as the simple feature -m- rendered pronounceable by the addition of an epenthetic vowel.

The question next arises what is represented by the writings im-ma and àm-ma. The commonest answer to this question (when it has been answered at all) has been that they derive from *i+b+a and *a+b+a. Now if we check which Akkadian forms are set against im-ma and àm-ma, we shall find that, almost without exception, they are *forms of the -t- infix themes with ventive suffix*. The exceptions are OBGT VIII 25 ff. and 34ff., where the -àm-ma- is to be regarded as part of a full spelling and not as the common chain -àm-ma-, i.e. ga-àm-ma-ši-íb- is written for *ga+ma+ši+b; and *ibid.* 49ff., where -àm-mu-e-ši-íb- occurs representing *a+mu+eši+b. In these cases ma and mu are the forms taken by m before ši and eši respectively, as will be shown below.

It will be demonstrated in full later that ba- is regularly set against the -t- infix themes. i-im and àm- are set against ventive forms, while im-ma and àm-ma are set against -t- infix themes with ventive suffix. From this it is a permissible conclusion to deduce that im-ma and àm-ma represent respectively i+m+ba and a+m+ba. This conclusion is also stated by Foxvog, as cited above, but without the argument leading up to it. Presumably the same conclusion may be drawn concerning the derivation of im-mi and àm-mi from i+m+bi and a+m+bi, but neither of these forms occurs in the paradigms under discussion.[38] This conclusion is at variance with that of Postgate.[39] The other forms set against a ventive all begin with mu-; however — and this is crucial — not all forms beginning with mu- contain the element under discussion, as is shown by the following table of forms grouped into types. Those in the lefthand column are set against ventive forms, those in the righthand are *not*:

1)	ga-mu-e-da hé-mu-e-da-	VI 49f		
	mu-e-ši-	VII 60f., 88f.	mu-ši-íb-	VIII 40
	ga-mu-e-ši- hé-mu-e-ši-	VIII 32f.		
	mu-e-	VIII 57		

35. *Das Sumerische*, p. 47 §33, 3 a β.
36. In 'About the Sumerian Verb', in *Towards the Image of Tammuz*, pp. 253ff.
37. In 'The Sumerian Ergative Construction', in *OrNS* 44 (1975), p. 400, n. 17.
38. They do, however, occur in the Ur paradigms. See §1.3 below. Edzard points out that the assimilaton of a plosive to a nasal is not elsewhere attested, and cites Akkadan *apparu*, derived from Sumerian ambar, where it is the nasal that assimilates to the plosive. But of course Akkadian may have been different in this respect.
39. *V.* 'Two Points of Grammar in Gudea', in *JCS* 26 (1974), pp. 16-54.

2)	mu- mu-un-	VIII 55f.	mu-(un-)	VI 124ff.
3)	-mu-un	VI 46, IX 55		
	-mu-ub	VI 51, VIII 28, IX 58		
4)	-mu-(un-)še-(en-zé-en)	VII 16, VIII 31, IX 61 etc.		
5)	-mu-un-na-ab ga-mu-un-na-ab- hu-mu-un-na-ab-	VI 31ff.		
	-mu-na-ab ga-mu-na-ab- hu-mu-na-ab	IX 25 ff.	mu-na-(an-)	VI 136ff., IX 132ff.
6)	mu-ri-(in/íb-)	VIII 58f., 62f., IX 128ff.		
	ga-mu-ri-íb- hu-mu-ri-íb-	VI 54f., VIII 29f.		
7)	-mu-na-ni-íb ga-mu-na-ni-íb- hu-mu-na-ni-íb-	VI 34ff., IX 28ff.	mu-na-ni-(in/íb-)	VI 139ff., IX 135f.
8)	ga-mu-ra-ab- hu-mu-ra-ab- ga-mu-ra-ni-íb- hu-mu-ra-ni-íb-	VI 42ff., IX 62f.	mu-ra-an- mu-ra-ni-in-	VI 214 VI 215
9)	-mu-ni-íb ga-mu-ni-íb- hu-mu-ni-íb-	IX 22ff.		VI 109ff., 127ff.
10)			mu-un-da- mu-da- mu-di-ni-(íb-)	VI 130 VI 131f. VI 133f.

In the forms in the lefthand column of type (1) mu- occurs for the phonetic reason that -m- followed by -e- always so appears in those circumstances. Similarly in the forms (2) mu- (1st person), (3) -mu-un/ub and (4) -mu-(un-)še-(en-zé-en) the form of the -m- combined with the 1st person marker produces (-)mu-. In types (5) mu-na-, (6) mu-ri- and (7) mu-na-ni-, it may be noted that the forms *ma-na-, *ma-ri- and *ma-na-ni- do not occur, at least not in the paradigm, and it may be supposed that in these cases the -m- *must* appear as mu-. This seems also to be the case with the determined forms of the infix -ši-: thus, ma-ši occurs, but with the third person infix -n- it becomes mu-un-še-.

Concerning forms of types (8) and (9) (with -ra- and -ni-) we may summarize the information available to us as follows:

type (8):

OBGT	VI	37	gar-ma-ra	*šuknam*
		42/3	ga-mu-ra-ab-gar	*luškinakkum*
			hu-mu-ra-ab-gar	*liškinakkum*, similarly 44f., IX 62f.
	IX	91f.	sá ma-ra-an-du_{11}	*ikšudakka*
			sá ma-ra-ni-íb-du_{11}	*ušakšidakka*

X	13	gub-ma-ra	*izizam*
	15	ga-mu-ra-ab-gub	*luzzizakkum*
	16	ga-mu-ra-ni-íb-gub	*lušzizakkum*
	62	ma-ra-an-gub	*izzizakkum*
	63	ma-ra-ni-in-gub	*ušzizakkum*

In other words, -m- marking the features set against the Akkadian ventive is altered before -ra- to -mu- when preceded by ga-, to avoid *ga-ma-ra-, and by hu-, to avoid *ha-ma-ra-: an example of 'vowel discord'.

type (9):

OBGT VI	22ff.	gar-ma-ni-íb	*šuškinam*
		ga/hu-mu-ni-íb-gar	*lušaškinam/lišaškinam*
	193	ma-ni-in-gar	*ušaškinam*
VIII	13ff.	kas_4 du_{11}-ga-ma-ni-íb	*šulsimaššu*
		kas_4 ga/hé-ma-ni-íb-du_{11}	*lušalsimaššu/lišalsimaššu*
IX	22ff.	sá du_{11}-ga-mu-ni-íb	*šukšidaššu*
		sá ga/hu-mu-ni-íb-du_{11}	*lušakšidaššu/lišakšidaššu*
	88	sá ma-ni-íb-du_{11}	*ušakšidam*
X	8	gub-mu-ni-íb	*šuzizam*
	53	ma-ni-in-gub	*ušzizam* (and contrast:
	35	mu-ni-in-gub	*ušziz*)

Apparently much the same principle is at work here. -m- appears as -ma- before -ni- except (usually) when preceded by ga- or hé- (which then appears as hu-). In this respect IX 22 and X 8 are divergent. VIII 14f. may be regarded as 'grammatical' rather than 'phonetic' writings.

We can now state the rules for the usage of -m-/ma-/mu- as generally observed in the verbal paradigms.

i) The element appears as -m- when it occurs after one of the prefixes i- or a-; or after the preformatives ga- or hé- (usually when followed by a consonant).

ii) If it is not preceded by a prefix or preformative it appears as ma-. (This ma- was listed by Falkenstein as a coalescence of the conjugation prefix mu- with a dative infix -a-).[40]

iii) This ma- appears as mu- if it is followed by -e-, -ri-, -na-, -nše- (but not -ši-) or the infix of the first person (whether folowed by a dimensional infix or not);

iv) or when preceded by ga- or hu- and followed by -ra- or -ni-.

It is essential to make the point that it is quite clear from the paradigms that this mu- is regarded as a separate element from the conjugation prefix mu-, which is formally distinguished from it by having a variant form occurring before -ni-, mi- (cf. VI 109, 127, 193). The -m- which is set against ventives never occurs in this form. This result is at variance with the contention of Postgate, based on evidence from literary texts, and the distinction between the two is ignored by Foxvog in his analysis of the paradigms thereby considerably weakening, not to say invalidating his argument. The two elements are incompatible with one another, as may be seen from the following diagram:

	-	ma-du	(m+du)
(i+du)	ì-du	i-im-du	(i+m+du)
(bi+du)	bí-du	im-mi-du	(i+m+bi+du)
(ba+du)	ba-du	im-ma-du	(i+m+ba+du)
(mu+du)	mu-du	-	
(mu+ni+du)	mu-ni-du } mi-ni-du	ma-ni-du	(m+ni+du)

40. *V. Das Sumerische*, p. 48 §33, 3 b 1 *a* and cf. Poebel, *GSG*, §563.

However, in the cases where -m- appears as mu-, it is usually impossible to distinguish between the two possibilities on graphic grounds. The analysis offered by Jacobsen, that -m- is reserved for 3rd person or no-person or 1st person plural goal, while -mu- is confined to 2nd person and 1st person singular and 2nd person plural, differs from ours in attributing a subtle difference of semantic nuance to what we regard as a purely morphophonemically conditioned feature.[41]

1.2.2 Themes

The themes of the Akkadian verb occurring in the paradigms OBGT VI-X are:

G (basic)	Gt (basic with -t- infix)
Š (causative)	Št (causative with -t- infix)
N (passive)	Nt (passive with -t- infix)

i.e. Gtn, Štn, Ntn (themes with the iterative -tan- infix) and all forms of D (with doubled middle radical) are absent. Collation of the text of OBGT II (see §1.1 above) makes it very unlikely that there is evidence for an equation, within the corpus of grammatical texts, of Sumerian reduplication with Gtn, although it is certainly found in bilinguals. Forms of the D theme do occur in OBGT III and XI, where they are normally set against Sumerian forms with reduplicated verb.

We shall deal first with the themes Gt and Št. It was said above that the Akkadian -t- themes were regularly set against Sumerian ba-. Out of 151 forms with ba- in OBGT IV-X, only 15 are not set against a form with infix -t-, i.e. there is a correspondence of almost 90%. Of those that remain (OBGT VI 58-63, 82-4, 88-90 and OBGT X 21-2 and 73), seven are set against Akkadian N themes and eight against Akkadian Š stative. These will be dealt with separately below. In order to proceed further, we must solve one problem: in Akkadian the perfect tense of the G theme and the preterite of the Gt theme have the same form, and it is impossible, except by circumstantial evidence, to distinguish them. The same is true of Š and Št, and of N and Nt (*v. infra*). It will be argued that the forms in the verbal paradigms are all preterites of the Gt, Št or Nt themes, and that the Akkadian perfect tense does not appear at all.

In the first place, it is inherently extremely unlikely that the same ambiguity existed in Sumerian as in Akkadian, viz. that the prefix ba- expressed some notion which corresponded both to the Akkadian perfect tense as well as something which corresponded to the reciprocal or separative or (in the case of the Št theme) passive sense of the Akkadian -t- themes. This distinction is, however, not made by von Soden.[42] The position held by Jacobsen is complicated by the fact that he regards the two uses of the -t- infix in Akkadian as essentially the same. He refers in the introduction to *MSL* IV (p. 6*) to 'the *t*-form, which seems roughly to denote participation in two contrasting spheres...' (and cf. p. 23*). The Akkadian forms are indiscriminately labelled 'perfect' (pp. 13*, 15*, 50*) or 'I.2', i.e. Gt, (pp. 18*, 34*, 47*). This is unsatisfactory, since the two uses of the -t- infix are in fact formally distinguished by the present tense of the Gt theme, and by the perfect tense of the same theme, where the -t- infix appears twice. We can fairly assume, then, that the ba- forms correspond to one or other of the two Akkadian possibilities, but not to both. Therefore the occurrence in OBGT VII of certain unmistakeable forms of the present tense of the *Gt theme* (52-9, 62-7, 145-54, 157-62, 203-210, 235-38, 265-70, 301-6) is in itself virtually sufficient to prove the point. The same is true of OBGT IX 103f., which must be emended to ik-ta-aš-<ša->da-ak-ka on the basis of the previous entry, *ikaššadakka* (101f.). This restoration was suggested above, p. 19.

41. In the Introduction to *MSL* IV, p. 6*, and, more fully, in *AS* 16, pp. 80f., n. 10. That is to say, for Jacobsen the vowel -u- following the element -m- connotes specifically "(ar)rest in/at the centre of the speaker's ken"; for me it is simply the form taken by the element -m- when followed by the -e- of the infixes for 2nd person singular and plural and by whatever is the notional infix for 1st person singular.

42. In 'Das akkadische t-Perfekt in Haupt- und Nebensätzen und sumerische Verbalformen mit den Präfixen ba-, imma- und u-', in *AS* 16 (1965), pp. 103-110.

Second, we have up till now several times mentioned the extremely systematic arrangement of the paradigms, and this may be seen to advantage in a text like OBGT VII, the more so if all the -t- forms are regarded as preterites of the Gt theme, in which case a symmetrical balance between present and preterite tenses results which would be destroyed if some of the preterites were re-labelled perfects. This balance may be seen in the earlier table (p. 13).

This conclusion is contrary to the views of the editors of *MSL* IV,[43] von Soden,[44] and Falkenstein.[45] It will follow from what was said earlier that -ma- in the groups (-)im-ma-, (-)àm-ma- and -em-ma- (also -mu- in (-)im-mu- and (-)àm-mu-) will also represent a form of ba- and thus be set against forms of the -t- themes. We must now consider the exceptions to this. Leaving aside those forms where the Akkadian has a form of N, Nt or Š stative, these are:

OBGT VIII	25	kas$_4$ du$_{11}$-ga-àm-ma-ši-íb	*šulsimaššum*
	26	kas$_4$ ga-àm-ma-ši-íb-du$_{11}$	(*lušalsimaššum*)
	27	kas$_4$ hé-em-ma-ši-íb-du$_{11}$	(*lišalsimaššum*)
	34	kas$_4$ du$_{11}$-ga-àm-mu-še	*šulsimam ana ṣērīya*
	35	kas$_4$ ga-àm-ma-ri-íb-du$_{11}$	(*lušalsimakkum*)
	36	kas$_4$ hé-em(text: a)-ma-ri-íb-du$_{11}$	(*lišalsimakkum*)
	49	kas$_4$ àm-mu-e-ši-íb-bé	*ilassumakkum*
	50	kas$_4$ àm-mu-e-ši-íb-bé-en	(*alassumakkum*)

VIII 34ff. should be compared with IX 64ff.:

64	sá du$_{11}$-ga-mu-še-éb	*šukšidam ana ṣērīya*
65	sá ga-mu-ri-íb-du$_{11}$	(*lušakšidakkum*)
66	sá hu-mu-ri-íb-du$_{11}$	(*lišakšidakkum*)

From these forms (which may be analyzed as e.g. ga+m+ri+b+du) it is clear that du$_{11}$-ga-àm-mu-še etc. do not in fact contain ba at all, but are simply deviant spellings, in the case of ga-àm/hé-em-ma-ri-íb- without vocalic assimilation. It is thus probable that the same is true of VIII 25-7, i.e. that these spellings represent not e.g. ga+m+ba+ši+b+du, but ga+m(a)+ši+b+du. Similarly VIII 49ff. may be compared with VII 60f.:

[mu-e-ši]-du	*illakakkum*
[mu-e-ši]-du-un	*allakakkum*

which represent m(a)+e+ši+du(+n). Thus VIII 49ff. probably represent not a+m+ba+e+ši+b+e(+n) but a+m+e+ši+b+e(+n).

These apparent exceptions to the principle that ba- (-ma-) is set against -t- themes do not, then, in fact contradict it. The other exceptions, where ba- or -ma- is set against non-indicative forms of the N theme (VI 58-72), preterites of the Nt theme (*ibid.* 160-5, 184-9 and 220) or statives of the Š theme (*ibid.*, 82-4, 88-90 and X 21-22), appear to reflect a quite separate use of the ba- which may be called stative. These forms are discussed below.

The rarest theme in the paradigms is the Nt. Von Soden specifically denied its existence.[46] Jacobsen marks the forms as IV$_2$, but since for him there is no real difference between the perfect tense and the -t- infix theme, there is for him no problem.[47] (Confusingly the same forms are described on p. 50* as I.2) The forms are as follows:

43. *V.* index *s.v. gamartum.*
44. In *AS* 16, pp. 103-111.
45. In *Grammatik der Sprache Gudeas von Lagasch* II (Rome, 1950), p. 185, n.3.
46. In *Grundriss der akkadischen Grammatik* (Rome, 1952), pp. 111f. §86b. But in the *Ergänzungsheft* (1969), p. 34** in paradigm 13, he allows it. In a stimulating recent article, 'Die sogenannten tan-Stämme des akkadischen Verbums und ihre semitischen Grundlagen', in *ZDMG* 131 (1981), pp. 9-27, G. Steiner puts the whole discussion on a new foundation.
47. Introduction to *MSL* IV, p. 47*.

OBGT VI	160	ba-gar	*ittaškan*
	161	ba-gar-re-en	*attaškan*
	162	ba-gar-re-en	*tattaškan*
	163	ba-na-gar	*ittaškan* <*šum*>
	164	ba-na-gar-re-en	(*attaškanšum*)
	165	ba-na-gar-re-en	(*tattaškanšum*)
	184	im-ma-[[an-]]gar	(*ittaškanam*)
	185	im-ma-gar-re-en	(*attaškanam*)
	186	im-ma-gar-re-en	(*tattaškanam*)
	187	im-ma-na-gar	*ittaškanaššum*
	188	im-ma-na-gar-re-en	(*attaškanaššum*)
	189	im-ma-na-gar-re-en	(*tattaškanaššum*)
	220	im-ma-ra-[[an-]]gar	*ittaškanakkum*

Quite clearly the features here set against the Nt theme (of which these forms are to be regarded as preterites) are the prefix ba- and the incorporation by suffix rather than by infix. Of course formally the preterite of the Nt is identical with that of the Ntn and with the perfect of the N theme (the same being the case with the D and Š themes), but it seems that we are dealing with a theme that has been especially concocted to set against certain Sumerian forms. We may legitimately conclude, from our earlier investigations, that ba- (-ma-) is here set against the infixed -t-; this then leaves the incorporation by suffix of the 'inert' as the feature marked by the use of an N theme. This accords exactly with what we should expect. (The form at 220, with infixed -n-, must be erroneous. im-ma-ra-gar, which occurs at 218, would be what we should expect here, while im-ma-ra-an-gar would make more sense at 218. Similarly the infixed -n- in 184 must have been erroneously introduced under influence from the preceding forms.) The likelihood of the occurrence of perfect tenses in the paradigms has already been shown to be minimal, and there is no feature present which could be equated with the -tan- infix of iteration. Thus these forms must be preterites of the Nt.

The forms set against the ordinary N theme are listed below. The restoration of *-šum* for *-šu* at VI 70 has already been discussed, above p. 19.

OBGT VI	58	gar-ba	*naškin*
	59	ga-ba-gar	(*lunnaškin*)
	60	ha-ba-gar	(*linnaškin*)
	61	gar-ba-na-ab	*naškinšum*
	62	ga-ba-na-gar	(*lunnaškinšum*)
	63	ha-ba-na-gar	(*linnaškinšum*)
	64	gar-àm-ma	*naškinam*
	65	ga-àm-ma-gar	(*lunnaškinam*)
	66	hé-em-ma-gar	(*linnaškinam*)
	67	gar-àm-ma-še-éb	*naškinaššum*
	68	ga-àm-ma-še-éb-gar	(*lunnaškinaššum*)
	69	hé-em-ma-še-éb-gar	(*linnaškinaššum*)
	70	gar-àm-ma-še	na-aš-ki-na-aš-šu <-um>
	71	ga-àm-ma-še-gar	(*lunnaškinaššum*)
	72	hé-em-ma-še-gar	(*linnaškinaššum*)
	221	ab-gar-re	*iššakkan*
	222	ab-gar-re	*iššakkan*
	223	an-na-gar-re	*iššakkanšum*
X	73	ba-ra-gub-bé	*innanziz*

Most of these are non-indicative forms. In some (67-69) there is a 3rd person singular infix which must mark the inert (since no other person is present). The feature against which the N theme is specifically set is then the prefix ba- (-ma-). This is the secondary, stative use of ba- noted above. This use has been called 'passive' by many grammarians, which is not really a suitable term for Sumerian. Further examples will be found among the forms set against the stative of the Š theme, discussed below under §1.2.4.

Finally the form ba-ra-gub-bé = *innanziz* (X 73) is completely mystifying. *innanziz* is unique, as *uzuzzum* does not normally have an N theme. It is analyzed by Poebel as 'the nasalising nif'al form of a secondary quadriliteral verb nz'z, derived from the old nif'al of **zâzu*'.[48] From the structure of the paradigm, we should have expected here ma-ab-gub-bé = *iz-za-a-az-za-am*.

We come now to consider the features which are equated with the Š theme in Akkadian. There are a great many such forms, and they will not all be quoted. Suffice it to say that with one exception they all contain the elements -ni-, bí- or -b-, and sometimes -ni-íb- or bí-íb-. (The exception is VIII 34, kas_4 du_{11}-ga-àm-mu-še = *šulsimam ana ṣērīya*, which is probably an error for du_{11}-ga-àm-mu-še-éb, as is shown by IX 64 sá du_{11}-ga-mu-še-éb = *šukšidam ana ṣērīya.*) In the Akkadian columns, forms such as *aškun* 'I placed' are contrasted with *ušaškin* 'I caused to place'. In the first of these the direct object is unspecified; in the second, both the direct object and what we may call the instrumental agent (the person whom I caused to do the placing) are unspecified. Since both of these would in Akkadian stand in the accusative case, forms like *ušaškiššu* or *ušaškikka* with accusative pronoun complements are technically ambiguous. Do they mean 'I caused (someone) to place him (it, you), ' or 'I caused him (you) to place (something, someone)'? This is one of the complications which face us. Consider these examples from letters of the period of the verbal paradigm texts.[49]

11, 11-13	ṭup-pa-ti ši-na-ti /a-na PN /šu-bi-il-ši-na-ti 'Send these tablets to PN', that is 'Cause (someone) to carry them'.
64, rev.5	šu-re-eš-š[i-n]a-ti-ma 'Escort them (the girls)', that is 'Cause (someone) to lead them'.
76, 6	m[a-a]s-sú-nu lu-ša-am-ši-šu-nu-ti-[ma] 'I want to make them forget their own country' lit. 'their country - I want to cause them to forget (it)'.

In general in the verbal paradigms, the latter interpretation is the only one possible with intransitive verbs (e.g. *ušalsimšu* 'I caused him to run'), while with transitive verbs the former is more likely; but sometimes it is not possible to know.

There are of course many verb forms listed to which no corresponding causative form is to be found. Our investigation will be confined in the main to those forms extant in both types, since it is thereby easier to isolate the elements associated with causation. In the Sumerian causative forms, as was said, the infix -ni- is the distinguishing mark of the vast majority which sets them aside from the non-causative forms. The traditional designation of this infix[50] is as a third person infix picking up nouns standing in the so-called locative-terminative case in -e. Many examples of the opposition between non-causative and causative may be cited. Also to be noted in the causative forms is a slight preference for marking the third person cause by -b- rather than -n-. This will be discussed later.

ma-ši-	ma-ši-ni-
ma-ši-in-	ma-ši-ni-in-
ma-ra-	ma-ra-ni-
ma-ra-an-	ma-ra-ni-in/íb-

48. In *AS* 9, p. 145. Two of the alleged occurrences of the N theme of *uzuzzum* listed by von Soden in *AHw* are to be assigned to the substantive *nanzazum*, see *CAD s.v.* The phrase *la na-an- za-az iluš i-di-i[š-šu]* (*PBS* 1/1 2:25; OB lit.) is more difficult. *CAD* (*s.v. ilu* p. 96) reads *nanzas* (for *nanzaz* + *šu* ?) and translates 'his god does not stand by him'. B. Groneberg too takes *nanzaz* here as a stative (*Untersuchungen zur hymnisch-epischen Dialekt der altbabylonischen literarischen Texte*, Münster 1972, p. 119); but this should probably be regarded as a deviant form of the G stative *nazuz, nanzuz*.

49. All taken from G. Dossin, *Archives royales de Mari*, I. Correspondance de Šamši-Addu (Paris, 1945).

50. See e.g. Poebel, *GSG*, sections 494-6; Falkenstein, *Das Sumerische*, p. 48, section 33, 3 b 2.

ma-	ma-ni-
ma-an-	ma-ni-in/íb-
mu-da-	mu-di-ni-
mu-da-an-	mu-di-ni-in/íb-
mu-na-	mu-na-ni-
mu-na-an-	mu-na-ni-in/íb-
mu-	mu-ni-
mu-un-	mu-ni-in-, mi-ni-in-
in-da-	in-di-ni-(íb-)
in-na-	in-na-ni-
im-ma-da-(an-)	im-ma-di-ni-in-
im-ma-na-	im-ma-na-ni-
im-ma-na-an-	im-ma-na-ni-in/íb-
im-ma-ra-(an-)	im-ma-ra-ni-in-
im-ma-	im-ma-ni-
im-ma-an-	im-ma-ni-in/íb-
ba-na-	ba-na-ni-
ba-na-an-	ba-na-ni-in/íb-
an-na-	an-na-ni-
ba-da-	ba-di-ni-
ba-da-an-	ba-di-ni-in/íb-
ba-	ba-ni-
ba-an-	ba-ni-in/íb-
i-ra-(an-)	i-ra-ni-in-
mu-ra-an-	mu-ra-ni-in-

The presence of -ni- appears generally to affect -da- to become -di- and sometimes mu- to become mi-, but there is no reason to suppose that these are anything but phonetically conditioned changes, *pace* Jacobsen's division into an a- and an i- series.[51] In the above causative forms (righthand column), the infix -n- seems to mark the third person agent or cause (English subject): this conclusion follows from the fact that it is absent in the parallel forms set against 1st and 2nd person Akkadian forms (i.e. forms with 1st or 2nd person subjects). Now, however, consider the following:

ga-mu-ra-ab-	ga-mu-ra-ni-íb-
ga/hu-mu-un-na-ab-	gá/hu-mu-na-ni-íb-
ga/hé-na-ab-	ga/hé-na-ni-íb-
ga/ha-ra-ab-	ga-ha-ra-ni-íb-
ga/hu-mu-ra-ab-	ga/hu-mu-ra-ni-íb-
ga-àm-	ga-mu-ni-íb-
hé-em-	hu-mu-ni-íb-
-ma-ab	-mu-ni-íb
-mu-na-ab	-mu-na-ni-íb
-ra-na-ab	-ra-na-ni-íb
-ma-ab	-ma-ni-íb

Once again certain phonetic changes appear to result from the presence of -ni-, e.g. -m- followed by -ni- apears as -mu-, once also as -ma-, but the principal difference is that in the non-indicative forms of whatever person, whether -b- is present in the non-causative form or not, -b- *does* appear in the causative. This is what Jacobsen called 'all-person -b-'.[52] In a causative verbal form, three persons (or two and one object) are present, what in English we should call, in the active form, subject or agent, instrumental agent and direct object. Clearly

51. In 'About the Sumerian Verb', in *Toward the Image of Tammuz*, pp. 259ff.
52. In the introduction to *MSL* IV, pp. 43*ff.

the -b- does not refer to the subject here (in Sumerian the cause). Nor does it refer to the instrumental agent, since that is the function of -ni-. Then it must refer to the object (inert): 'let me cause him to place (*it*)'. It is interesting that not all of the Akkadian forms set against those just listed bear the accusative suffix *-šu*. The conclusion from this must be that in these forms (presumably in fact in all the non-indicative forms) a form of incorporation is used in which the inert is incorporated by infix, and therefore cause, where marked, by suffix; rather than that evidently used in the indicative forms set against Akkadian preterites, where the *cause* is incorporated by infix (and the inert by suffix).

ga-na-ab-gar	= *luškunšum*
I desire + for him + it + be placed	= let me place (it) for him
ga-na-ni-íb-gar	= *lušaškiššum*
I desire + for him_1 + thro' him_2 + it + be placed	= let me cause (him_2) to place (it) for him_1.

Before we go on to discuss the other means of marking causation in Sumerian, there are certain forms that need explaining:

OBGT VI	25	gar-ma-da-ab	28	gar-ma-ni-íb
	26	ga-àm-da-gar	29	ga-ma-ni-íb-gar
	27	hé-em-da-gar	30	hé-ma-ni-íb-gar
	7	gar-ra-an-da	10	gar-ra-ni-íb
	8	ga-an-da-gar	11	ga-ni-íb-gar
	9	hé-en-da-gar	12	he-ni-íb-gar
X	3	gub-an-da	4	gub-an-ni-íb

The above all exhibit the same peculiarity: in the causative forms (righthand column), although -ni- is introduced, -da- disappears. The non-causative forms are set against *šukuššu, šuknaššu, izissu* etc., so -da- is quite clearly equated with the third person singular pronoun complement *-šu* representing the person or thing placed (the inert). In the corresponding causative forms (*šuškiššu, šuškinaššu, šuzissu* etc.) the *-šu* still represents the inert him (it) which is 'caused to be placed'; but in the Sumerian this now appears as the infix -b-. -b- cannot in the circumstances represent anything else. So -(n)da- is used in the non-causative forms, perhaps for some sort of emphasis, and in non-indicative forms the infix -b- is used to mark the inert.

One further group of forms can be eliminated from the discussion. These are the forms set against the Š theme of the stative (VI 82-4, 88-90, 94-6; X 20, 22). They will be discussed below under tenses (§1.2.4). Essentially, the stative form of the Š theme is not properly causative in meaning, and so we should not expect to find any specifically causative elements in the Sumerian.

In discussing causatives in which the causative aspect is not signalled by -ni-, certain factors must be taken into account. One, alluded to above, is the nature of the meaning of the Akkadian verbs against which they are set. Causatives occur with the verbs *šakānum* (OBGT VI), *lasāmum* (VIII), *kašādum* (IX) and *uzuzzum* (X), but not with *alākum* (VII). Of these, *alākum*, *lasāmum* and (one would have thought) *uzuzzum* are intransitive, and the others transitive, although *uzuzzum* is treated sometimes as if it too were transitive. This makes a difference to the meaning of the causative forms, especially to that of those with suffixed accusative pronouns. Consider the following:

iškun	'he placed'
ušaškin	'he caused (someone) to place'
ikšud	'he reached'
ušakšid	'he caused (someone) to reach'
ilsum	'he ran'
ušalsim	'he caused (someone) to run'
izziz	'he stood', 'he was standing'
ušziz	'he caused (someone) to stand'

and:

iškunšu	'he placed him (it)'
ušaškinšu	'he caused (someone) to place him (it)'
luškikka	'let me place you'
lušaškikka	'let me cause you to place' (VI 52)
ikšussu	'he reached him (it)'
ušakšissu	'he caused (someone) to reach him'
lušalsimšu	'let me cause him to run'
izzissu	meaning?
ušzissu	'he caused him to stand'

Even within the same verb, variation may be found: VI 11 ga-ni-íb-gar = *lušaškiššu* 'let me cause him to place', 115 in-di-ni-íb-gar = *ušaškiššu* 'he caused (someone) to place him'.

Another factor is the nature of the Sumerian verbs involved. gar and gub are simple verbs; but kas_4...du_{11} and sá...du_{11} are verbal phrases in which a noun carrying the verbal idea is closely associated with a verb of general meaning ('do' or 'effect' running or reaching). In one type of incorporation these verbs habitually mark the presence of the noun in the verbal complex by the 3rd person infix -n-/-b-. Thus VIII 38 kas_4 ab-bé-en = *alassum* 'I run' is literally 'running — I do it'. Similarly IX 96 sá an-e-en = *akaššad* 'I reach' is literally 'reaching — I achieve it'. This is bound to affect the incorporation of other elements in the sentence, as will be seen.

The following causative forms are *not* constructed with -ni- (causatives in the righthand column):

OBGT VI	103ff.	bí-(in-)	106ff.	bí-íb-
VII	58f.	mu-ri-(in-)	62f.	mu-ri-íb-
	60f.	im-ma-ri-(in-)	64f.	im-ma-ri-íb-
IX	79ff.	bí-(in-)	82ff.	bí-íb-
	120f.	im-ma-ri-(in-)	122f.	im-ma-ri-íb-
	128f.	mu-ri-(in-)	131f.	mu-ri-íb- (131 mu-ri- exceptionally)

A consideration of these suggests that the infix -ni- cannot be used when bí- or -ri- is already present; that is to say, that -ni-, bí- and -ri- are features of the same *rank*, to use Jacobsen's terminology.[53] In these cases, the only possible recourse in Sumerian is to the second type of incorporation, with inert appearing as -b-.

OBGT VI	1	-ra (i.e. -i)	4	-bí-íb
	2	ga-	5	ga-bí-íb-
	3	hé-	6	hé-bí-íb-
VIII	1	-ga-ab	7	-ga-bí-íb
	2	ga-ab-	8	ga-bí-íb-
	3	hé-éb-	9	he-bí-íb-
	19	-ga-àm-še	25	-ga-àm-ma-ši-íb
	20	ga-àm-ši-	26	ga-àm-ma-ši-íb-
	21	hé-em-ši-	27	hé-em-ma-ši-íb-
IX	1	-ga-ab	7	-ga-bí-íb
	2	ga-ab-	8	ga-bí-íb-
	3	hé-éb-	9	hé-bí-íb-
	16	-ga-àm[[-me]]	19	-ga-àm-mi-íb
	17	ga-àm-	20	ga-àm-mi-íb-
	18	hé-em-	21	hé-em-mi-íb-
X	1	-ba (i.e. -i)	2	-bí-íb
	26	í-	27	bí-in-, 28 bí-íb-
	67	in-	69	bí-íb-

53. *V.* 'About the Sumerian Verb', in *Toward the Image of Tammuz*, p. 245.

If we consider the structure of some of these non-causative prefix chains (lefthand column) it will be apparent that if -ni- were added it would be in initial or virtual initial position (preceded only by the modal preformatives ga- or hé-). Instead bí- is used. We can therefore tentatively formulate a rule that bí- is an allomorph of -ni- in initial position. Since the writing -mmi- represents -m + bi, we can assume that bí- is inserted for -ni- after -m- also.

Finally we have to consider how causation is expressed when -ni-, bí- or -ri- is already present, e.g. VI 103f. In these, the cause is marked by an infix (long vowel, -e- or -n-). The inert is therefore notionally marked by a suffix, but as there is no suffix of the third person, it is not apparent. (I placed [it], I did [running], I effected [reaching]). In the corresponding causative forms, the infix is regularly -b- whatever the subject of the Akkadian forms. (The two or three exceptions to this, IX 127, 131, 136, are probably irregularities.) This indicates, as has been said before, that the infix no longer refers to the cause of the action, but that a different form of incorporation must be operating, in which the infix marks the inert. It has already been shown that in these causative forms the instrumental agent is marked by the infix -ni-, where this is present. We conclude that where the infix is not present, or where it is already present in the non-causative in a form such as bí- in some other function, the instrumental agent is not marked. The cause will now notionally be expressed by the suffix, but it will be noted that for some reason the cause is not marked, so that in the indicative forms of this type there is no variation in the Sumerian for the different persons of the Akkadian verb. The exceptions which prove this rule are VI 107-8 and 110-11. In the non-indicative forms, of course, the preformatives ga- and hé- make the person of the cause clear.

So sometimes the difference in the mode of incorporaton is all that distinguishes a causative from a non-causative. Consider now these forms from OBGT VIII:

7	kas$_4$ du$_{11}$-ga-bí-íb	*šulsim*	'cause (someone) to run'
10	kas$_4$ du$_{11}$-ga-ni-íb	*šulsimšu*	'cause him to run'
8	kas$_4$ ga-bí-íb-du$_{11}$	(*lušalsim*)	'let me cause (someone) to run'
11	kas$_4$ ga-ni-íb-du$_{11}$	(*lušalsimšu*)	'let me cause him to run'

This makes it look as if another difference between -ni- and bí- is one of meaning: that -ni- is more definite and perhaps less remote than -bí-. Now, could the same distinction be drawn between -n- and -b-? Jacobsen's distinction between 'singular ergative -n-' and 'plural (or neuter) -b-', presumably derived from the possessive suffixes -ani 'his, her' and -bi 'its, their', seems inappropriate here, although he was able to cite ample evidence for the observance of their distinction in literary texts.[54] Consider:

OBGT IX	120 sá im-ma-ri-in-du$_{11}$	*iktašdakkum*	'he reached you'
	123 sá im-ma-ri-íb-du$_{11}$	*uštakšidakka*	'he caused (someone) to reach you'
			OR 'he caused you to reach someone/something

i.e. literally:

120 'reaching + at you + by him + was effected (+ it)', and

123 'reaching + at you + it + was effected (+ by someone, caused by him)'

OR

123 'reaching + thro' you + it + was effected (+ caused by him)'

(The bracketed elements are not expressed in the Sumerian.) This makes it look as if Sumerian is being made to say 'he effected reaching at you' for 'he reached you' but '...effected reaching at you' for 'he caused (someone) to reach you' or, taken the other way, '...effected reaching through you', for 'he caused you to reach (someone, something)'.

All in all, the Sumerian of the causative sections of the paradigms is complicated and awkward. We can only say that the Babylonian grammarians seem to have tried to force Sumerian into a straitjacket by devising un-idiomatic forms which would correspond to those of the complex and productive causative system possessed by their own language. Sumerian

54. *V.* introduction to *MSL* IV, p. 40* and *AS* 16 pp. 93f., n. 16.

has no specific 'causative' morphemes, but expresses instrumental agency where necessary by means of instrumental or locative infixes. Often it does not incorporate into the verb all the persons present in an action.

1.2.3 Moods

It is not necessary to devote much space to describing the use in the paradigms of the various Akkadian moods. The forms occurring are indicative, imperative, volitive, cohortative and optative. Without exception, Akkadian optatives (*li-* etc) are set against Sumerian forms with hé- (ha-, hu-); Akkadian volitives and cohortatives against Sumerian forms with preformative ga-; and Akkadian imperatives against Sumerian forms of the 2nd person imperative. All other forms are set against Akkadian indicatives.

1.2.4 Tenses

We come now to investigate the patterns according to which the various Akkadian indicative tenses were equated with certain Sumerian verbal constructions in the paradigms, and the regularity with which these patterns are maintained. By 'tenses' are here meant the Akkadian present-future, preterite and stative. The use of the word tense is in no way tendentious. It is used simply as the normal and convenient term. The perfect tense does not occur in the texts; at least, it has been shown that those forms with -t- infix which occur are to be regarded as preterites of the themes with -t- infix, not perfects of the themes without infix. The occurrence of the various tenses in our corpus is as follows:

G	present	preterite	stative
Gt	present	preterite	
Š	present	preterite	stative
Št	present	preterite	
N	present (OBGT VI, NGBT VIII)		stative (NBGT VIII)
Nt		preterite (OBGT VI)	
D	present (OBGT III)	preterite (OBGT III)	stative (OBGT III)

Forms of the N, Nt and D are, as indicated, confined to a certain few texts, including some outside the group of big paradigms on which we have so far concentrated our attention, so examples will be taken from these also (viz. OBGT III, NBGT VIII).

It is most convenient to deal first with the stative. Certain problems arise here in connection with the interpretation of the Akkadian forms. According to von Soden,[55] the stative of the basic (G) theme expresses an intransitive or passive state or condition, as *paris* 'it is decided', *dummuqat* 'she is made good' etc. In the case of verbs which are normally transitive, it can also have a transitive sense, as *ahiz*, not 'he is in the possession of (someone)' but 'he has in his possession', *kašdū* 'they have reached, obtained', *lamdū* 'they have learnt, they know'. In general, the stative of other themes is used only when those stems already have a specific nuance semantically different from that of the G theme, as *šūṣâku* 'I have leased' from *waṣûm* 'to go forth'. The phrase *(bukānam) šūtuq* 'it has been caused to pass over (the *bukānum*)', very common in commercial documents to denote completion of a contract, may be compared. The transitive sense can also be present as *puhhurūšunūti* 'they have collected them together', *šaṣṣurāti* (Old Assyrian) 'you are having (so-and-so) watched'. For the passive meaning of the N stem, the G stative is generally used, as *immahiṣ* 'he was struck', *mahiṣ* 'he is struck', though the N stative may be used where a specific nuance exists or where the N form is basic; otherwise it may be used as a stylistic variation, thus *nalbušāku* = *labšāku* (in its reflexive sense only ['I get dressed, wear'], not in its transitive ['I clothe']). The Š theme is described by von Soden as forming in some verbs a factitive form from the (intransitive) sense of the G stative, as *šakin* 'it is situated', *šuškunum* 'to site, settle'; *tariṣ* 'it is extended', *šutruṣum* 'to extend'. The question to which it is difficult to find an answer is whether the stative *šuškun* then means very much different from *šakin*.[56] These very forms occur in our texts. The forms at present under consideration are as follows:

55. *V. GAG*, §77, pp. 100f.

56. The article by M.B. Rowton, 'The use of the permansive in Classic Babylonian', in *JNES* 21 (1962), pp. 233-303, while collecting together much material, is not organized in such a way as to answer this question.

OBGT VI	79	an-gar	*šakin*
	80	an-gar-re-en	(*šaknāku*)
	81	an-gar-re-en	(*šaknāta*)
	82	ba-ab-gar	*šuškun*
	83	ba-ab-gar-re-en	(*šuškunāku*)
	84	ba-ab-gar-re-en	(*šuškunāta*)
	85	an-da-gar	*šakiššu*
	86	an-da-gar-re-en	*šaknākšu* (text: ša-ak-na-ak-ku)
	87	an-da-gar-re-en	*šaknāssu*
	88	ba-da-ab-gar	*šuškunšu*
	89	ba-da-ab-gar-re-en	(*šuškunākšu*)
	90	ba-da-ab-gar-re-en	(*šuškunāssu*)
	91	an-na-gar	*šakiššum*
	92	an-na-gar-re-en	(*šaknākšum*)
	93	an-na-gar-re-en	(*šaknāssum*)
	94	an-na-ni-íb-gar	(*šuškunšum*)
	95	an-na-ni-íb-gar-re-en	(*šuškunākšum*)
	96	an-na-ni-íb-gar-re-en	(*šuškunāssum*)
	97	ab-gar	*šakin*
	98	a-gar	(*šaknāku*)
	99	e-gar	(*šaknāta*)
	208	ma-gar	*šaknam*
	209	a-ra-gar	*šakikkum* (text: ša-ak-na-ak-kum)
	210	a-ra-gar-re-en	*šaknākkum*
IX	105	sá an-du$_{11}$	*kašid*
	106	sá a-du$_{11}$	[[ka]] (*kašdāku*)
	107	sá e-du$_{11}$	(*kašdāta*)
X	20	an-gub	*nazuz*
	21	ba-ab-gub	*šuzuz* (text: šu-zi-iz)
	22	ba-da-ab-gub	*šuzussu*
	23	an-na-gub	*nazussum*
	24	an-na-ni-íb-gub	*šuzussum*
	25	ab-gub	*nazuz*
III	58-9	gi-dub-ba-zu e-da-gál	*našiāta*
	60	mu-da-gál	*našiāku*
	61	an-da-gál	*naši*
	62	nu-e-da-gál	*ul našiāti*
	63	nu-mu-da-gál	*ul našiāku*
	64	nu-an-da-gál	*ul naši*
	151	al-húl-húl-[en]	[*ubbuṭ*]*āku*
	152	nu-húl-húl-[en]	[*ūl*]*a ubbuṭāku*
	160	al-gar-gar$^{ga\text{-}ga\text{-}ra}$	*nuppuh*
	161	nu-gar-gar	*ūla nuppuh*
	164	al-zi-in-zi-im	*nuṭṭup* (text: nu-ṭù-úh)
	165	nu-zi-in-zi-im	*ūla nuṭṭup* (text: ú-la nu-ṭù-úh)
	166-7	al-zi-in-zi-im-me-en	*nuṭṭupāku*
		nu-zi-in-zi-im-me-en	*ūla nuṭṭupāku*
	168	al-gú-gú	*pussul*
	169	al-sa-sa	*zuqqut*
	170	šu an-tál	*qātam pete*
	171-2	šu-ni al-íl	*qātāšu zanbilā*
	191	da-ra an-šub	*baṭi*[*l*]
	192	da-ra e-šub	*baṭ*[*lāta*]
	193	da-ra a-šub	*baṭ*[*lāku*]

IV	iv 4'	sá ab-du$_{11}$	*kašid* (text: ši id ka)
XII	13	ka-mu šu àm-bar	*pīya wuššur*
	14-15	ka-mu ab-ša$_6$-ge	*pīya ṭâb*
	16-17	ka-mu al-ša$_6$-ša$_6$	

(I take 16-17 as a correction of the irregular ab-ša$_6$-ge. Hence the blank in the right-hand column.)

NBGT VIII	2	[da]-da-ra a-dù	*nenzuhāku* (text: šu-zu-ha-ku)
	3	da-da-ra e-dù	*nenzuhāta* (text: šu-zu-ha-ta)
	4	da-da-ra an-dù	*nenzuh* (text: nen-su-uh)

There is clearly an equation here between the Akkadian stative and a Sumerian prefix whose form for the moment can be listed as a-. There are exceptions to this, principally in the Š forms; and as we shall see, the prefix a- is also translated by the Akkadian present tense.

The full form of the prefix, when it stands alone before the verb, appears to be al-. This is shortened to a- before:

-n- -b- -m- -nda- -nna- -ra-
and -first person infix-.

Before the 'infixes' -e- and -eda- it disappears; and it is incompatible with
nu-
ma- (= -m- initially)
and mu-da- (= -m- + first person infix + da).

In view of the fact that -e- and -e-da- are ordinarily *only* infixes it is better to regard e- and e-da- as writings for *a-e and *a-e-da-. ma- and mu-da- are prefixes, and nu- a preformative, and a- is of the same rank as both.

We may then state the prefix as al- before the verb itself, a- before infixes (with the proviso that *a-e- is written as e-) and add that it is incompatible with nu- and initial forms of -m-.[57]

Apart from the cases where al- is absent because of the presence of nu- or -m-, there are a number where not al- but ba- occurs in the Sumerian. These are all set against forms of the Š stative and were mentioned above in §1.2.2, p. 28, and again on p. 32 (for absence of causative element). These forms share with certain others set against Akkadian N themes a ba- which is not represented by an infixed -t- in the Akkadian. We concluded that here a different use of ba- is reflected from the 'separative' ba- of ba-gen = *ittalak* 'he went away'; it is the ba- of ba-hul 'it was destroyed', i.e. a stative ba-.[58] This is well known from literary and historical texts, and has been called passive; but passive is not an appropriate term for the Sumerian. The fact that it can also occur in ba-ab-gar = *šuškun* ('he has been placed, is standing') suggests that the precise nuance expressed is a state resulting from the action of *some agent unknown or unmentioned* as opposed to, say, Akkadian *šakin* 'is situated' which leaves the question of agency out of it altogether. This squares exactly with what we know from pairs of year names such as

mu ^{d}amar-^{d}suen ur-bí-lum^{ki} mu-hul-a 'Year when Amar-Suen destroyed Urbilum'
mu ur-bí-lum^{ki} ba-hul 'Year when Urbilum was destroyed'.[59]

It is possibly for this reason, the suggestion of the presence of an agent, that the stative of the Š theme is used in the Akkadian. It is clear, anyway, from what we already know of Sumerian, that *šuškun* in the Akkadian of our texts must be passive, and *cannot* be intended to mean 'he is settling, has sited' (transitive). Now suffixed forms of these statives also occur. The paradigm of *uzuzzum* (OBGT X) makes sense if we can understand it as meaning 'stand over, guard', as Poebel has suggested.[60] But what are we to make of these forms:

---

57. But cf. nu-ul-til (translated as *ul ašib*) in a 1st millennium text (bilingual cult song), *4R* 11 39f.
58. The term 'stative' is here borrowed from Akkadian grammar. I use it to mean 'describing a state or condition'.
59. *V.* A Ungnad *s.v.* 'Datenlisten' in *RlA* II pp. 131-195, esp. p. 143, no. 69.
60. In *AS* 9, pp. 192-6.

OBGT VI	85	an-da-gar	*šakiššu*
	86	an-da-gar-re-en	*šaknākšu*
	87	an-da-gar-re-en	*šaknāssu* (i.e. *šaknāt(a)* + *šu*)
	88	ba-da-ab-gar	*šuškunšu*
	89	ba-da-ab-gar-re-en	*šuškunākšu*
	90	ba-da-ab-gar-re-en	*šuškunāssu*

—if, as has been demonstrated, these statives (or at least certainly the Š ones) are to be understood as intransitive or passive: 'he is situated (him)', 'you have been placed (him)' etc.? The equation of -da- and -nda- with the suffixed *-šu* elsewhere in this text and in OBGT X has already been described (*supra* p. 20) and the use of the feature in these intransitive forms must be the result of a desire for completeness. It is difficult to see how it could make sense in Akkadian.

The forms of verb used in the examples listed above are gar, du_{11}, gub, gál, húl-húl, gar-gar (for the commoner kár-kár), zi-in-zi-im, gú-gú, sa-sa, tál, íl, bar, $ša_6$-$ša_6$ and dù, i.e. apparently all simple "*hamṭu*" forms, sometimes with free reduplication (represented by the Akkadian D theme). *Hamṭu* is certain in the cases of du_{11} (IX 105ff.) and húl-húl (III 151ff.); for gar the question is not entirely clear, since the text OBGT VI does not use the form gá-gá at all. (The terms *hamṭu* and *marû* are discussed in detail in sections 3.6 and 4 below).

The type of incorporation used depends to some extent on the meaning of the verb. First, attention may be directed to those forms which are translated by Š statives but which have in Sumerian not ba- but *a- with infix -ni-* (OBGT VI 94-6, X 24). These are almost certainly forms concocted so as to make them different from the forms equated with the corresponding G stative forms, as the infix -ni- is here clearly taken as an equivalent of the Š theme even though, as has been demonstrated, the specifically causative sense of the Š theme is absent from the statives which occur here.

The types of incorporation used are three. First, the personal element may be infixed. This is found in the following cases:

OBGT VI	97	ab-gar	*šakin*
	98	a-gar	*šaknāku*
	99	e-gar	*šaknāta*
IX	105	sá an-du_{11}	*kašid*
	106	sá a-du_{11}	*kašdāku*
	107	sá e-du_{11}	*kašdāta*
III	191	da-ra an-šub	*baṭil*
	192	da-ra e-šub	*baṭlāta*
	193	da-ra a-šub	*baṭlāku*
NBGT VIII	4	da-da-ra an-dù	*nenzuh*
	2	da-da-ra a-dù	*nenzuhāku*
	3	da-da-ra e-dù	*nenzuhāta*

If the infix here represented the inert, the cause would be represented by a suffix, which in the third person would be -e. Thus here the infix must represent the *cause* and these forms must mean 'he puts', 'I put', 'you put', 'he reaches' etc. If these forms are correct Sumerian and if the translation of them by Akkadian statives is correct, then these must be *transitive statives*. However, it should be noted that while Sumerian da-da-ra...dù and da-ra...šub, being compound verbs, are constructed in Sumerian with both cause and inert (where the inert is the nominal part of the compound), they are rendered, because of their meaning, by the Akkadian statives *nenzuh* 'he is girded' and *baṭil* 'he is idle, has stopped' (intransitive).

Second, the personal element may be suffixed, with no infix. These occur as follows:

OBGT VI	85	an-da-gar	*šakiššu*
	86	an-da-gar-re-en	*šaknākšu*
	87	an-da-gar-re-en	*šaknāssu*
	91	an-na-gar	*šakiššum*

	92	an-na-gar-re-en	*šaknākšum*
	93	an-na-gar-re-en	*šaknāssum*
	209	a-ra-gar	*šakikkum*
	210	a-ra-gar-re-en	*šaknākkum*
III	164	al-zi-in-zi-im	*nuṭṭup*
	165	nu-zi-in-zi-im	*ūla nuṭṭup*
	166-7	al-zi-in-zi-im-me-en	*nuṭṭupāku*
		nu-zi-in-zi-im-me-en	*la nuṭṭupāku*

Here we may conclude that these forms are suffixed to mark the person of the inert, as, if the cause were intended, the third person would end in -e. From the arrangement it is clear that the forms without endings are to be taken as third person. The sense of the statives by which these are translated must therefore be intransitive, 'he is situated', or passive, 'he is torn out'.

Third, forms may carry both an infix and a (clear) suffix. Such are:

OBGT VI	79	an-gar	*šakin*
	80	an-gar-re-en	*šaknāku*
	81	an-gar-re-en	*šaknāta*
	82	ba-ab-gar	*šuškun*
	83	ba-ab-gar-re-en	*šuškunāku*
	84	ba-ab-gar-re-en	*šuškunāta*
	88	ba-da-ab-gar	*šuškunšu*
	89	ba-da-ab-gar-re-en	*šuškunākšu*
	90	ba-da-ab-gar-re-en	*šuškunāssu*
	94	an-na-ni-íb-gar	*šuškunšum*
	95	an-na-ni-íb-gar-re-en	*šuškunākšum*
	96	an-na-ni-ib-gar-re-en	*šuškunāssum*
X	21	ba-ab-gub	*šuzuz*
	22	ba-da-ab-gub	*šuzussu*

From the arrangement, again, it is clear that the forms without the ending are to be understood as third person singular inert. The possible significance of the infixed cause has already been discussed. However, its use in the forms an-gar, an-gar-re-en = *šakin*, *šaknāku/šaknāta* is not clear: we should have expected al-gar, al-gar-re-en.

The remaining cases are all rendered by Akkadian third person singular forms and either have neither infix nor suffix (in which case they may be taken as third singular inert; these are not listed) or are exceptional, as follows:

OBGT X	20	an-gub	*nazuz*
	25	ab-gub	*nazuz*
III	170	šu an-tál	*qātam pete*
IV	iv 4'	sá ab-du$_{11}$	*kašid*

The paradigm of *uzuzzum* treats the Akkadian as if it were a transitive verb and the Sumerian forms are regularly infixed for what must be cause, so I assume these are so also. The other two forms may be compared with OBGT IX 105, III 191, and NBGT VIII 4 (discussed above), i.e. they carry an infix for cause and a (notional) suffix for inert, and šu an-tál is translated by the intransitive Akkadian *qātam pete* (literally) 'he is open as to the hand', 'he is liberal'.

In summary, Sumerian forms translated by Akkadian statives may be listed as follows:

a) Forms with prefix a- and a cause infix. These are set against the transitive sense of the stative, although in the case of compound verbs, equation with a stative of intransitive meaning may be more appropriate.

b) Forms with prefix a- or al- and an inert suffix. These are set against statives of the more usual intransitive or passive meaning.

c) Forms with prefix ba-, or a- (with or without -ni-), third person cause infix, and inert suffix. These are generally set against forms of the Š stative and are presumably to be understood as expressing a state resulting from the action of some (unspecified) third person. They may be compared with certain rare classical Greek perfects. The normal Greek perfect expresses a state resulting from the action of the person concerned, as οἶδα I know (because I found out), ἥκω I am here (because I came), τέθνηκα I am dead (because I died). The rare cases are likewise active in form, but the meaning is different: πέπηγα I am fixed (because someone has fixed me), διέφθορα I am undone (because someone has destroyed me), τέτηκα I have melted (intransitive), cf. τέτηχα I have melted (transitive). The genuineness of this last group of Sumerian forms, especially those with infixed -ni-, is suspect.

So far as can be determined, the use of the *hamṭu* base with all these forms is regular.

In investigating the forms set against Akkadian preterite and present, we shall again be looking at three criteria:

a) choice of verbal base i.e. *hamṭu* or *marû*, where appropriate,
b) form of incorporation used, and
c) choice of prefix.

Inprimis, we may look at a special use of the Akkadian present, when it is preceded by *lā* and functions as a 2nd or 3rd person negative imperative: 'don't...' or 'he is not to...'. These forms are absent from OBGT VI-X, the big paradigms. They occur as follows:

OBGT III	89	na-ab-dím-me	*lā ippeš*
	92	na-ab-dím-e-ne	*lā ippešū*
	93	na-an-[na-]ab-dím-e	*lā ippessum* (text: [[ni]]-ip-pe-su-um)
	98	na-an-na-ab-dím-e-ne	*lā ippešūšum*
	157	na-an-ha-ha-e-ne	*lā utebbeṭū*
	158-9	nam-mu-un-ha-ha-en[61]	*lā tutebbeṭanni*
	163	na-an-gar-gar	*lā inappah* (text: i-na-pi-ih)
	228-9	sag si-sá na-an-na-ak-en	*lā tešêr*
	237	na-an-ni-ib-ti-ti	[*lā*] *ureššešu*
OBGT V	4	na-an-na-te-ge$_x$-dè-en	*lā teṭehhišum*
	5	nam-ma-te-ge$_x$-dè-en	*lā taṭehhiam*
XV	8	na-an-na-ab-gur-re	*lā tutâršum*
	30	a-ša-an-gàr nam-ak	*lā tušaggaranni*
	32	la-ba$^{!}$an-gi$_4$-gi$_4$-me-a[61a]	*lā tumteki*
NBGT VIII	5	zà na-ba-e-dù	*lā tennezzih*
	6	zà na-mu-ni-dù	*lā innezzih* (text: en-ne-ez-zi-ih)

The Sumerian is na- with cause suffixed (-e(n), -e or -ene) and *marû* verb. ha-ha 'to burst (out laughing?)' is treated as *marû* of húl-húl 'to be joyful' and te-g 'to approach' is here used with -ed- which requires the *marû* form. The exceptions to this are:

OBGT III	163	(cited immediately above)
XV	30, 32	
NBGT VIII	5, 6	

The form la-ba$^{!}$-an-gi$_4$-gi$_4$-me-a looks altogether confused. The forms na-an-gar-gar and nam-ak carry no suffix, while na-ba-e-dù and na-mu-ni-dù appear to be infixed instead. But as NBGT VIII is only a practice tablet we need not pay too much attention to the forms therein.

For the ordinary present tense, we may look first at OBGT VI-X.

---

61. Thus Poebel's copy (*PBS* V 142) *pace* the printed text in *MSL* IV.

61a. See p. 157.

OBGT VI. Present forms occur only at 221-227:

221	ab-gar-re	*iššakkan*
222	an-gar-re	*iššakkan*
223	an-na-gar-re	*iššakkanšum*
224	an-na-ab-gar-re	*išakkanšum*
225	in-gar-re	*išakkan*
226	in-da-gar-re	*išakkanšu*
227	bí-ib-gar-re	*ušaškan*

As will become evident, the first three examples here must be inaccurate, manufactured forms. Apparently the compiler, wishing to find a Sumerian form corresponding to the present tense of the N theme, has fused two rules-of-thumb: 'the prefix a- followed by an inert infix gives a stative sense which can be rendered by the Akkadian N theme' and 'forms with a cause suffix -e can be set against an Akkadian present'. The result should have been a transitive present. Conversely we might simply assume that the spelling iš-ša-ak-ka-an in 221-3 (but not 224) is a scribal error for i-ša-ak-ka-an. In the other forms here (224-7) note a) use of prefix a- and b) marking of cause by suffix. Peculiar to this paradigm (and one entry in OBGT V, 10) is the use of the *hamṭu* gar instead of the expected *marû* gá-gá.

OBGT VII This text lists present tenses systematically throughout. Note here a) use of prefix a- (confined to present tense forms) and b) use of *marû* du (sing.) and re$_7$ (plur.), even with a-. The subject (in Sumerian inert) is marked by suffix in all forms.

OBGT VIII and IX Note a) use of prefix a-, b) use of *marû* base e (in kas$_4$...e), also with prefix a- and c) marking of cause by suffix, inert by infix.

OBGT X Present tenses occur at 66-74. Note a) use of prefix a- (once only but absent from the preterite forms) and b) marking of cause by suffix, inert by infix.

Other occurrences of present tenses are:

OBGT III	86	ab-dím-me-en	*eppeš*
	87	nu-ub-dím-me-en	*ūla eppeš*
	99	mu-ub-dím-e	*ippešam*[!] (text: i-pu-ša-am)
	100	nu-<mu->ub-dím-e	*ūla ippešam*[!] (text: i-pu-ša-am)
	104	ab-tum$_x$-tum$_x$-me-en	*anāku uṣâp*
	105	ab-tum$_x$-tum$_x$-e	*šū uṣâp*
	154	al-húl-húl-e-ne	*utebbeṭu*
	155	nu-húl-húl-e-ne	*ūla utebbeṭu*
	230	sag si-sá al-ak-en	*išêr*
	231	sag si-sá nu-ak-e	*ūla išêr*
	232	mu-un-ti-ti	*ureššeanni*
	233	nu-mu-un-ti-ti	*ūla ure[ššeanni]*
	234	an-ni-ib-ti-ti	*urešši[šu]* (*pace* translation)
	235	nu-un-ni-ib-ti-ti	*ūla [ureššišu]*
	242	KA-zu-sa$_6$ an-tuku	a *surram īšu*
			b *rīdam īšu*
	243-4	KA-zu-sa$_6$ a-tuku	a *surram anāku īšu*
			b *anāku īšu*
	245	KA-zu-sa$_6$ e-tuku	b *rīdam tīšu*
	247	KA-zu-sa$_6$ nu-tuku	b *ul īšu*
OBGT IV	iii 6'	sá ab-bé-e-ne	*ika[ššadū]*
	7'	sá nu-ub-bé-e-ne	*ul ik[aššadū]*
OBGT V	6	nu-mu-ra-te-ge$_x$-dè-en	*ūla eṭehhiakkum*
	10	in-da-gá-re-e-en	*tašakkaššu* (text: ta-ša-ka-áš-um)
	14	al-gub	*izzaz*
	15	al-gub-bé-en	*azzaz*
	16	nu-gub	*ūla izzaz*

Here again the same features are evident. The use of the *marû* base is clear in OBGT IV iii 6'-7' and V 6. Where inert alone is present (as at OBGT V 14-16) it is marked by suffix. The forms OBGT III 242-7 follow rather the pattern established for forms set against transitive stative, and the use of the (strictly speaking *preterite* tense) forms *išu* and *tīšu* in the Akkadian column here should perhaps not be pressed too hard.

The results are largely as expected, except for the novel feature that where a verb with prefix a- is set against a present rather than a stative it is constructed in Sumerian, so far as can be determined, with the *marû* base. The exceptions to this are OBGT III 154-5, where we should have expected al-ha-ha-e-ne, nu-ha-ha-e-ne (or else al-húl-húl-eš and equation with statives). This is perhaps explained by the presence immediately before of just such stative forms, opposite al-húl-húl-en, nu-húl-húl-en (151-2).

Thus, in summary, the following features are set against the Akkadian present tenses:

a) use of prefix a- with *marû* form (as well as other prefixes),
b) use of *marû* form where appropriate and
c) incorporation of cause where present by suffix.

The use of the prefix a- with *marû* forms, corresponding to Akkadian present, will be found extensively in the grammatical texts from Ur.

For forms of the preterite we look first at OBGT VI-X.

OBGT VI In general any prefix except a- may be used (ì-, bí, mu/mi-, ba-, ma- or im-ma-). The simple gar is used, and cause is incorporated by infix, inert (as for example in the forms corresponding to the passive Nt theme, as ba-gar-re-en *attaškan* 'I was placed') by suffix. Exceptions to this are:

106	bí-íb-gar	*ušaškin*
107	bí-íb-gar-re-en	(*ušaškin*, 1st person)
108	bí-íb-gar-re-en	(*tušaškin*)
109	mi-ni-in-gar	*ušaškin*
110	mi-ni-in-gar-re-en	(*ušaškin*, 1st person)
111	mi-ni-in-gar-re-en	(*tušaškin*)

These forms were discussed above, p. 33 f. Apparently they employ exceptionally the inverted form of incorporation, possibly so constructed in order to bring out a causative sense which cannot be conveniently expressed in Sumerian.

OBGT VII The bases gen (sing.) and su_8 (pl.) are used; a- is avoided.

OBGT VII and IX The base du_{11} is used, a- is avoided and cause is marked by infix, except at VIII 62-5 and IX 122-3, 126-7, 130-1 where, as at VI 106-111, the inverted incorporation is used and the cause is not marked. (Above, p. 34, IX 127, 131 and 136 were regarded as errors for forms with infix -b-).

OBGT X a- is avoided and cause is marked by infix.

Other occurrences are as follows:

OBGT IV	i	3	ì-zi-ge-en	*etbi*
		4	nu-zi-ge-en	*ul etbi*
		5	ì-zi-ge-en	*tetbi*
		6	nu-zi-ge-en	*ul tetbi*
		7	ì-zi	*itbi*
		8	nu-zi	*ul itbi*
		9	[ba-zi-]ge-en	*ettebi* (text: e te et bi)
		10	[la-ba-zi-g]e-en	*ul ettebi* (e te et bi)
		11	[ba-zi-g]e-en	*tettebi*
		12	[la-ba-zi-g]e-en	*ul tettebi*
	iii	8'	sá ba-an-ne-eš	*iktaš[dū]*
		9'	sá nu-un-ne-eš	*ul ik[šudū]*
OBGT V		2', 9'	in-na-te-e-en	*teṭhišum*
		3	in-na-te-en	*eṭhišum*

Here we may note a) use of *hamṭu* plural base e in OBGT IV iii 8'-9' and b) marking of cause by infix (-n-) with plural marker suffixed (-eš). In OBGT V 2, 3 and 9 the *hamṭu* te is used. In the forms of zi(g) and te no cause is present and so the inert is regularly marked by suffix.

So, in summary, the following features are set against the Akkadian preterite tense:

a) Use of prefix a- is excluded.
b) Where appropriate, *hamṭu* base is used.
c) Where present, cause is incorporated by infix.

The findings of this investigation which are new concern the use in our texts of the prefixes a- and stative (not separative) ba-. These may be represented diagrammatically as shown below. This argues strongly against an overall equation *marû* = durative, *hamṭu* = punctive. It should follow from this that the common ba-hul of year names (see above, p. 37) represents a notional form ba-n-hul with infixed cause and *hamṭu* verb, 'someone has destroyed', '... was destroyed (by someone unspecified)'. The natural Akkadian equivalent would appear to be a Š stative with passive sense. This seems perfectly plausible. If ba-hul represents a notional ba-n-hul, it is true that one might expect to find occasional writings of ba-an-hul. Against this argument, it would need to be maintained that ba-hul became a completely stereotyped writing.[62]

prefix	infix	verb	suffix	set against
a-	inert	*marû*	cause	transitive present
a-	-	*marû*	inert	intransitive present
a-	cause	*hamṭu*	-	G stative, transitive if appropriate (otherwise intransitive)
a-	-	*hamṭu*	inert	G stative, intransitive or passive sense
a- } ba-	(-ni-) cause	*hamṭu*	inert	Š stative (rarely G), passive sense
cf.				
ba-	-	*marû*	inert	Gt present, intransitive
ba-	cause	*hamṭu*	(inert)	Gt preterite, intransitive

1.3 The verbal paradigms from Ur

In addition to the version from Ur of the paradigm of the verbs 'to go', which has already been described (above, §1.1), two other verbal paradigms from Ur are known.[63] The transliterated texts are presented below as appendices 5.1.2 and 5.1.3. These paradigms are discussed separately because, owing to their condition of extreme textual corruption, they are best interpreted in the light of the foregoing analysis of the paradigms from Nippur, rather than *vice versa*.

First the text UET VII 102 is dealt with. It falls into thirteen sections, as follows:

1. lines	i 1-17	de$_6$ = *wabālum*, 'to bring':	singular forms
2.	18-34	"	plural forms (mainly)
3.	35-49	še(g) = *magārum*, 'to agree':	basic forms
4.	50-ii 10	"	forms with suffix *-šu*
5.	11-24	"	forms with suffix *-ka* (lx *-ninni*)
6.	25-39	gíd = *maṣûm*, 'to reach, to suffice':	basic forms
7.	40-54	"	forms with ventive and suffix *-kum*
8.	55-iii 7	"	forms with suffix *-šum*

62. Cf. the remarks of Edzard on forms of this sort, in ' "Du hast mir gegeben", "ich habe dir gegeben". Über das sumerische Verbum sum', in *WdO* 8 (1975-6), pp. 159-177, esp. pp. 169, 176 ff.

63. *V.* O.R. Gurney, *Ur Excavations Texts* VII (London, 1974), nos. 102 and 99.

9.	9-22	ta_{12} = *ezēbum*, 'to abandon, to leave':	basic forms
10.	23-27	"	forms with ventive suffix
11.	38-52	"	forms with suffix -*šu*-[*um*]
12.	iv 1-27	è = *šūlûm*, 'to raise':	various forms
13.	28-49	gùr = *našûm*, 'to lift, to bear':	various forms.[64]

Of these, sections 3 to 11 show a fixed order of forms, which is listed below. Certain errors occur in the text, viz. ii 33-4 give preterite forms for present, 42 preterite for present, iii 3 a Gt form for a G form, iii 35 present for preterite, 37 present for preterite and 43-4 present for preterite. Otherwise the pattern is followed exactly. The forms given are:

imperative 2nd person plural
cohortative 1st person plural
present 2nd person plural
present 1st person plural
present 1st person plural negative
preterite 1st person plural
preterite 1st person plural negative
Gt preterite 1st person plural
present 3rd person plural
present 3rd person plural negative
optative 3rd person plural
optative 3rd person plural negative (vetitive)
preterite 3rd person plural
preterite 3rd person plural negative
Gt preterite 3rd person plural

(Imperative, cohortative, optative are the individual persons of the forms so far grouped together as 'non-indicative'.) Within this pattern can be seen a double arrangement, schematically:

present	1pl and 3pl (and 2pl)
present negative	1pl and 3pl
preterite	1pl and 3pl
preterite negative	1pl and 3pl
Gt preterite	1pl and 3pl
non-indicative	1pl and 3pl (and 2pl)
non-indicative neg.	3pl

Thus in contrast to the Nippur paradigms, those from Ur list plural forms almost exclusively. The Sumerian entries against which these are set contain many mistakes, some of which can be recognized simply on grounds of inconsistency in what is otherwise a hypercorrect class of text. Of the three verbs in the central portion of the text, ta_{12} = *ezēbum*, 'to leave, to abandon', is the most correct and will be used as a model for correcting the other two.[65] Two sets of features will be taken into consideration: first, the choice in Akkadian of verbal form (number, tense, person, mood, whether affirmative or negative), to which correspond the variation in the Sumerian verbal base used (*hamṭu* or *marû*) and the suffixed elements of incorporation together with the preformative; and second, the suffixed Akkadian elements, ventive or personal, which appear in Sumerian in the pre-verbal chain. In the

64. It is possible that è is written for e_{11} and that *šūlûm* and *našūm* are here to be understood in their mathematical senses of 'to subtract' and 'to multiply'. So also *maṣûm* and *ezēbum*. Cf. the choice of verbs in the paradigm OBGT IX.
65. On the verb ta_{12} (tag_4), see now M.A. Powell, 'Ukubi to mother...with an excursus on the verb taka: da_x-da_x(TAG_4)' in *ZA* 68 (1978), pp. 163-195.

Sumerian forms considerable inconsistency is found in the marking of the elements set against Akkadian ventive and personal suffixes; in the case of the simple verbal forms, however, it is usually possible to attempt a restoration of the correct form. The latter will be dealt with first.

The form of verb set against *ezēbum* varies between ta_{12} and the reduplicated ta_{12}-ta_{12}, as follows:

imperative (2nd person) cohortative (1st person) preterite	ta_{12}
optative (3rd person) present	ta_{12}-ta_{12}

The suffixes used are:

imperative (2nd person plural)	-(b)zen
1st person plural	-enden
2nd person plural	-enzen
3rd person plural	(-ta_{12})-eš/(ta_{12}-ta_{12})-ne

The only exception to this is iii 27 where the second -ta_{12}- is omitted. In iii 28 and 29 the forms]-ta_{12}-dè-en-dè-en are found. Against Professor Gurney's suggestion that this might mean that the scribes were reading]-kid-dè-en-dè-en, we may cite iii 10-12 -ta_{12}-ta_{12}-a-[an-] and 41-2 -ta_{12}-ta_{12}-an- as evidence of vowel harmony conditioned by the -a- of ta_{12}, and therefore iii 28 and 29 should be regarded as errors.

We can now apply these results to the paradigms of gíd = *maṣûm*, 'to reach, to suffice'. This evidently contains more mistakes. The two forms of the Sumerian verb are written gíd and gíd-i; when gíd is followed by a suffix, the -d- may be written in, as one might expect, so that it appears as gíd-dè-, and when gíd-i is followed by a suffix beginning with the vowel -e-, the -i- is written as -a-, so that gıd-da- results. Thus the correct forms of the verb with their suffixed element of incorporation should appear as follows:

imperative 2pl	gíd-an-zé-en, gíd-àm-zé-en, gíd-mu-zé-en
cohortative 1pl	-gíd-dè-en-dè-en
present 2pl	-gíd-da-en-zé-en
present 1pl	-gíd-da-en-dè-en
preterite 1pl	-gíd-(dè-)en-dè-en
present 3pl	-gid-i-ne
optative 3pl	-gíd-i-ne
preterite 3pl	-gíd-(dè-)eš

If the damaged portions of the text are overlooked, out of 27 remaining forms, the scribe has got 15 wrong!

For the Sumerian equivalent of the verb *magārum*, 'to agree', the problem is less complicated in that the Sumerian verb še(-g) does not have two forms; however, that section of the text is less well preserved. The seemingly bored or careless scribe has indiscriminately put 1st person plural endings on the forms ii 18-21 as well as on the four preceding forms, and seems to have done the same at i 43-7 as well, although in both cases he has got the corresponding Akkadian more or less right.

The reconstruction of the correct forms of the pre-verbal chains is much more difficult. These consist of the preformatives ga- and hé- for the equivalents of cohortative and optative, na- for negative optative (vetitive), nu- for negative indicative, with prefix ba- for the Gt theme and ì-, mu- or a- variously for indicative (present or preterite, although a- is confined to present); and the various elements set against the Akkadian suffixes ventive, *-šu*, *-šum*, *-ka*, *-kum*, *-ninni* (1 ×) and *-šu(-um)*. There are large gaps, but some of the pre-verbal chains may be presented thus in tabular form:

(basic forms, i.e. without any suffixes)

	maṣûm	*ezēbum*
cohortative 1pl		ga-ab-
present 2pl		mu-ni-ib-
present 1pl		mu-ni-ib-
present 1pl negative		nu-mu-ni-ib-
preterite 1pl	mu-un-	ì-
preterite 1pl negative	nu-mu-un-	nu-ì-
Gt preterite 1pl	ba-an-	ba-
present 3pl	mu-un-	mu-ni-ib-
present 3pl negative	nu-mu-un-	nu-mu-ni-ib-
optative 3pl	hé-	hu-mu-ni-ib-
vetitive 3pl	na-an-	nam-mu-ni-ib-
preterite 3pl	mu-un-	in-
preterite 3pl negative	nu-mu-un-	nu-un-
Gt preterite 3pl	ba-an-	ba-an-

These forms are all comprehensible, although the use of the infix -ni- in some of the forms set against the (in Akkadian, transitive) verb *ezēbum* is difficult to account for. In the paradigm of *ezēbum* there is a section of forms which have just the ventive suffix, against which we would expect, in the Sumerian, -m-/ma-/mu-. The Sumerian has:

imperative 2pl	ta_{12}-ma-ab-zé-en
cohortative 1pl	ga-àm-ab-
present 2pl	àm-mi-ib-
present 1pl	àm-mi-ib-
present 3pl	àm-mi-ib-
present 3pl negative	nu-àm-mi-ib-
optative 3pl	hé-em-
vetitive 3pl	na-àm-
preterite 3pl	im-ma-an-
preterite 3pl negative	nu-um-ma-an-
Gt preterite 3pl	im-ma-an(text: -in)-

These are as expected. -m- + -ba- gives -mma-. The forms with -mmi- are presumably derived similarly from -m- + -bi-, and -bi- will here be the 3rd person singular locative-terminative infix (which appeared as -ni- in the basic forms).

Ventive forms also occur in the paradigm of *maṣûm*, this time with the addition of the suffix *-kum*. For *-kum* we should expect -ra-. The forms (omitting 2nd person forms, as the combination would be impossible) in the Sumerian column are:

cohortative 1pl	ga-
present 1pl	àm-
present 1pl negative	nu-àm-
preterite 1pl	mu-ši-
preterite 1pl negative	nu-mu-ši-
Gt preterite 1pl	ba-ra-
present 3pl	mu-ra-
present 3pl negative	nu-mu-ra-
optative 3pl	hu-mu-ra-
vetitive	nam-mu-ra-
preterite 3pl	mu-ra-
preterite 3pl negative	nu-mu-ra-
Gt preterite 3pl	im-ma-ra-

These again are as expected, with the following exceptions: the form for Gt preterite 1pl should be im-ma-ra-; the forms set against cohortative 1pl, present 1pl and present 1pl negative contain no element corresponding to *-kum* (perhaps for semantic reasons: it is difficult for 'us' to reach 'hither' 'to you' - but the same should be true for the Akkadian), and for preterite 1pl and 1pl negative the element -ši- is used, which is properly a 3rd person element. It may be that mu-ši- is here written for mu-e-ši-, which does occur elsewhere as an equivalent of *-kum* (e.g. in OBGT VII).

A second person singular suffix (*-ka*) is also found in the paradigm of *magārum*, 'to agree'. The forms are (once again without 2nd person forms):

cohortative 1pl	ga-mu-ri-ib-
present 1pl negative	nu-mu-un-
preterite 1pl	i-
preterite 1pl negative	nu-un-
Gt preterite 1pl	ba-e-
present 3pl	mu-e-
present 3pl negative	nu-mu-e-
optative 3pl	hé-
vetitive 3pl	na-an-
preterite 3pl	mu-e-
preterite 3pl negative	nu-mu-e-
Gt preterite 3pl	im-mu-<e->

(-e- can be restored in this last, since -mu- is a form of ba- occurring after -m- and before -e-).

This is all rather confusing. -e- (normally marking a cause of the second person) occurs in some of the forms, but others have no mark of the second person at all. The form *ī nimgurka* is set against ga-mu-ri-ib-še-ge-en-dè-en: this at least is what we should expect, since ga- appears to require that sort of incorporation in which the inert is marked by infix and the cause by suffix, leaving only the possibility of dimensional infix (the slot called prefix by Foxvog)[66] to mark what must here be the 'person agreed with' - 'let it be agreed upon with you by us'. But otherwise the Sumerian of this section does not seem very consistent.

The suffix *-šu* is presumably to be restored in the damaged parts of the section i 50-ii 10. Of the Sumerian forms, only the following survive:

present 3pl	an-na-ab-
present 3pl negative	nu-an-na-ab-
optative 3pl	hé(text: ga)-en-na-ab-
vetitive 3pl	na-en-na-ab-
preterite 3pl	in-
preterite 3pl negative	nu-in-
Gt preterite 3pl	ba-an-na-

Where the personal suffix has any corresponding feature in the Sumerian, it is -na- 'to him', presumably again representing the 'person agreed with'.

-na- also occurs in some of the forms of gíd = *maṣûm* where the Akkadian has the suffix *-šum*, at ii 55-61. However, in other forms, -ni- occurs. The surviving forms are as follows (here the whole verbal complex is quoted):

imperative 2pl	gíd-mu-zé-en
cohortative 1pl	ga-mu-gíd-en-dè-en
present 2pl	mu-ni-ib-gíd-<da->-en-zé-en
present 1pl	mu-ni-ib-gíd-<da->en-dè-en
present 1pl negative	nu-mu-ni-ib-gíd-<da-> en-[dè-en]
preterite 1pl	mu-un-na-gíd-[en-dé-en]
preterite 1pl negative	nu-mu-un-na-gíd-[en-dè-en]

66. In 'The Sumerian Ergative Construction', in *OrNS* 44 (1975), p. 400.

It will be noted that -ni- occurs when the form of incorporation whereby -b- is infixed to mark an inert 'it' is used - 'to him it is stretched out by us'; and that further this is accompanied by the extended form of the verb, gíd-i. The standard form, used when set against Akkadian preterite or 1st person cohortative, has -na- instead of -ni-ib-. We were earlier (above, p. 46) puzzled by the appearance of -ni- in certain forms corresponding to basic, i.e. non-suffixed, *ezēbum* (iii 8-22), and it will be of interest now to observe that -ni- occurs in precisely those forms which use the extended form of the verb, viz. those set against Akkadian present and 3rd person optative (and vetitive), and is absent when the simple verb is used. The same will be found to be true of the distribution of the occurrence in section iii 23-27 of -mmi- (-m- + -bi-) with the exception of the 3rd person plural optative and vetitive (iii 33-4), where the text has hé-em-ta_{12}-ta_{12}-ne and na-àm-ta_{12}-ta_{12}-ne. Another exception to the above general principle appears to be iii 7: [ba-?]-ni-ib-gíd-[?]-eš = *imtaṣûšum*.

Finally we must describe the passage iii 38-52, which is as follows:

imperative 2pl	ta_{12}-an-na-ab-zé-en
cohortative 1pl	ga-àm-ab-
present 2pl	mu-un-na-ni-ib-
present 1pl	mu-un-na-ni-ib-
present 1pl negative	in-na-ni-ib- (expected: nu-mu-un-na-ni-ib-)
preterite 1pl	in-na-an-
preterite 1pl negative	nu-in-na-an-
Gt preterite 1pl	ba-an-na-
present 3pl	mu-un-na-ni-ib-
present 3pl negative	nu-mu-un-na-ni-[ib]-
optative 3pl	hu-mu-un-na-[ni-ib-]
vetitive 3pl negative	nam-mu-na-an-[ni-ib-]
preterite 3pl	in-na-an-
preterite 3pl negative	nu-in-na-an-
Gt preterite 3pl	[ba]-an-[na-an-]

Here the following points may be noted:

1) Once again the construction with -ni-ib- is found in those forms only which use the extended form of the verb (i.e. Akkadian present and 3rd person optative and vetitive).

2) Instead of ga-àm-ab- we would have expected ga-na-ab-.

3) Otherwise the infix -na- occurs throughout. Unfortunately the righthand part of the column is broken away and the Akkadian suffix occurs only in iii 43, 45 and 46, where it is *-šu-* but with space for another sign. In view of -na- it seems likely (although unusual) that the text had a syllabic spelling of *-šum* 'to him, (for him)'.[67]

4) In this section (as opposed to the section ii 55-iii 7), where -ni-ib- occurs, it occurs in addition to -na- rather than instead of it.

There remain the outer sections of this text. The first two sections give forms of de_6 = *wabālum*, 'to bring', although the Sumerian de_6 is preserved only in lines i 15-17. These forms, of which the first group (i 1-17) are singular and the second (i 18-34) plural, bear the ventive suffix together with *-kunūšim* (alternating with *-niāšim* in 2nd person forms), with the following exceptions, all in the second group:

i 18	*bilāniāšim*	omits the ventive suffix
20	*tablāniāšim*	" " " "
22-26	*tubbalanniāšim*	give singular forms for plural
	ubbalakkunūšim	
	[*ul*] *ubbalakkunūšim*	
	[*ublak*]*kunūšim*	
	ul [*ublakku*]*nūšim*	
34	*itbalūniāšim*	omits the ventive suffix and has *-niāšim* for *-kunūšim* (cf. i 17)

67. *Cf.* OBGT V 2 [te-eṭ-ḫ]i-šu-u[m].

The verbal forms listed are much the same as in the central sections of the text. There is one discrepancy between the two sections of *wabālum*, in that i 3 gives a present tense (apparently) while i 20 gives a Gt imperative. In view of i 5, it is likely that i 3 is an error for the Gt imperative. The pattern of these sections may be compared with that of the central sections, which list more 1st person forms. Only parts of the Sumerian remain, and of 25 of which elements can definitely be recognized, 15 can confidently be said to be wrong. The Akkadian forms are listed below, compared with the forms occurring in the central sections of the text.

wabālum	*magārum, maṣûm, ezēbum*
imperative 2sg/pl	imperative 2pl
volitive 1sg/cohortative 1pl	cohortative 1pl
Gt imperative 2sg/pl	
Gt volitive 1sg/cohortative 1pl	
present 2sg/pl	present 2pl
present 3sg/pl	present 1pl
present 3sg/pl neg	present 1pl neg
preterite 3sg/pl	preterite 1pl
preterite 3sg/pl neg	preterite 1pl neg
Gt preterite 1sg/pl	Gt preterite pl
present 3sg/pl	present 3pl
present 3sg/pl neg	present 3pl neg
optative 3sg/pl	optative 3pl
vetitive 3sg/pl	vetitive 3pl
preterite 3sg/pl	preterite 3pl
preterite 3sg/pl neg	preterite 3pl
Gt preterite 3sg/pl	Gt preterite 3pl neg

It will be seen that there is a certain amount of repetition in the paradigm of *wabālum*. Whether this is due to faulty memory on the part of the copyist at the beginning of a text one cannot say.

Of the Sumerian columns of the last two sections of the text, virtually nothing survives: although enough for us to suspect errors at iv 38 (where a form ending in -eš is expected), 41 (should be -en-dè-en) and 44 (should be -eš). The paradigm of è = *šūlûm*, 'to raise', may be divided into four sections as follows:

1) iv 1-5: singular forms with ventive suffix, of which iv 4 (from the arrangement of the surviving signs) is probably a negative form, and iv 5 a form of the Št theme.

2) iv 6-12: 3rd person plural forms with ventive suffix: present (with negative), optative (with vetitive), preterite (with negative) and Št form. Note here the curious form of vetitive, *[ul li]šēlûnim* (restoration from iv 19) for the expected *lā išellûnim*.

3) iv 13-20: singular forms with suffix ventive +*-šunūšim* (*-šum* in 16): 3rd person present (with negative), Št optative (also occurring at 20), Š imperative, 1sg volitive and 3rd singular optative (with irregular vetitive).

4) iv 21-27, of which only a few syllables remain in lines 21-23, suggesting plural forms with suffix ventive +*-kum*.

The final section, concerned with the verbs gùr = *našûm*, 'to lift, to bear', is the least organized of all parts of this text. It may be divided into two portions, iv 28-38 and 39-end, of which the second lists forms with the ventive suffix (with the exception of iv 41). Thus

iv 28-38	iv 39-end
present 3pl	imperative 2pl, ventive + *-ni*
present 3pl negative	present 3pl, ventive + *-ni*
stative 3pl	stative 1pl
stative 2pl	present 3pl, ventive
Gt preterite 2pl	vetitive 3pl, ventive

Gt preterite 2pl
present 2pl negative
present 2pl negative
N volitive 1sg
optative 3pl
Gt preterite 3pl

Gt preterite 3pl, ventive
optative 3pl, ventive
optative 3pl, ventive + *-ni*
preterite 3pl, ventive
pl, ventive
pl, ventive
+ at least four more lines.

This text has some very curious features. However, one of the problems facing us in the interpretation of it is the large number of errors. Quite clearly it was copied by an incompetent: but was it also compiled by an incompetent? It is of course difficult to know whether we are dealing with one single text or three separate texts (sections 1-2, 3-11 and 12-13). The impression one gets is that at some earlier stage in the transmission, the central sections of this text were quite carefully organized. The ingenuity of the organization is the principal parameter by which we can estimate the reliability of a text of the list literature. None the less there are certain usages which suggest that the middle section of the text, as well, was composed rather mechanically. The use of personal dimensional infixes and personal infixed and suffixed elements is somewhat irregular. As has been suggested, it is to some extent conditioned by the meaning of the verbs concerned. Consider *magārum*. The Akkadian accusative suffixes presumably represent the 'person agreed with'. In the Sumerian, in the section where the Akkadian has *-šu*, these appear, except in two instances (ii 8 and 9), as -na-. Corresponding to this in the section with *-ka*, there is in one instance -ri-, which is at least comprehensible and not without parallel; but in the remainder the cause infix -e- has been appropriated (in the cases where the 2nd person is marked at all) to mark the person agreed with. This would be explicable, perhaps, in the *marû* forms where the cause is normally marked by a suffix, but among these, -e- is used only on two occasions out of seven (ii 18 and 19); but it is perplexing in the *hamṭu* forms, where it occurs four times out of seven (ii 17, 22-24). The paradigm of *ezēbum* is, as has been said, the best organized: here, the forms of incorporation vary regularly between (for *marû* forms) -ni-+ reduplicated verb + cause suffix, i.e. you, we, they abandon it there, and (for *hamṭu* forms) -n-+ standard base + plural marker, i.e. you, we, they abandon. -n- occurs of course only in 3rd person forms, although exceptionally (and probably incorrectly) it also occurs at iii 43-4 in 1st person forms (but not at ii 13-15 or iii 45). This -n- appears again exceptionally in *hamṭu* 1st person plural forms at ii 30-32, but not at corresponding places in the same paradigm.

A second factor indicating a mechanical method of compilation is the spelling of certain preverbal chains: spellings such as nu-in- or nu-i- directly following in- or ì-, and nu-an- directly after an-; similarly na-en-na-ab- directly after ga-en-na-ab- (itself erroneous for hé-en-na-ab-). A further example is the vetitive *ul lišēliaššunūšim* at iv 19, irregularly formed by simply prefixing *ul*, 'not', to the optative. (Apparently the same construction was used at iv 9.) In this latter case, since there is no reason to assume that Babylonian was not the native language of the compiler, or scribe, we should assume a deliberately unidiomatic form intended in some way to illustrate the composition of the (unfortunately missing) Sumerian form.

On the whole, then, interesting as this text is in that it illuminates the thought processes of the ancient grammarians, as far as its content is concerned it is to be regarded as less reliable than the texts from the Nippur scriptoria.

It will be convenient to describe here also the fragmentary text UET VII 99. The transliterated text is appendix 5.1.3 below. It is part of a paradigm of kú = *akālum*, 'to eat', and nag = *šatûm*, 'to drink'. In the righthand column of the first double column, a few present tense forms of *akālum* survive, some with the suffix *-kum*, 'to you', whatever that means when suffixed to 'to eat'. The second column of the fragment contains the following forms of nag = *šatûm*:

2	in-nag-eš	[*ištû*]	preterite 3pl
	nu-un-nag-eš	*ūla* [*ištû*]	preterite 3pl negative
	i-nag-dè-en	*ništi*	preterite 1pl

nu-nag-dè-en	*ūla ništi*	preterite 1pl negative
al-nag-nag-ne	*išattû*	present 3pl
nu-nag-nag-ne	*ūla išattû*	present 3pl negative
i-nag-zé-en	*taštiā*	preterite 2pl
i-nag-dè-en	*ništi*	preterite 1pl
ba-e-nag	*taštati*	Gt preterite 2sg
la-ba-e-nag	*ūla taštati*	Gt preterite 2sg negative
ba-e-nag-zé-en	*taštatiā*	Gt preterite 2pl
[ba-nag-dé-]en	*ništati*	Gt preterite 1pl

The corrections nu-nag-dè-en for la-ba-nag-dè-en and i-nag-zé-en for i-nag-nag-ne are easily made by inspection. nag (*hamṭu*) here varies with nag-nag (*marû*). Furthermore, the form of incorporation using infixes to mark the person of the cause (although a suffix is added to mark the number) is here seen quite clearly in a form like ba-e-nag-zé-en. In other respects this text follows the Nippur usage in its structure and rationale.

2 *Grammatical Vocabularies, Analyses and Epitomes*

2.1 Grammatical vocabularies, analyses and epitomes

The second class of text is the grammatical vocabulary. These differ from the first class in that the content does not consist of verbal forms. Instead, pronominal, prepositional and adverbial expressions are listed, arranged usually in paradigmatic groups in which one element is systematically varied. 'OBGT I', the fragments OBGT Ia and Ib, and OBGT XVIII (which comes from Boğazköy, date approximately 14th-13th cent. B.C.) are of this type, as also the first portion of MBGT (Middle Babylonian grammatical text) II.

It should be pointed out here that 'OBGT' I is to be separated into two texts, OBGT I(A) and OBGT I(B). A (= CBS 19791) is a tablet of 16 double columns, c. 1200 lines, columns i-iii and xii-xvi are completely destroyed. B (= CBS 6509) is the lower righthand corner of a much smaller tablet preserving A ix 657-'660e' followed *directly* by A xii c. 869-'880c', thus:

B obv. 1'	]	⌜a-li⌝ [at]-⌜ta⌝	= A ix 658
2'	]	a-li a-na-ku	656,657
3'	]-⌜dè⌝-en	a-li ni-nu	659
4'	]-⌜en⌝-zé-en	a-li at-tu-nu	660
5'	]- e - ne -ne	a-li šu-nu	653,654,655 (Sum. difft)
6'	]lú me-en-dè-en	a-li ni-šu-ni	–
7'	]un-en-zé-en	a-li ni-šu-ku-nu	–
8'	]⌜x⌝-⌜gá?⌝-ne-ne	a-li ni-šu-šu-nu	–
(end of col.) 9'	]-⌜mu⌝	a-li ki-im-ti	–
			(cf. iv 256]⌜ki⌝-im-ti-šu-nu)
rev. 1	]	(vacat)	?
2	]	(vacat)	?
3		k]i-a-am-ma	866,871
4	]⌜a⌝	ki-i ki-a-am	–
5	]⌜a⌝	ki-i ki-a-am	–
6	]x	ki - a - am	? 869,870
7	]x	aš-šum ki-a-am	? 876-8
8	]	ki-a-am ma-ṣi-a-am	–
9		]x ki-a-am	?
10		]ki-a-am-ma	?873,875
11		]x na ù ta	–
12		]x li-im ù ta	–
13		](damage)	?

Thus although B certainly more or less duplicates A for two passages totalling 18 out of the 102, only in lines 659 and 660 does it seem fairly certain that both tablets had the same Sumerian as well as the same Akkadian.

The order of persons in A, col. ix, is 3sg. 3pl. 1sg. 2sg. 1pl. 2pl;
in B, obv., is 2sg. 1sg. 1pl. 2pl. 3pl.

It seems clear that B is not 'another text' of A. Either it consists of two passages excerpted from A and badly quoted with lines in the wrong order (A is notably *well* organised, in its earlier stages, at least), or more likely it is a different text of the same general type.

In A, cols. vi, vii, viii, the order is regularly 1pl., 2pl., 3pl. (x, xi, xii are non-pronominal). A col. iv has different material; col. v has forms set against *annûm*; cols. vi, vii, viii have forms with *nīnu, attunu, šunu*; col. ix has mixed personal pronouns; col. x interrogative adverbs; col. xi temporal adverbs; almost all col. xii has forms of *kīam*. Thus although well-organised A may represent a compilation. It seems clear that B is not 'another text' of A. Either it consists of two passages excerpted from A and badly quoted with lines in the wrong order (A is notably *well* organised, at least in the earlier portions), or, more likely, it is a different text of the same general type.

Mr. D.A. Kennedy kindly made his copies of MBGT II available to me. It comes from Ugarit, dating from about 1200 BC, and the obverse of 'OBGT XIV' is an excerpt from it. The first half (lines 1-111) is a mixture of grammatical vocabulary and grammatical analysis, while the remainder (112-259) lists general vocabulary in the manner of a commentary on a literary text. Particularly interesting in the first portion is the systematic inclusion (set against Sumerian -še) of the Akkadian demonstrative *anmû* 'this' alongside the normal *annû* (set against -e). (Note also the hitherto unattested demonstrative *ullallû*: lú-lú-ri = ul-la-lu-ú (line 22, cf. 28, 34, 80, 89, 99, 111; meaning perhaps 'some person over there').) *Anmû* is elsewhere attested only in texts from OB and MB Alalakh, and one letter from Ugarit (see *CAD s.v.*). This suggests strongly that MBGT II is not entirely derivative from Babylonian tradition but includes at least some material especially characteristic of the western dialects of Akkadian. Thus it seems that there was a productive tradition of redacting grammatical texts at Ugarit in the Middle Babylonian period.

It is the systematic variation that marks this class of text out as 'grammatical' rather than as mere lexical vocabularies. As a sample of this the passage OBGT I 373-418 may be considered. This consists of five sections, each of which shows emphatic forms of the three plural personal pronouns in turn. The five sections demonstrate different ways in which each of these emphatic sets of forms can be constructed in Sumerian with various affixes which render them free-standing: the suffix -àm (385-394), -àm with the verbal prefix ì- (395-400), the particle na-nam (401-409) and the prefix ì- with the infixed conjunction -nga- (410-418). A thoughtful and more extended exposition of this whole text will be found in Jacobsen, 'Very Ancient Linguistics, Babylonian Grammatical Texts', pp. 45-49.

Mention may be made here for completeness' sake of the remaining texts published in *MSL* IV. OBGT XII, NBGT IV, OBGT XIII, XV and XVII are not grammatical texts. OBGT XII may well be a commentary. The content of the first part of NBGT IV is closely related to it; while the latter part, although listing entries of a type common in grammatical vocabularies, lacks the systematic organization characteristic of a grammatical text. OBGT XIII, XV and XVII are probably commentaries. OBGT XVI and NBGT VII are too poorly preserved to classify.

The content of 'NBGT' III is in part typical of a grammatical vocabulary, and in part (columns iii and iv) typical of a grammatical analysis, the third type of text, described below. This text is particularly important historically, since its script (as noted by the editors of *MSL* IV (p. 158), and as I was able to see from excellent photographs kindly provided by Dr. Liane Jakob-Rost) is clearly *not* neo-Babylonian. It is an earlier Babylonian 'library' hand, obviously later than Old Babylonian but with certain sign-forms which appear archaic by comparison with Kuyunjik Babylonian script. It can thus certainly be placed between about 1600 and 800 BC, and along with the Ras Shamra text MBGT II (see above) and 'Examination Text A' (see section 2.6 below) represents the earliest evidence for grammatical 'analysis'. Little information can be retrieved about the archaeological context of its discovery. Dr J. Marzahn of the Vorderasiatisches Museum, Berlin, was kind enough to inform me that according to the finds journal the tablet was found on 5th January 1906 in square cC 6II at the western limit of the excavated area. This would fall approximately within Ditch IV (*Tal* IV). The nearest excavated buildings are the dwelling houses built over the terrace of the Palace of Tukulti-Ninurta I, which are unlikely to date from earlier than 1100 (in particular houses 27-30, see C. Preusser, *Die Wohnhäuser in Assur*, in WVDOG 64 (Berlin, 1954), chapter 4, esp. p. 36f.; plates 9; 13f, g; 10a, b). NBGT V is like an analysis but may have more in common with a sign-list (see in particular rev. col. i lines 2-7), as may IXb. NBGT IXa cannot be classified. Further grammatical vocabularies, all Babylonian, are as follows:

Ni 4125 and Ni 4143 in Kramer, Çig and Kızılyay, *İSET* 1, nos. 74 and 77 respectively (pp. 132 and 135) appear to contain passages of a grammatical vocabulary with verbal forms. These were kindly brought to my notice by C. Wilcke. For transliteration of these and some of the other texts following, see appendix 5.3 below.

N1761 is another fragment joining the tablet CBS 6568 (OBGT Ia) + UM 29-16-30 (OBGT Ib) + CBS 6563 (unpubl.).

N4217 has some forms of sìg = *mahāṣum*, and reduplicated forms of verbs, recalling the OBGT III texts. Transliterations of this and the texts following, all unpublished, were generously communicated to me by M. Civil. It is possible that N4217 joins OBGT III(A) or (B).

N6939. What is preserved includes grammatically varied forms of si-sá...ak.

Ni9688 lists phrases using the words dub-sar and nam-dub-sar. Lines 8-10 may be compared with OBGT III(B) 58-64.

Ni10269 lists verbal imperatives. Cf. OBGT XI.

N3077 and N3125 are probably also pieces of grammatical vocabularies, but are too fragmentary to be worth transcribing.

VAT 244, published by G.A. Reisner, 'The Berlin Vocabulary V.A.Th.244', in *ZA* 9 (1894), pp. 149-164, is a neo-Assyrian copy of a grammatical vocabulary of mixed type, copied from originals from Borsippa (see Hunger, *Kolophone*, no. 413).

These grammatical vocabularies are only important for the present inquiry inasmuch as they and the paradigms described in Chapter 1 above are the two types of text from which the third type is derived. This, as explained in the Introduction, is the grammatical analysis, a reduction to analytic form of the content of paradigms and vocabularies. No complete grammatical analyses remain, but, in addition to the passages of analysis in the Ras Shamra text MBGT II and in 'NBGT' III, described above, two epitomes of analyses survive in late copies. The structure and content of these and certain other texts relevant to the inquiry will now be investigated.

2.2 Structure and content of the epitome NBGT I

The study of the arrangement of material in these texts gives crucial clues as to how particular lexical items were regarded by the compilers. For NBGT I this work has already been done briefly by Jacobsen,[68] but the following treatment differs in certain details from his. He regards the text as consisting of a basic 'core' section dealing with personal pronouns, with a number of additional sections dealing with a variety of verbs, conjunctions and other words (202-256, 308-321, 395-462) which, he conjectures, represent additions to the original composition. However, closer scrutiny of the text reveals that it is even less homogeneous than Jacobsen supposed. The section 35-46 may also be non-pronominal, and so strictly is the section 85-101. The essentially modern distinction made by Jacobsen between 'bound' and 'free' forms is, within the context of this analysis of the arrangement of NBGT I, unreal.[69] Except in the first section (1-101), which lists only bound forms infixed or prefixed before the verbal base, the 'bound' and 'free' forms are never contrasted by the arrangement of the text. Furthermore the structure of some of the later sections (notably 322-394) is different from that of the earlier ones, and no homogeneous section is ever actually broken up by an 'inserted' section, which all suggests that we are dealing with a text which is a complete compilation from a number of sources, and not a single composition concerning pronouns, with accretions. The colophon affords little help, merely telling us that the tablet is part of the first section (*pirsu*) of a longer tablet entitled from its first line ù = *anāku*. *Pirsu* is the name usually given to a smaller division of a series than the principal one into tablet-lengths i.e. in an edition using tablets of a

68. In 'Very Ancient Linguistics: Babylonian Grammatical Texts', in Dell Hymes, ed., *Studies in the History of Linguistics: Traditions and Paradigms* (Bloomington and London, 1974), pp. 54-61.
69. *loc. cit.*, fold-out table between pp. 58 and 59.

smaller size than the numbered 'tablets' of the standard version; the series of which ù = *anāku* is a tablet is identified as tuš = *wašābu hamṭu ša ištēn*. The tablet was written at Nippur, in the 17th year of Darius (504 BC), and copied from an original from Ur. In all probability the text was further tampered with *after* its compilation, since certain entries occur which are quite out of place or irrelevant, and we may assume that at least when it was originally put together it was well organized. (Cf. OBGT VII for an example of admirable economy and exactitude.) More than this about its history we cannot say. The tablet series tuš = *wašābu* must have been very long indeed. NBGT II uses some of the same material: the relationship between the two will be discussed later.

The first part of the text lists Sumerian elements which are affixed to the verbal complex. These are set against the nominative and accusative cases of the Akkadian singular personal pronouns. First are given, in the Sumerian, so-called *rīqu* forms (1-34). This term is taken by Jacobsen to mean 'without final consonant expressly indicated by writing', and contrasts with *malû*, 'with final consonant expressly indicated by writing'. The words are discussed below in section 3.2. Four forms are listed in the Akkadian, the pronouns *anāku*, *atta*, *šū* and *šuāti*, nominative of the 1st and 2nd person and nominative and accusative of the 3rd. As will become clear, this unequal distribution is possibly the result of contraction of material arising from the epitomizing of the text. Apparently the Sumerian verb made no distinction between persons in whatever respect is intended, since ù a i e are given in all four cases; and of the extra entries given for *šū* and *šuāti* (ul al il ša ši na ba ab ta), some at least do not conform to the proposed distinction between *rīqu* and *malû* (since ul al il and ab all end in a consonant), while il occurs in no attested prefix or suffix chain to my knowledge. This leads us to suspect that 13-21 and 26-34 were not part of the original section and must have been mistakenly and misleadingly added later; or else that the grammatical terms *rīqu* and *malû* were added to the section later.

Before the *malû* forms corresponding to these are given, there is a short section as follows (35-46):

35	[	a-na]-⌜ku⌝ ma-⌜lu-ú⌝
36	[	]
37	[	]
38	[	]
39	[	]
40	[	]
41	[	]
42	[ú	m]a-ri-tum KI.TA
43	[a]	
44	i	
45	e	
46	-ne	

The editors, followed by Jacobsen,[70] evidently suspect that this broken passage obscures a (possibly incomplete) section going through the personal pronouns again, and restore *anāku* in line 35. In view of the presence of *marītum* in 42 and the shortness of the section, too short to go through all the pronouns, we would very tentatively propose to read ha-an-ṭ]⌜u⌝ instead in line 35, a possibility which seems consonant with the traces on the tablet. This would then not be a pronominal section at all. The occurrence of feminine forms such as *marītum* is discussed below in section 3.6. Jacobsen's fold-out table[71] is misleading here. 1-46 is not all *rīqu* if *malû* is read in 35. The only indication of 'aspect' in the whole text is *marītum* in 42, so there can be no grounds for a division of the elements in the text into items distinguished by aspect.

At 47-84 the *malû* forms are given. This time both nominative and accusative forms are given for each person in the Akkadian column. un an in en are listed in each case, and in addition:

---

70. *loc. cit.*

71. *loc. cit.*, between pages 58 and 59.

ab	mu	u$_8$	for *anāku*
	mu		for *yâti*
ab		u$_8$	for *atta* and *kâta*
ab	ub	u$_8$	for *šū*
ab	ub	íb	for *šuāti*

These forms are presumably infixes occurring directly before the verb. Extremely noticeable here is the apparently random use of AN.TA, MURU$_4$.TA and KI.TA, as may be seen from the following table:

		under *rīqu*	under *malû*
Sumerian forms set against	*anāku* are designated	MURU$_4$.TA	AN.TA MURU$_4$.TA
	yâti		AN.TA KI.TA MURU$_4$.TA
	atta	KI.TA	KI.TA
	kâta		MURU$_4$.TA KI.TA
	šū	KI.TA	AN.TA MURU$_4$.TA
	šuāti	AN⌜TA MURU$_4$.TA⌝[72]	AN.TA MURU$_4$.TA

The following section (85-101) may be described as, strictly speaking, not concerned with pronouns, since, after the first four entries (which in any case set ub against *anāku*, *atta* and *šū*, with íb as well), there is no division by person. The section is concerned instead with the terms *šushurtum* and *riātum*. The text has at this point been misleadingly rationalized by the editors in such a way as to give the impression that line 89 consists of a Sumerian entry 'ta' with the remainder as the Akkadian equivalent. Almost certainly the 'ta' must be the TA of the MURU$_4$.TA in 88 mistakenly repeated by the scribe, being thus part of the Akkadian entry to go opposite the previous Sumerian one, ub (line 87). There was not room opposite ub (87) for the whole entry, which spilled over into a second line (88). The colon after the 'ta' in 89 shows that what follows is a separate line, and this is then the entry which belongs opposite the Sumerian of 88, íb. The tablet actually looks like this (collated):

85	ub	ana - ku šu - ús - hur - tum	
		ma - li-tu MURU$_4$ - tú	
86	ub	at - ta šu-ús-hur-tum MURU$_4$.TA	
87	ub	šu - u šu - ús - hur - ti	
88	íb	ma-li-tú AN. TA	MURU$_4$. TA
89	TA:šu-ús-hur-tú ríq-tim AN. TA		MURU$_4$. TA

and this may be interpretatively transcribed as:

85	ub	*anāku šushurtum malītu* MURU$_4$-tú
86	ub	*atta šushurtum* <*malītu*> MURU$_4$.TA
87	ub	*šū šushurti malītu* AN.TA MURU$_4$.TA
88/9	íb	*šushurtu riqtim* AN.TA MURU$_4$.TA

Another possibility is that there has been a greater omission, perhaps due to compression of the material, between lines 88 and 89. Following this, u/a/i/em me u/a/i/en-ga and ma-ra/da/ta/da-ta appear with the term *riātum* and AN.TA MURU$_4$.TA set against them.

The section 102-124 lists free-standing forms of singular pronouns and forms of the copula. This time the accusatives of *anāku* and *atta* are given, but not of *šū* (constrast 1-34); but only minor differences exist between the forms, which are as follows:

anāku	gá-e	gá-a-me-en	me-en	ì-me-en
yâti	gá-e	gá-e-me-en	me-en	ì-me-en
atta	za-a	za-a-me-en	me-en	ì-me-en
kâta	za-e	za-a-me-en	me-en	ì-me-en
šū	e-ne	[e-ne-me-a]	[me-a]	ì-me-⌜a⌝ al ì ab-ta

72. Evidently so read by Thureau-Dangin, *RA* 32 (1935), p. 92.

These seem to be i) free-standing form of pronoun (the spellings gá-a and za-a are not significant and represent contracted forms of gá-e and za-e), ii) free-standing form with suffixed copula, iii) suffixed form of copula, and iv) verb 'to be', i.e. free-standing form of copula. In addition for the 3rd person are given some prefixes which are set against Akkadian statives and thus might be translated 'he is...'. This section is therefore properly concerned with expressing the notion of the copula and the free forms of the pronouns (i) are probably listed here because of their possibilities of use in predicative functions ('I am ...', 'you are...' etc.).

The next section (125-201) is the only part of the text dealing with plural pronouns. It falls into three portions, dealing with first, second and third persons plural in that order. In each case, free-standing forms, possessive and conjugative suffixes and dimensional infixes are given. The three portions are not, however, perfectly symmetrical, as may be seen by comparing only the entries in the Akkadian column:

nīnu AN.TA	*attunu* AN.TA	*šunu marītum*
	attunu KI.TA	
	šunu	
nâti	*kunūti*	*š[unū]t[i* ? .T]A
ana niāti	*ana kunūti* AN.TA	*šunūti* AN.TA
	ana kunūti	

Under the 1st person plural (125-140) are listed opposite *nīnu* the basic form of the 1st person plural infix -me-; the free forms me-en-dè and me-en-dè-a (? with suffixed copula) and the incorporating suffix -u/a/i/en-dè-en. For *nâti* (accusative) the same forms are given, all with the suffix -a; it is not clear whether these are datives or genitives or nominalized forms.[73] The dimensional infixes me-šè, me-da and me-ta (i.e. the basic personal infix inflected in various dimensional cases) are grouped together against *ana niāti*. We shall often find this particular shorthand of using Akkadian *ana* ('to') for the Sumerian dimensional cases in general. It may be compared with the use of the term 'oblique' in Indo-European grammars.

For the second person (141-170) are listed the infix -e-ne- and, curiously, the form e-ne-ne as *attunu*, whether AN.TA or KI.TA with the suffix -u/a/i/(e)n-zé-en as *attunu* AN.TA. After a sort of footnote (148) reminding us that -e-èš is *šunu* (3rd person plural, and surely out of place), the section proceeds with the forms for *kunūti* (with the addition of -e-zé-en-na), all with suffixed -a as with the forms for the accusative *nâti* above. The dimensional infixes are given in the form

$$\left.\begin{array}{r}\text{-e-ne-}\\ \\ \text{-u/a/i/en-ne-}\end{array}\right\} \;-\; \left\{\begin{array}{l}\text{-še-}\\ \text{-da-}\\ \text{-ta-}\end{array}\right.$$

with the -šè- and -da- forms marked AN.TA and the -ta- unspecified.

For the third person (171-201) are listed the suffix -e-ne and free-standing form e-ne-ne (for a-ne-ne), with the form u/a/i/en-n[e-ne], as *šunu marītum* (presumably suffix). Another four forms and -meš are given against *š[unū]t[i* ? .T]A. The 'accusative' forms (with suffixed -a) and the dimensional infixes -u/a/i/en-ne-šè/ta/da (+-e-ne-šè/<?ta>/<?da>-) are here lumped together under the heading *šunūti* AN.TA.

This whole plural pronouns section is somewhat confusing and difficult to understand. In the first place we may note the irregular application of the terms AN.TA, MURU$_4$.TA and KI.TA, already observed in earlier sections of the text. Second, the reasoning is far from clear which led the Babylonians to equate the relationship between Sumerian pronouns and possessive and incorporating suffixes, and the same forms with suffixed -a, with the relationship between the nominative and accusative cases of the Akkadian personal pronouns. The Akkadian forms are here being used more as labels to separate different sets of Sumerian forms than as genuine possible renderings. Finally, the 2nd and 3rd person plural sections show a number of curious confusions and similarities:

---

73. Thureau-Dangin in *RA* 32 (1935), p. 103, took them as datives.

attunu	e-ne e-ne-ne u/a/i/en-zé-en	*šunu*	e-ne e-ne-ne u/a/i/en-n[e-ne]
kunūti	e-ne-a e-ne-ne-a e-zé-en-na u/a/i/en-zé-en-na	*šunūti*	e-ne-a e-ne-ne-a u/a/i/en-ne-ne-a
ana kunūti	e-ne-šè u/a/i/en-ne-šè e-ne-da u/a/i/en-ne-da e-ne-ta u/a/i/en-ne-ta	*šunūti*	e-ne-šè u/a/i/en-ne-šè <?e-ne-da> u/a/i/en-ne-da <?e-ne-ta> u/a/i/en-ne-ta

For comparison, the corresponding section in NBGT II (206-55) has:

kunūti	e-ne	*šunu*	e-ne e-ne-ne ì-ne-ne u/a/i/en-ne
kunūšim	e-ne-a	*ana šunūšim*	u/a/i/en-ne-ši/da/ta
attunu	me-en-zé-en u/a/i/en/b-zé-en		

This seems inexplicable. In NBGT I, there is a deep-rooted corruption in the text at this point.

The following section (202-238ff.) is concerned with a number of different particles. The Sumerian conjunction ù, suffixes -bi and -bi-da and infixed verbal conjunction -nga- are set against Akkadian *u* 'and'. ù/a/i/e is given against *lū*: these may be the various forms taken by the suffix -e generally used to mark the third person singular after the optative preformative hé-. Opposite the Akkadian relative and genitive preposition *ša* are given ša (phonetic for šà), nì, the suffixes -e and -a after -k, the latter plus copula (-kam), the comitative -da (possibly in its possessive use, as with the verb gál) and final vowel (marking the genitive after a variety of vowels?). For *ina* and *ana* are given different Sumerian case-suffixes: -(k)a, -(n)e, -da, -ta, -ù/a/i/e, -(u/a/i/e/)r, -ra, together with the puzzling u_8, ši, ša and ki (which may be the ki of ki....ta). The heading of the next section (241-256) is destroyed. The section ends with the Sumerian verbal prefix ba- (not the suffix -ba, as assumed by Jacobsen),[74] described as *gamartum*, which, it will be argued below (section 3.4), denotes the Akkadian -t- themes and not the perfect tense. A short section of possessive forms follows (258-266):

yā'um	-mu	-mu	nì-gá
kû	-zu	-za	nì-zu
šûm	-ni <-bi>	-na -ba	?

The form -bi and the 3rd person singular possessive pronoun are missing from the section. The first Sumerian column of the above diagram lists the possessive suffixes, and the second the genitives (or locatives) of the possessive suffixes, and the third the possessive pronouns. The Akkadian forms are possessive pronouns. In lines 259-60 we expect -gá and nì-mu and it appears that the nì has got copied onto the wrong line, so that -mu is erroneously repeated in 260 (i.e. lines 258-260 should read -mu, -gá, nì-mu).

The next section (267-307) is exceptionally well organized. It gives forms against which are set the datives of the Akkadian singular pronouns after the preposition *ana* and includes (as noted before) other dimensional cases in the Sumerian. The forms given are the possessive suffix with locative or genitive case ending ('in my...', 'of my...'), the dative of the free form, and the dimensional cases of the infixed forms. In the case of the 1st and 3rd persons, the suffixed and free forms are given before the dimensional cases (the free form of the 3rd person is missing); the 2nd, however, has them the other way round and starts off with some extra 2nd person dative infixes, for which the corresponding 1st and 3rd person forms (not listed) would presumably be -ma- and -na-. The forms may be tabulated thus:

	1st person	2nd person	3rd person
poss. suff. + loc.	-gá	-zu-a/-za	-bi-a/-ba -ni-a/-na

74. *loc. cit.*, p. 57.

free form + dat.	gá-ra	za-ra	e-ne-ra
terminative infix	-mu-ši-	-e-ši-	-u/a/i/en-ši- -u/a/i/eb-ši-
comitative infix	-mu-da-	-e-da-	-u/a/i/en-da- -u/a/i/eb-da-
ablative infix	-mu-ta-	-e-ta-	-u/a/i/en-ta- -u/a/i/eb-ta-
dative infix		-e-a- -ra-da- -a-ra- -e-ra-	
	<-ma->	-ri-, -ra-	<-na->

The remainder of the text (308-462) falls into three clear sections (308-321, 322-394, 395-462), not two as assumed by Jacobsen.[75] The first of these is a section of adverbs and similar words which may be compared with NBGT II 13-45.

The penultimate section (322-394) gives Sumerian forms set against the prepositions *eli* ('over, against'), *qadu* ('with' [adnominal]) and *ittum* ('with' [adverbial]) and various combinations of these with the singular pronouns. The forms listed may be divided into verbal infixes and free-standing forms (whether cases of the free forms of the pronouns or prepositional phrases including them).

First is *eli* (322-52):

	infixed		free-standing			
eli	da	ta	<ra>	diri	ugu	<su>
1ps	-mu-da	-mu-ta-	gá$^{!}$(mu)-ra	diri-mu-šè	ugu-mu-šè	su-mu-šè
2ps	-e-da-	-e-ta-	za - ra	diri-zu-šè	ugu-zu-šè	
3ps	-u/a/i/en/b-da	</ta->	e-ne-a-ar	diri-ni-šè	ugu-ni-šè	
	-mu-da-			diri-na	ugu-na	
				diri-bi-šè	ugu-bi-šè	
				diri-ba	ugu-ba$^{!}$(bi-zu)	

There appear to be one or two errors, as indicated. 3rd person ablative-instrumental forms are wanting.

This is followed by *qadu* (353-377):

	infixed		free-standing		
qadu	da	<ta>	-bi-a-da,	-bi-da	-bi-ta
1ps	-mu-da-	-mu-ta-	gá-a-da		gá-a-ta
2ps	<-e-da->	-e-ta-	za-a-da		za-a-ta + -zu-da (= *ramanīka*)
3ps	-u/a/i/en/b-da/ta-		<e-ne-da>		<e-ne-ta>

Again the initial portion listing just the preposition does not correspond exactly with the subsequent combinations of it with the persons.

Finally *ittum* is listed (379-94). Apparently there are errors and omissions here too:

	infixed		free-standing			
ittum	da	ta	á		ki$^{!}$(ta)	
1ps	-mu-da-	-mu-ta-	<a-mu-da	a-mu-ta>	ki-mu-ta	<ki-mu-da>
2ps	-e-da-	-e-ta-	a-za-da	a-za-ta	<ki-zu-ta	ki-zu-da>
3ps	-an$^{!}$(da)-da-	-an-ta-	<e-ni-da>	e-ni-ta	ki-ni-ta	ki-ni-da

75. *loc. cit.*, p. 57: 308-402, 403-462.

Note here the phonetic spellings e-ni-ta (for á-ni-ta) and a-za-d/ta for á-za-d/ta, with vocalic assimilation of -zu- to -za-. Thureau-Dangin wanted to read za-a-da and za-a-ta here, but the context makes it clear that a-za-da and a-za-ta are correct.[76]

The final section (395-462) is concerned with adverbs, conjunctions and other particles, among which we may note the following: u/a/i/en-ga, given earlier opposite *u* (205-8), is here set against *appūna*, 'moreover'. This is further evidence of compilation. 399-402 gives evidence for the 'abilitative' function of the comitative case noted by Gragg.[77] It is interesting to observe the principles of arrangement at 403ff. Line 404 is erroneous, but the Sumerian lú in 403 appears to have suggested the next line, 405, in which ga is set against *Akkadian lu*. In 414 the ul in the lefthand column is an erroneous anticipation of Akkadian *ul* in 415. 415-25 lists Sumerian negatives, 426-30 interrogatives. The remainder (436-462) is taken up with particles such as ma-a, *-man*, *-mi* and *manma*. ma-a is presumably Akkadian *mā* 'indeed' and not the enclitic *-ma*.

2.3 Structure and content of the epitome NBGT II

Most of the exemplars of NBGT II are from Nineveh. The best preserved was copied from an original from Babylon. The text can be divided, for descriptive purposes, into six sections: but this is partially due to the existence of two lacunae of approximately 11 and 63 lines respectively, so that there may originally have been more distinct sections. The problems of analysis are slightly more complicated here than in NBGT I owing to the dependence of the text on three exemplars rather than on one, and the consequent difficulty in one or two cases of deciding between variant readings. Since the exemplars overlap in only a few places, it is impossible to decide on grounds of frequency of error which of the manuscripts is more likely to be correct.

The initial section (1-12) gives various forms of the bases of Sumerian verbs set against the Akkadian *alāku, uzuzzu, babālu, qabû* and *ašābu*. See p. 99 and pp. 128 ff. It is perhaps no accident that four of the five verbs here chosen are also used in extant verbal paradigm texts. The section is concerned with a biaxial division into the distinctions *ša ištēn* / *ša mādūti*[78] and *hamṭu* / *marû*, although the information presented is not sufficient to make both distinctions in all the verbs. In Sumerian the first three verbs are all written with the same sign (and the plural forms of the first two with the double form of the sign). The reading of the Sumerian equivalent of the singular, *hamṭu* form of *babālu* is not clear: the gloss to the sign was read di-e by the editors of *MSL* IV, but Deimel prints ki-e, presumably following Langdon.[79] The correct reading is probably de_6. The information in this section may be tabulated as follows:

	ša ištēn		*ša mādūti*
alāku	gen, du		re_7, su_8-bé
uzuzzu	gub		súg
babālu	de_6		túm
qabû		? du_{11}, e ?	
ašābu	tuš		dúr-ru-un

	hamṭu		*marû*
alāku	gen, re_7		du, su_8-bé
uzuzzu	gub		súg
babālu	du_6		túm
qabû	du_{11}		e
ašābu	tuš	dúr-ru-un ?	

76. In *RA* 32 (1935), p. 107; cf. *CAD* 'I' *s.v. idu* A, lexical section, p. 10b.
77. G.B. Gragg, *Sumerian Dimensional Infixes*, AOATS 5 (Neukirchen-Vluyn, 1973), pp. 53-66.
78. For readings of these terms see section 3.6 below.
79. A. Deimel, *Sumerisches Lexikon* (Rome, 1928-33), *s.v.* DU; S. Langdon, 'Assyrian Grammatical Texts', in *RA* 13 (1916), pp.91-97.

The entry tuš = *ašāb ištēn hamṭu* should be compared with the colophon of NBGT I, where the tablet series to which it belongs is identified as tuš = *wašābu hamṭu ša ištēn*, in the interests of the relative content of the two texts.

The next section (13-45) lists a variety of particles, conjunctions and prepositions which may be compared with NBGT I 202-40, 308-21 and 403-62.

The third section occupies from 46 probably to 73, since it is likely that nothing is missing from the beginning of the section starting in 74. The righthand entries in the present section are three in number, of which the second, as will be shown, is almost certainly applicable only to the entry immediately opposite it to the left and does not cancel the heading *ana ina* KI.TA in line 46. The third heading survives only as [ ].TA KI.TA[ ], which is unfortunately unintelligible. The heading *ana ina* KI.TA tells us that listed here are Sumerian dimensional case endings which can be summarized by Akkadian *ana* 'to' or *ina* 'in'. The similar use of *ana* in NBGT I may be compared. Since some of the case-endings are single-phone morphemes (i.e. -š or -r or -a) and since the cuneiform writing system cannot write anything shorter than a syllable, the consonant morphemes are here presented together with some of the sounds with which they may come into contact. We have already seen this procedure in NBGT I. Here we have:

(-u)š (-a)š (-i)š for the terminatives;
(-ú)r (-a)r (-i)r for the dative (after a vowel);
-ta for the ablative;
-ra for the dative;
(-r)á (-k)a (-n)a -a for the genitive (or locative);

and we may perhaps conjecture that the list continued with forms such as (-g)a (-g)á (-l)a (-l)á and possibly -e (-k)e$_4$ (-n)é etc. Note that the spelling úr for -r after -u is quite idiomatic. The second heading appears opposite line 53. Whether the reading of D, šá ki-ma A i-te-ner-ru-bu should be preferred to that of C, šá KI.TA i-te-ner-ru-[bu] is not clear, since no satisfactory explanation has so far been produced for either. Against Shaffer's hypothesis that we should understand by the reading of D "-ta- which is *infixed* in place of" (or even "corresponding to") "the case-ending -a",[80] we may object that the section up to this point has listed suffixes not infixes, and that if this head were thought to cancel completely the previous head *ana ina* KI.TA, we should expect *it* to apply to entries subsequent to itself as well. Whatever we may say about ta, and even ra and an, it is clear that rá(DU) and ka never occur as infixes, whereas they do occur as suffixes; and it would make no sense to say of a (58) that it was 'infixed in place of a'. It is precisely because the entries after 53 can be understood as a continuation of those before it that we cannot accept an interpretation of *ītenerrubu* in 53 that cancels the sense of 46. Nor is there any reason to consider the possibility that 53 is entirely out of place. Instead we offer the following solution. The entry is to be understood as a supernumerary comment about the nuance of one suffix in a section of suffixes; -ta- "when it occurs in its locative sense", i.e. when it is 'like' or used 'instead of' -a, as opposed to its equally common ablative sense, may be equated with Akkadian *ana* or *ina*. The strictly ablative sense of -ta is more likely to be equated with *ištu*. Thus on this occasion an Akkadian entry occurs which does *not* cancel altogether the sense of the previous head, but merely adds a comment about *one* of the elements in a list. It seems likely that the scribe of C misread -ma A as TA: not difficult in the Assyrian script.

The fourth section probably begins where the lacuna ends, in 74. The Akkadian entry appears on the tablet in line 74, not in 75 where it is printed in *MSL* IV. The fourth sign is badly damaged but may have been ši i.e. a-na ⌜ya-ši⌝ [x?]. The section tails off into the second lacuna at 117, which lasts until a new section begins in 181. This fourth section gives the

80. *V*. A. Shaffer, 'TA *ša kīma* A *ītenerrubu*: a study in native Babylonian philology', in *OrNS* 38 (1969), pp.433-46.

impression of having been compressed: it is not well organized as it stands, and there is some evidence of confusion on the part of the scribe. The Sumerian forms listed are pronominal elements occurring directly before the verb:

u/a/i/e u/a/i/em u/a/i/eb u/a/i/en u/a/i/em-ta

In addition mi occurs at 78. It may be conjectured that the righthand heading in 94 is out of place, almost certainly the result of compression:

91	ub	*šū ša šushurti*
	ab	
	ib	
94	eb	*anāku* „

The Akkadian entries in this section read as follows. There is damage all down the righthand side of the tablet and it is not possible in every case to know whether some writing has been lost or whether the broken area was blank. Only in 111 is it clear from the tablet (if not from the copy) that there was no more writing on that line.

74 *ana yâši*
79 „
83 *gamart*[*u*
86 *šū ša e*[*līti*
87 *u šushurti e*[*līti*
88 AN.TA *u* [MURU$_4$.TA
91 *šū sa šushurti*[
94 *anāku* „ [
95 *anāku yâti ša* [*malīti*
99 *atta kâ*[*ti*
100 *ša malīt*[*i*
103 *anniš*
107 *šū ša ri*[*qti*
108 AN.TA MU[RU$_4$.TA
111 *šuāti*
115 *anāku u*[

The entries at 86-88, 99-100 and 107-108 are meant to be read together. These all seem difficult to understand at first. What, for example, is meant by *anākū yâti* or by *atta kâti*? Some of these become clearer when the passage is compared with the following: NBGT I 1-12, 22-25, 47-101. In the present section, NBGT II 102-117 is clearly closely related to NBGT I 1-12 and 22-25, where the *rīqu* forms of the pronominal infixes were listed according to the unequal distribution of cases *anāku, atta, šū, šuāti*. Here we have *anāku, šū* and *šuāti*; and *šū* is designed *ša riqti*. However, *anniš* 'hither' remains mystifying (103-106). Next NBGT II 95-102. which seem to fall together as a paired sub-section, should be compared with NBGT I 47-84. It is probably not going too far to say that the former is a direct though incomplete condensation of the latter passage, which lists *malû* forms set against the nominative and accusative of the Akkadian pronouns. Certainly they are derived from the same original material. In the NBGT II passage, the only persons given are *anāku*/*yâti* (combined) and *atta*/*kâti* (also combined), with the entries shortened in both cases. We can confidently restore *malīti* in 95. Lines 91-94 may be compared with NBGT I 85-89, which read:

85	ub	*anāku šushurtum malītu* MURU$_4$-tú
86	ub	*atta šushurtum* <*malītu*> MURU$_4$.TA
87	ub	*šū šushurti malītu* AN.TA MURU$_4$.TA
88/9	íb	*šushurtu riqtim* AN.TA MURU$_4$.TA

Thus NBGT II 91-94 probably represent the *šushurtu malû* forms. The fact that AN.TA (88) directly follows *elīti* (86 and 87), for which, as will be shown, it is the logographic writing, is further evidence of condensation. Finally the forms mu u/a/i/(e)m mi at 74-77 may be compared, as may also u/a/i/(e)m (83-85), with NBGT I 90-93: u/a/i/(e)m and me, which are described as *riātum* AN.TA MURU$_4$.TA. *Gamartum*, as will be shown, denotes the Akkadian -t-theme forms, and the forms listed here are probably intended to refer to those prefix chains beginning im-ma- and àm-ma- which in the verbal paradigms are set against Akkadian -t-forms.

This section tails off into a lacuna of approximately 63 lines, of which only the entries ub and ab are preserved, suggesting that the present subject matter continued for most if not all of the lacuna. The fragment K.14991, part of Rm 361 (text C) but not joining it, belongs in the lacuna at approximately lines 139-51, see *MSL* V pp.195ff. Recognizable are AN].TA KI.T[A (obv. 4'), ⌜a⌝-ṣe-e-x[(*aṣṣēr*?) (rev. 3), AN.TA (rev.5, 7) and šu-ús-hur-[tú (rev. 6), but, *pace* Landsberger, I cannot see [ga-m]ar-t[u] in obv. 5.

At 181 begins a long section dealing with the free-standing forms, possessive and incorporating suffixes, and infixed forms of the personal pronouns. It is summarized in the table below. The first person plural is given first (181-94). Against *nīnu* are set the basic form of the infix -me-, the prefix chain mu-un-, the free form me-en-dè-en and the incorporating suffix -u/a/i/en-dè-en. Against *niāti*, the accusative, is set a form of the infix with suffixed -a

Table to show the content of the section NBGT II 181-255

	free forms	suffixed forms (in sg., possessive, in pl., incorporating)	infixed (and prefixed) forms
1sg	gá-ra	-mu	
	ana yâšim	*yâum*	
	gá-da	-gá	
	ittīya	*ana yâšim*	
2sg		-zu	-e- *atta, kâšam*
		kûm	-e-šè- -e-da- -e-ta- -e-ra- *ana kâši*
		-zu-a, -za	-e-da- *tele'i*
		ana kâšim	-e-da- *ittīka*
3sg		-ni, -bi	-ši-
		šûm	*ana šuāšum*
		-ni-a, -bi-a / -na, -ba } *ana šuāšum*	
1pl	me-en-de-en	-u/a/i/en-dè-en	-me- -me-a- mu-un-
	nīnu	*nīnu*	*nīnu* *niāti* *nīnu*
			-me-šè- -me-da- -me-ta- -me-a- *ana niāšim*
			-me-da- *nile'i*
			-me-da- *ittīnī*
2pl	me-en-zé-en	-u/a/i/en/b-zé-en	-e-ne- -e-ne-e-a-
	attunu	*attunu*	*kunūti* *kunū[ti]*
3pl			
	e-ne-ne / ì-ne-ne }	-e-ne	-u/a/i/en-ne-
	šunu	*šunu*	*šunu*
			-u/a/i/en-ne-ši-
			-u/a/i/en-ne-da-
			-u/a/i/en-ne-ta-
			-u/a/i/en-ne-a- *ana šunūšum / šunūti*

(Falkenstein's 'dative-locative' infix),[81] which may be compared with NBGT I 132; the phrase *ana niāšim* does duty for the various dimensional cases in their infixed forms. Finally two other uses of the comitative case are noted.

There follows the treatment of the first person singular (195-98). The change of number was apparently missed at first by the scribe, who continued to write *niāšim* (1st person plural) for *yâšim* etc. (lines 196, 198). Only the possessive suffix and declined forms of it and of the free-standing pronouns are given. That gá in 196 is the locative (or possibly the genitive) of -mu, contracted from -mu-a, and not the uninflected form of the free-standing pronoun, is likely both because it is set against *ana yâšim* and not *anāku*, and because of the parallel with the succeeding paragraph 217-26. *ana* is here again used to mean 'dimensional cases', 'oblique'. The text then moves on to the infixed forms of the second person singular (199-205). (The overall arrangement of this section is considered below). The lefthand entry in 199 is to be transcribed:

-tum. -e-

The reading íb can make no sense in this context. The *-tum* is probably the end of whatever the last word of the preceding righthand Akkadian entry was in the full version of the text from which this condensed section is derived. We must assume that there was not room for it in its proper place. The TA at NBGT I 89 may be compared. The Sumerian entry in 199 is then -e-, which is written on the far right of the column, well away from the -tum, although this is not clear from the printed text. Against it is set *atta kâšam*, a type of heading which we earlier regarded as indicative of condensation (cf. NBGT II 94-102). Note that here nominative and dative (*kâšam*) occur together; earlier nominative and accusative were combined. The dimensional cases of the infix (= *ana kâši*) follow, with other uses of the comitative. 206-216 is occupied with the second person plural. The infix -ene- is set against *kunūti* (or *-ku[nu]*, following B) and its dative-locative form (e-ne-e-a, not e-ne-a [collated]) probably also against *kunūti* (*pace* the editors' suggestion *kunū⌜šim⌝*: cf. NBGT I 149), followed by the free form me-en-zé-en and the incorporating suffix -u/a/i/en/b-zé-en (*attunu*).

After this the second person singular section is continued, with the possessive suffix -zu (Akkadian *kûm*, the possessive pronoun) and its locative or genitive in contracted and uncontracted forms. The same forms are then given for the third person singular animate and inanimate respectively (220-22, 224-26). After -na (*ana š[uāšum]*) has been added -ši-, probably by a scribe mistaking the locative of the possessive suffix for the dative infix -na- and deciding to insert another infix which could also go opposite *ana šuāšum*.

The final and by far the longest part of the section (227-55) deals with the 3rd person plural. It is split up by a lacuna of about nine lines of which three can confidently be restored. Opposite *šu[nu]* (possibly *šu[nūti]*, cf. NBGT II 206) are given the incorporating suffix -e-ne-, the free form e-ne-ne and the form ì-ne-ne, with the basic form of the infix, -u/a/i/en/ne-. The dimensional cases of the infix are then listed, opposite *ana šunūšim*. Since the terminatives are given in 234-37, the comitatives in 244-47, ablatives in 248-51 and dative-locatives in 252-55 (where they are set against *šunūti*; there is no trace of the ditto [for *ana*] in C), it is difficult to imagine which other infixes could have filled the gap.

This section of pronouns appears to have been put together, then, possibly from a larger work. There are many indications of condensation. It may also have been rearranged at some point. This may have been accidental, or it may have been a result of the epitomization. The evidence for this is the imbalance between the sub-sections, which was first noticed by Langdon, who suggested that the 1st person singular section was out of place and properly

81. *Das Sumerische* p.48.

belonged with the 2nd and 3rd person singular sections.[82] The content of the whole section is shown by the table on p. 66, while the following demonstrates the present order of the material:

1pl. 1sg. 2sg.(infixes) 2pl. 2sg.(suffixes) 3sg.(suffixes) 3pl.

It may be conjectured that this represents an original arrangement:

[1sg.(infixes)] 1pl. 1sg. 2sg.(infixes) 2pl. 2sg.(suffixes) 3sg.(suffixes) 3pl. [3sg.(infixes)]

and that the beginning and end of the section have somehow gone missing, or, alternatively:

1pl. 1sg. 2sg.(infixes) 2pl. 2sg.(suffixes)↓ 3sg. 3pl.↓

which would produce the symmetrical pattern:

1pl. 1sg. 2pl. 2sg. 3pl. 3sg.

The order of pronouns here, 1st, 2nd, 3rd, is found elsewhere in grammatical epitomes and grammatical vocabularies, and differs from the orders preferred by verbal paradigms, 3rd, 1st, 2nd or 2nd, 1st, 3rd.

We come now to consider the final portion of the text (256-79), a list of various Sumerian pre-verbal chains with Akkadian equivalents. This section also gives indications of having once been perfectly symmetrical and well organized; through faulty and probably uncomprehending copying it has been confused to the point where it is actually unintelligible. We begin by proposing our emendations, which are to the Akkadian entries only. In 274 beneath šu-a-šum appears, in small writing, :ti. This colon sign is normally used to introduce a variant reading, which the scribe, working from two exemplars and unable to decide between two alternatives, did not wish to exclude. The implication is that his alternative text read

a-na-ku šu-a-ti šu-a-ti ù a-na-ku šu-a-ti

which makes very little sense. What seems more likely is that the text originally had 𒁁-ti, i.e. TIL-ti (= *gamarti*) as in 262, and that this was originally not in line 274 but opposite the Sumerian entry in line 271. A second possible but by no means so necessary or defensible emendation concerns lines 274 and 277, which actually read:

274 a-na-ku šu-a-ti šu-a-ti
ù a-na-ku šu-a-šum
:ti
277 a-na-ku šu-a-ti šu-a-ti
a-na šu-a-šu! (collated) u ga-mar-tum

Instead of introducing *-ku* in 277, with the editors, it would be preferable to exclude the *-ku* from the second *anāku* of 274, and read *ana šuāšum* (as an error of homoeotopy). *Ana šuāšum* makes better sense opposite the dative infix -na-.

The arrangement of this section will be seen from the following schema, incorporating the proposed emendations. It should be noted that two of the paragraphs, the first and the third (256-61 and 265-70) are double, i.e. they list two forms for each person instead of one. The second -ni- in the entries set against Akkadian 1st person singular (*anāku*) should be read as -i-, since -ni- is not, as far as our knowledge goes, ever associated with a 1st person singular agent, nor are the prefix chains in question ever attested, so far as I know; whereas the form with a long vowel spelling is known to be associated with the 1st person singular, and is attested, in other spellings at least (cf. 256-57 and 262 of the present text). The rulings of the tablet, which become intermittent after line 271, can be discounted as without special significance.

82. In *RA* 13 (1916), p.96.

256/7	bí-, bi-i-	*anāku šuāti*
258/9	^{bi}bí-, bí-e-	*atta šuāti*
260/1	bi-in-, bí-in-	*šū šuāti*
262	ba-a-	*anāku šuāti gamarti*
263	ba-e-	*atta šuāti gamarti*
264	ba-an-	*šū šuāti gamarti*
265/6	i-/mi-ni-ì-	*anāku šuāti šuāti*
267/8	i-/mi-ni-e-	*atta šuāti šuāti*
269/70	i-/mi-ni-in-	*šū šuāti šuāti*
271	ba-ni-i-	*anāku šuāti šuāti gamarti*
272	ba-ni-e-	*atta šuāti šuāti gamarti*
273	ba-ni-in-	*šū šuāti šuāti gamarti*
274	in-na-ni-ì-	*anāku šuāti šuāti u ana$^{!}$ šuāšum*
275	in-na-ni-e-	*atta šuāti šuāti u ana$^{!}$ šuāšum*
276	in-na-ni-in	*šū šuāti šuāti u ana$^{!}$ šuāšum*
277	ba-na-ni-ì-	*anāku šuāti šuāti ana šuāšu u gamartum*
278	ba-na-ni-e-	*atta šuāti šuāti ana šuāšu u gamartum*
279	ba-na-ni-in-	*šū šuāti šuāti ana šuāšu u gamartum*

The Akkadian headings here may be divided into four:

i) *anāku, atta, šū* clearly refer to 1st, 2nd and 3rd person singular forms of the verb, marked in the Sumerian by the infixed long vowel, -e- and -n- respectively.

ii) The designations *šuāti* and *šuāti šuāti* alternate as the infix -ni- is either absent or present. Thus they apparently distinguish between non-causative and causative forms.

iii) *ana šuāšum* is clearly equated with the dative infix -na-.

iv) *gamarti, gamartum* appears to be connected with the presence of the prefix ba-. It is dealt with more fully below, §3.4.

2.4 The text NBGT IX and its commentary

It is likely that if only one version of this text survived it would be described as a practice tablet. The content is mixed and confusing. However, fragments of two versions exist, both carefully written tablets from the library of Ashurbanipal. Exemplars A_1, A_2 and A_3 are fragments of the same tablet, although they do not join. Their column lines are drawn exactly alike. It is extremely likely that B and C are fragments of a second tablet. The widths of the columns are exactly the same on C as on B with the exception of the lefthand margin, which is a little further to the left on C, judging from the photograph, and the hand is apparently identical. Consequently we must assume that we are dealing with a text of the literary tradition, i.e. a tablet that was copied for reading, even though the text itself might be a collection of excerpts. This view is supported by the existence of a tablet in a later, neo-Babylonian script, which is a *ṣâtu* commentary apparently on our text, or on texts on which ours was also based. This commentary has been edited by Leichty.[83] The arguments against its being a commentary on NBGT IX are, first, the confused and derivative nature of our text, not the sort of text on which a commentary would normally be written, and, second, the fact that the entries in the commentary do not always occur in the same order as the entries in the other text to which they are supposed to refer.[84] It is then perhaps wiser to describe both text and commentary merely as deriving from the same material.

The two versions of NBGT IX overlap in two places only: the first part of B is identical with A_1; the end of it with A_2. The setting out of the fragments in *MSL* IV is slightly

83. In 'Two Late Commentaries', in *AfO* 24 (1973), pp.79-82.

84. Though this is sometimes so in commentaries, cf. E. Reiner, *Šurpu*... (Graz, 1958), pp.50f.

confusing. There are no grounds for calculating the rather exact figures given for the numbers of missing lines. In any case the figures given do not make sense. The colophon on the reverse of A_1 is omitted entirely.

The text may be described as follows. For convenience' sake the line-numbering of *MSL* IV is retained. A_3 does not overlap with any other piece. It consists of portions of four adjacent columns, two on either side of a righthand edge. The latitudinal curvature makes it likely that these are columns ii, iii, iv and v of a six-column tablet. Longitudinally it is virtually flat, suggesting that it comes from the middle of a tablet. A_1 curves latitudinally to a left edge and longitudinally to what must be close to an upper edge. The preserved surface of A_2 betrays no trace of curvature. C is clearly a lower lefthand corner. Thus we have:

	version 1		version 2
col. i	(near beginning)	A_1 obv.	(overlapping A_1 and A_2) B
	(middle)	A_2	(bottom) C
col. ii	(middle)	A_3 obv.	
iii	(middle)	A_3 obv.	
iv	(middle)	A_3 rev.	
v	(middle)	A_3 rev.	
vi	(colophon; bottom)	A_1 rev.	

The variants between the two versions where they overlap are only slight. Owing to the heterogeneity of the content the analysis must be done fragment by fragment. There are seven unconnected fragmentary sections of text altogether, of which the first is formed by the overlap of A_1 obv., A_2 and B. Although written throughout in four sub-columns, the text is essentially a *two* or *three* sub-column text. Sub-columns iii and iv are read straight across. In general where there is a lefthand entry of only one sign it is written in sub-column ii. But the first fragment is not clear in this respect. How are the two occurrences of HA, written, exceptionally, at the far right of sub-column i (B, lines 32 and 59 [in fact 60]), to be explained? And what does KÚR MIN mean (57)?

The first fragment has in sub-columns iii and iv a number of entries characteristic of the righthand column of a grammatical epitome, down as far as line 56, NI.GI RI ⌜x⌝ (it is not clear from the tablet that this last sign is BI), but sub-column ii at lines 34-37 has signs arranged as if in a sign-list: LÚ LU (collated) LA LI. There can be no connection between the two sets of entries here. ÈM.KÚŠ (line 39) appears in the commentary, line 4, where it is glossed *šushurtum*. Possibly it is to the DUR of line 42 (or line 218) that the commentator refers in line 1, explaining it as *qablû*. li-la!-a in 50 he has never heard of (even if he has read it correctly) (commentary, line 5). NÌ.TIL RI IŠ (55) can probably be correctly so restored from the commentary, line 5, but beyond the first NÌ.TIL (= *gamartum*) it is not comprehensible. The remainder of this passage (collated) reads:

	version 1			version 2			
57			[	KÚR	MIN	DÙ.LUH	57
58			[			DAM A RA [x	58
60		Ù	x[	HA		DAM DU[	59
61	ŠE	GU.SUM	an-[		ŠE GU.SUM	an-[	61
62			NÌ[			NÌ[	62
63		UL	DA_5?[		UL	x[	63
65	ZA	U	AN[			x[	64
66			DAH[		HA	[	65
67			x[	[			67

Does it say in line 61 ŠE *mihiltum* (GU.SUM) *an[nītum]* 'this sign is ŠE', as suggested by the commentary, line 3? Does it refer to dù-luh, 'terrifying' (also mentioned in the commentary, line 6)? What is the meaning of DAM A RA[x]?

The next fragment is C. DAM A RA appears again. The remaining entries are more characteristic of a grammatical epitome, as are the passages from columns ii and iii, in that there is only one lefthand sub-column (viz. ii, and i is blank), and the entries in this sub-column are mu, ar, ni, ir, bi — easily recognizable as grammatical elements. The entries in the righthand sub-column are also of a familiar type, although KAS_4 LÁ MA in line 116 is inexplicable. Line 118 reads TIL-tum: ya-ši (collated; correct in CT XI 42). aṣ- in 202 is perhaps the beginning of *aṣṣēr*. *ra'i* (119) also occurs in the commentary, line 11. The sign at the end of 125 appears to be TA; that at the end of 216 could be -tum or -šum. Sub-columns i and ii in 220 are destroyed and may not have been blank.

The passage from column iv continues in the same vein. It looks odd because of the way it is written, but all the equations are familiar from elsewhere:

	lū; *ša* ⸢x⸣; *šū*[ ]; *ša* NÌ.⸢SUD⸣ [x]
ga-nam	*pī*[*qa*]; *min*[*di*]; *u*[*qa*]; *tūša*[*ma*]; *appū*[*na*]
-dam	*mā* KI.[TA]; *ša* KI.[TA]; *ana* KI.[TA]; *anāku*; *šushurtum* (⸢NIGÍN⸣ (collated))^{tum} KI
á-še	(erasure)*inimma*; *lūman*; *anumma*
u_4-ta	*appiš* RI; *ana irat*; *allapak*; *ina qabal*; *ištu* [*ūm*]

Various entries in the commentary can be connected with this passage: *uqa* and *tūšama* (line 15), *lūman, anumma* and *ana irat* (16) and u_4-ta = *allapak* (17).

It is impossible to ascertain what the text as a whole was used for, or why, if it is a collection of excerpts, it was copied. It was perhaps used for teaching purposes. Other examples of mixed sign-lists and grammatical texts which may be compared are NBGT III, V, IXa and IXb. Its principal interest for us lies only in the occurrence in it of a number of grammatical terms.

2.5 The Eme-sal Vocabulary

This is a short three-tablet series, entitled dím-me-er = dingir = *ilum*, of some 489 entries, surviving in a number of copies from the neo-Assyrian period. It is a vocabulary of Eme-sal, the 'women's dialect' of Sumerian, arranged in three columns of Eme-sal, Eme-gi (standard dialect) and Akkadian respectively. The chief passage of interest for our investigations occurs at the beginning of the third tablet:

[ma]	[D]U	a-la-ku
[de-de]	du	KI.MIN ma-ru-u
[d]e	gen	KI.MIN ha-am-ṭu

<ga->ga[85]	túm-ma	*babālu*!(text: KI.MIN) ma-ru-u
ga	de_6	KI.MIN ha-am-ṭu
er	de_6	KI.MIN KI.MIN

er	de_6	ta-ba-lu KI.MIN
er	de_6	le-qú-u KI.MIN

85. It appears that the scribe actually wrote ga here and not ga-ga, since elsewhere in sections with a mixture of single-sign and multiple-sign entries, the single-sign entries are written on the far left, but here both ga's (4 and 5) and er (6) are written on the far right of the column, implying that this was a section of single-sign entries only. But clearly ga-ga was intended.

9 er	de_6	šu - lu - u ša *titāpī*(BARÁ.$MUNU_{?7}$)[86] KI.MIN
10 er-er	túm-túm	KI.MIN ša *titāpī*(BARÁ.$MUNU_{?7}$)[86] ma - ru - u
sag er-er	sag túm-túm	qúl-lu-lu ma-ru-u
múš ga	múš túm	na-pár(D: par)-ku-u ma-ru-u
múš nam-ba-an-ga-ga	múš nam-ba-an-túm-ma	a-a ip-pár-ku

This passage is discussed in Chapter 4, p. 127 ff.

Hamṭu and *marû* occur again at III 76 ff. There seems to be some confusion here. The text should say

ma-ma	gá-gá	*šakānu marû*
ma-al	gál	*šakānu marû*
mar	gar	*šakānu hamṭu*

In certain circumstances gál might be equated with *šakānu*. The alternation of inim gar and inim gál, both meaning 'to sue', in legal documents, might be instanced. But the *grammatical* counterpart of gá-gá is not gál but gar.

Marû also occurs at III 82, where it appears to be entirely out of place, and at II 90, where it occurs in its other sense, 'fattened' of sheep. This may be etymologically unconnected with the verb *marû* 'to be slow' and the grammatical term *marû* 'slow', although the scribe of manuscript D of the third tablet of this text evidently felt able to write the grammatical term with the logogram for 'fattened', ŠE. Perhaps he knew no better.

2.6 The dialogue dub-sar dumu-a-ni ab-dim_4-e-dè

This composition, published by Sjöberg as 'Examination Text A',[87] is regarded by its editor as not being of Old Babylonian date but as none the less reflecting the curriculum of the scribal colleges of that period.[88] The earliest manuscripts date from perhaps as early as 1000 BC, certainly no earlier. A senior scribe taxes his son (or pupil) with his ignorance and indolence and puts to him a whole series of questions to which, it may be supposed, he could be expected to know the answers.

The text contains a number of grammatical terms. Consideration of the text as a whole suggests that the senior scribe's questions were not systematic but rather random. However, each time a question is asked, the various parts of it appear to be concerned with the same subject. Thus from the position of the grammatical questions in the examination, no conclusion can be drawn; on the other hand, we can happily be fairly certain that the whole section lines 16-17 was concerned with that topic, and that the topic was confined to that section.

This section is preserved in only two manuscripts, the neo-Assyrian B (which has both lines) and N, dating from the Seleucid era (which has only 16). These read as follows:

86. This sign seems to be most like $MUNU_7$ with the last few strokes written superscript. D has $MUNU_4$ in 9. The printed text has BARA in 9, BÁRA in 10; the tablet BARÁ in both places.
87. In *ZA* 64 (1975), pp.134-76.
88. *V. AS* 20, p.160, and also the introduction, see above, pp. 5f.

B, line 16, Sumerian column:

]nì-nigin muru$_4$-bi [x x]-lá
nu-tu]ku peš - a - bi x[ ]MIN

Akkadian column:

uh-hur-ta a-tar-ta ga-[mar-]ta šu-ús-hur-ta qab-ta
ma-ra-a ha-an-ṭa šá[x x]a? la i-šu-u šul-lu-šu [MIN?]

N, line 16 (N has an interlinear Akkadian version):

nì-t]il-la-a nigin[
]ga - mir - tim[

B, line 17, Sumerian column:

e]-ne ra uš aš eš[an]
]EŠ GIŠ IG[I
]DA ì - zu-[ù

Akkadian column:

a-na-ku at-ta šu [a-na uš a]š? eš an
]x[ ] ⌜an⌝ x x

At the end of line 16, MIN stands for Sumerian i-zu-ù, Akkadian *tīde*, 'Do you know...?' If we set the Sumerian and Akkadian of both mss. of line 16 against one another, we get:

uhhurta atarta/gamirti/gamarta? šushurta qab<lī> ta
nì-t]il-la-a nigin/nì-nigin muru$_4$-bi
marâ hanṭa ša[ ]*a lā išu šullušu* (*tīde*)?
[še? ul$_4$]-lá[nu-tu]ku peš-a-bi x (i-zu-ù)

Gamartum (here with the variant spelling *gamirtum*), *šushurtum*, *qablītum* (the correction is easily made), *marû* and *hamṭu* are terms which are already familiar from the grammatical epitomes. Sjöberg suggests restoring ul$_4$ (known as the Sumerogram for *hamṭu*) in the gap after lá.[89] Better would be the restoration ul$_4$]-lá, still leaving space in the lacuna for ŠE, if that is the correct Sumerian for *marû*.[90] What is to be restored directly after that ('that which has no ...') it is impossible to deduce. The reference to triplication of the verb[91] is perhaps more likely to be connected with a similar reference in this text (line 15) and with the apparent practice of learning and reciting things in threes noted by Sjöberg elsewhere.[92] May it not also possibly refer to the grouping in verbal paradigms of forms into threes, each of three persons?

Line 17 appears to refer to the contents of grammatical analysis texts. -ra is doubtless the dative postposition and -uš/aš/eš forms of the terminative.

The importance of this text for us is twofold. First, it gives further evidence for the spelling and for the Sumerian equivalents of the grammatical terms already known, as well as two new terms, *uhhurtum* and (*w*)*atartum*. Second, if Sjöberg is right to regard the content of the text as reflecting the curriculum of the scribal colleges of the Old Babylonian period (an institution which seems to have died out at the end of that period), it provides valuable proof that the

89. *loc. cit.*, p.142.
90. *V.* section 2.5 above, Eme-sal vocabulary III 10.
91. Assumed by Sjöberg, *loc. cit.*, p.159.
92. In *AS* 20, p.164 and n.20. Cf. also Civil's description of the series erim-huš = *anantu* and an-ta-gál = *šaqû* in *AS* 20, p.126.

grammatical terms and type of analysis familiar to us from other texts surviving only in late copies (and hence the grammatical theory on which they were based) date back at least to the Old Babylonian period a thousand years earlier; thereby upholding the view expressed by Jacobsen in 'Very Ancient Linguistics: Babylonian Grammatical Texts', that the 'bold and radical step' required to analyse the paradigms and vocabularies into their elements had already been made at that early date.[93]

2.7 The text K4808 and its duplicates

When he published it in 1883, Haupt described this fragmentary composition, of which the text is presented below as appendix 5.2, as being part of a five-column vocabulary. It is fairly clear, however, that whatever the text is, it is not a vocabulary or sign-list. Nor is it a practice tablet, for such tablets do not, of course, get copied several times. It seems possible that it is a commentary of some sort, albeit a rather unusual one, since the central (third) column, which seems to contain the entries according to which the others are arranged, lists words which might all come from the same text. These are:

2	*erba*	come in!
5	*tišab*	sit down!
8	*namru etellu*	brilliant prince
10	*šupših*	pacify!
12	*lurēška* (*lurīška*?)	I will exult in you (I will cause you to rejoice)
15	*luppaliska*	I will look to you
18	*lu'udka*	I will praise you
20	*lussukka*	I will choose you
22	*amru hassu*	perceptive and wise
25	*lē'ûm*	puissant
28	*bān kala*	creator of everything
31	*ēpiš mimma šumšu*	maker of all things
33	*mudû*	wise
36	*mušēpiš*	who causest to be done
39	*tašme*	you heard
40	*usa*[	

The choice of vocabulary and the forms of expression are highly reminiscent of the private 'prayers of humble access' collected together in the series called šu íl-la 'lifting of the hand',[94] but I cannot find any one text there which contains this sequence of words and phrases.

The second column normally contains a logographic writing of the principal word in the third column entry. Thus there are:

5	TUŠ	for	*ašābu*
8	ŠÈR	for	*etellu*
15	IGI	for	*naplusu*
18	ÁR	for	*na'ādu*
20	SUH	for	*nasāqu*
31	NÌ	for	*mimma*
33	ZU	for	*mudû* and
36	DÙ	for	*epēšu*.

93. *loc. cit.*, p.54.

94. *V.* E. Ebeling, *Die akkadische Gebetsserie "Handerhebung"...* (Berlin, 1953), and O. Loretz and W.R. Mayer, *Šu-ila-Gebete, AOAT* 34 (Neukirchen-Vluyn, 1978).

In line 22, ban is probably an error for AN which is recorded as a logographic writing for *šutaqtû* and appears as such in columns iv and v (line 24), or else it is an error for PÀ. Similarly e in line 28 is probably an error for AG (=*epēšu*) which occurs in columns iv and v (line 27). UR in line 39 is difficult; it may perhaps be connected with an entry in the Eme-sal Vocabulary iii.21 (*MSL* IV, p.28) where úr-da (ur$_5$-da) is given as = *šemû*; or possibly the scribe has simply written the taš of *tašme* in the wrong place before writing it in the right place.

The entries in the first column normally re-appear in the fourth column except that in lines 10 and 12 the first (and second) columns are blank. In certain cases it is possible to explain these, as for instance, in line 8: ar. This is rendered in column v as *namāru* and may be regarded as a logographic writing for the *<nam>ru* of column iii.[95] So the section lines 8-9 is fully explicable. Apparently the fifth column is meant to explain the fourth, and this does indeed make the text resemble a vocabulary.

However, in the remaining sections, the entries in the first columns, repeated in the fourth column of each section, bear no relation to the second or third column entries. In line 10 SÌG occurs in the fourth column, explained by *pašāhu* in the fifth, although the first and second columns are blank; this clearly reflects the *šupših* of column three.

Just as the largely inexplicable first column entries reappear on the first line of the fourth column, so the second column entries normally reappear on the second line of the fourth column, or, if it is a three-line section, on the third line. The exceptions to this are lines 2-4, where KU$_4$, the logographic writing of the third column entry, appears on the second line of a three-line section, and lines 12-14, where LI similarly appears on the second line; likewise lines 22-24; and lines 25-27, where the second column entry DÙ reappears on the third line of the fourth column, but the logographic writing for the third column entry, *lē'ûm*, actually occurs on the *second* line of the fourth column. In those sections which have three lines, the extra entry in the fourth column appears to be quite unconnected with the rest of its section.

As has been said, the fifth column is apparently intended to 'explain' the fourth, even though the Akkadian reading of the fourth column entries is already clear enough from the third column (although, admittedly, the fifth column gives the verbs in the infinitive form). This is clear enough in the case of about half the entries, viz.

2	ag	=	*e[pēšu]*
3	ku$_4$	=	*erē[bu]*
6, [34]	e$_4$	=	*pašāhu* (written for e$_{11}$)
7	tuš	=	*ašābu*
8	ar	=	*namāru*
9	šèr	=	*etellu* EME.SAL
10	sìg	=	*pašāhu*
13	li	=	*râšu*
17	igi	=	*amā[ru]*
19	ár	=	*na'ādu*
21	suh	=	*nasāqu*
23	pà	=	*amāru*
24	an	=	*šutaqtû*
26	ú	=	*lē'ûm*
27	dù	=	*mudû*
30	ag	=	*e[pēšu]*
32	nì	=	*mimma [šumšu]*

95. For AR = n[a]-ma-rum see *Ugaritica* 5 (1968), p.239 r. 14' (S^a-type vocabulary).

— even though the presence of the entries in lines 2, 6, 24 and 27 is difficult to explain at all.

The remaining fourth and fifth column entries are:

4	um	=	*riā[tum]*
5	ma	=	EŠ NÌ.[ ]
11	ba	=	MÌN *ina:ana*
12	ra	=	*anāku* NIGÍN AN
14	tum	=	*atta* NIGÍN SIG
15	bí	=	EŠ NÌ BA
16	e	=	NÌ.KÚŠ SIG-*tum*
18	tum	=	*atta* NIGÍN AN (D *add.*:SIG)
20	si	=	*kâšu*
22	ba	=	*lī- ša mā*
25	ru	=	AN $MURU_4$ SIG
28	um	=	*riyātum*
29	da	=	*kala* (B: ka-[, D: ka!-la; Lambert's trans. has il-la)

The last of these probably refers to the *kala* of line 28, but seems corrupt; it need trouble us no further. Many of these entries contain grammatical terms familiar from other texts: AN, $MURU_4$; SIG evidently appears here for KI; *lī-*, *ša mā, riātum* (with the useful new spelling ri-ya-a-tum); while *anāku, atta, kâšu, ina* and *ana* are ubiquitous in the grammatical epitomes. The reading of EŠ NÌ[ ] and of EŠ NÌ BA are unknown to me.

The equation um = *riātum* is known from other texts; -ba = *ana* or *ina* is comprehensible; tum (ÍB) = *atta* may actually be derived from NBGT II 199, where the *-tum* was regarded as intrusive and incorrect; but the remainder of the 'equations' in the above list seem incomprehensible. However, the portions of text 12-14 and 18-21 do offer some clue as to the principle of composition. In lines 12-14, against *lurēška* are set *anāku - râšu - atta*, suggesting that this is some sort of grammatical analysis. If so, it is analysis of Akkadian, which is a novelty. Similarly against *lu'udka* in 18 is set *atta*, although with AN, 'prefixed' added, which it is not; and against *lussukka* in 20, *kâšu* (which is, however, dative whereas *-ka* is an accusative suffix). The presence in these lines of NIGÍN and NÌ.KÚŠ, which, it is suggested below, are used to refer to non-indicative forms (such as *lurēška, lu'udka* and *lussukka* are), is interesting.[96]

All in all, this is a puzzling text. Professor Lambert suggested to me that an acrostic might be involved. The entries in the first column, read downwards, do spell out some Akkadian words:

lines 2, 5, 8	*[n]agmar* (?) 'it is finished'
lines 12, 15, 18	*rabītum* 'great' (fem.)
lines 22, 25, 28	*barûm* 'seer'
lines 31, 33, 37	*balāṭa* 'life'.

But we were unable to explain the connection of those syllables with the rest of the text. What we may be dealing with here is some sort of cryptographic numerological or 'graphological' speculation in which words and syllables were lifted from ancient, perhaps ill-understood texts, re-arranged and invested with some intrinsic, maybe magical or philosophical value of their own. For our study of grammatical terminology, the value of this text lies in the spelling of *riātum—riyātum—*that it offers and in the evidence that SIG and SIG-tum are alternative logographic writings of whatever the term was which is elsewhere written KI or KI.TA.

96. *V.* section 3.3 below.

3 *Grammatical Terms*

3.1 AN.TA, MURU$_4$.TA and KI.TA

We come now to investigate in detail the technical grammatical terms occurring in the texts described in Chapter 2. The terms AN.TA, MURU$_4$.TA and KI.TA, meaning literally ‘at the top’, ‘in the middle’ and ‘at the bottom’, and others similar to them in form and meaning, occur extensively throughout the epitomes and in certain other texts. It seems certain that they are related and should be treated together. The traditional interpretation of them has always been ‘prefix’, ‘infix’ and ‘suffix’, and it is hoped to show that while this is in principle correct, the picture is in fact somewhat more complicated. A key passage for their interpretation[97] is a sentence of Esarhaddon in which it is explained how Marduk altered the length of time that Babylon was destined to lie in ruins by reversing the figure of 70 to make 11. In cuneiform writing these figures are written  and  respectively, and Esarhaddon says *eliš ana šapliš ušbalkit* ‘he turned them upside down’. This reflects the original downward direction of cuneiform, and shows how ‘top’ and ‘bottom’ may refer to what we should call the beginning and end of a word.[98]

The occurrences of the terms in their commonest forms (AN.TA, MURU$_4$.TA and KI.TA) as well as in other forms *outside* the epitomes are mostly in difficult or confused contexts and are therefore of little help in elucidating the meaning of the terms. However, they are most helpful in suggesting the correct Akkadian readings for them.

Thureau-Dangin[99] proposed to read them as adverbs in *-iš* and this is perhaps supported by an-ta = e-liš and ki-ta = šap-liš in Examination Text A (but in a non-grammatical context),[100] and by a similar entry in ur$_5$-ra = *hubullu*.[101] But the evidence of other sources suggests overwhelmingly that, as grammatical terms, they should be read as adjectives, and the apparently feminine forms as feminine adjectives or as abstract nouns.[102] The forms (excepting the regular AN.TA, MURU$_4$.TA and KI.TA) occur as follows:

AN	K4808 lines 12, 18, 25 (see appendix 5.2)
e-lu-u	Leichty’s commentary (see section 2.4 above), obv.10
e-lu-ú	" " , obv. 11
e-li-ti	NBGT II 86, 87
MURU$_4$	K4808 line 25

97. Pointed out by Shaffer in *OrNS* 38 (1969), p.435, n.4.
98. *V.* H. Hirsch in *AfO* 21 (1966), p.34. The usage in Old Babylonian mathematical texts may be compared in which *šapal* is used to mean, in effect, ‘to the right of’, as is clear from Neugebauer and Sachs, *Mathematical Cuneiform Texts, AOS* 29 (New Haven, 1945), p.42, line 5, see *ibid.*, n. 125^b.
99. In *RA* 32 (1935), p.100.
100. *V. ZA* 64 (1975), p.140, line 14.
101. At tablet II, lines 228ff., in *MSL* V (Rome, 1957), p.68.
102. The question of these forms is discussed below in section 3.6, pp. 100 ff.

muru$_4$-bi (= qab-<li->ta)	Examination Text A, 16
MURU$_4$-ú	S^{a} Voc F 10' (*MSL* III 57); Leichty's commentary, obv. 1
MURU$_4$-tú	NBGT I 85
KI	Aa II/6 ii 3 (*MSL* XIV 291)
SIG	K4808 lines 14, 25
SIG-tu[m]	K4808 line 16

We propose the readings *elû* (*elītu*), *qablû* (*qablītu*) and *šaplītu*). There is no syllabic evidence for the reading *šaplû* in grammatical texts, but the following passage from a commentary on the Weidner god list, in which the word *šaplû* is apparently used by the commentator to refer to the feminine ending of a word, seems to suggest that it is the correct reading:[103]

line 13: [^{d}n]a-na-a : NA : na-bu-ú : A : ši-i ⌜šap⌝-lu-u : šá-niš etc.

This would imply a reading *šaplītum* for SIG-tu[m].

There follows an inventory of all occurrences of these terms in NBGT I and II.

AN.TA

NBGT I	125-31	me me-en-dè me-en-dè-a u/a/i/en-dè-en	ni-nu AN.TA
	141-45	e-ne e-ne-ne u/a/in-zé-en	at-tu-nu AN.TA
	156-65	e-ne-še u/a/i/en-ne-šè e-ne-da u/a/i/en-ne-da	a-n[a] ku-nu-ti AN.TA
	181-201	e-ne-a e-ne-ne-a u/an-ne-ne-a e-ne-šè u/a/i/en-ne-šè/ta/da	šu-nu-ti AN.TA
	390	an$^{!}$-da	it-ti-šú AN.TA
	436-38	DU ù ši	ma-a AN.TA
NBGT II	15-16	nu-uš	lu-ma-an AN.TA ú-ul AN.TA
	17-18	nu-ub-da	a-di-ni AN.TA la-ma-an AN.TA
	23	u$_4$-ta	ap-piš AN.TA
	31	mu	„ (aš-šum) AN.TA
	41	en-na	a-di AN.TA
	42	ga	lu-ú AN.TA
	43	hu	lu-ú AN.TA
	44	ha	lu-ú AN.TA
	45	hé	lu-ú AN.TA

103. The passage was kindly brought to my attention by Professor Lambert, and will be published by him in a forthcoming edition of the god lists.

MURU$_4$.TA

NBGT I	1-4	ù/a/i/e	a-na-ku ri-qu MURU$_4$.TA
	85	ub	ana-ku šu-ús-hur-tum ma-li-tú MURU$_4$.-tú
	86	ub	at-ta šu-ús-hur-tum <*malītu*> MURU$_4$.TA
NBGT II	199	[[tum]] e	at-ta ka-šam MURU$_4$.TA

KI.TA

NBGT I	5-8	ù/a/i/e	at-ta ri-qu KI.TA
	9-12	ù/a/i/e	šu-u ri-qu KI.TA
	42-45	[ù/a/]i/e	[m]a-ri-tum KI.TA
	59-64	u/a/i/en	at-ta ma-lu-u KI.TA
		ab	
		u$_8$	
	146-47	e-ne	at-tu-nu KI.TA
		e-ne-ne	
	257	ba	*gamartum*! KI.TA(see p. 85)
	310-12	ke$_4$-eš	aš-šum KI.TA
		nam	
		ke$_4$-nam	
	439-54	um/àm/im	ma-a KI.TA
		me/ma	
		dam/da-àm	
		nam	
		na-nam	
		u/a/i/en-ga	
		ab-ga	
		i-me	
		i-me-a	
	460	giš	ma-an KI.TA
	461	e-še	mi-i KI.TA
NBGT II	13	e-še	mi-i KI.TA
	14	giš-en	ma-an KI.TA
	19-20	nu-me-a	šá la KI.TA
			ba-lum KI.TA
	21	na-an-na	e-la KI.TA
	22	u$_4$-da	šum-ma KI.TA
	29	ke$_4$-eš	aš-šum KI.TA
	30	ka-nam	„ KI.TA
	32-33	ta	iš-tu KI.TA
			i-na a-na „
	195	mu	ya-u-um KI.TA
	208-16	me-en-zé-en	at-tu-nu KI.TA
		u/a/i/en-ze-en	
		u/a/i/eb-zé-en	

AN.TA MURU$_4$.TA

NBGT I	22-25	ù/a/i/e	šu-[a-t]i AN.⌈TA MURU$_4$.TA⌉ [104]
	47-53	u/a/i/en	a-na-ku ma-lu-ú AN.TA MURU$_4$.TA
		ab	
		mu	
		u$_8$	

104. Evidently so read by Thureau-Dangin in *RA* 32 (1935), p.92.

	71-77	u/a/i/en		[šu]-u ⸢ma-lu⸣-ú AN.TA MURU$_4$.TA
		ub/ab		
		u$_8$		
	78-84	u/a/i/en		šu-a-ti ma-lu-ú AN.TA MURU$_4$.TA
		u/a/íb		
	87	ub		šu-ú šu-ús-hur-ti ma-li-tú AN.TA MURU$_4$.TA
	88-89	íb	[[ta]]	šu-ús-hur-tú ríq-tim AN.TA MURU$_4$.TA
	90	u/a/im		ri-a-tum AN.TA MURU$_4$.TA
		me		
		u/a/i/en-ga		
		[ma-]ra		
		ma-da		
		ma-ta		
		ma-da-ta		
	313	mu aš		aš-šum AN.TA MURU$_4$.TA
	316	u$_4$-ta !(text: da) [105]		ap-piš AN.TA MURU$_4$.TA
NBGT II	86-90	u/a/i/en		šu-ú šá e-li-ti [
		ab		u šu-ús-hur-ti ⸢e-li-ti⸣[
				AN.TA u [MURU$_4$. TA]
				(restored on the basis of NBGT I 71ff.)
	107-110	ù/a/i/e		šu-ú(ša ri-i[q-ti]
				AN.TA MURU$_4$[. TA]
	188	me-a		ni-ya-ti AN.TA MURU$_4$.TA
	189-92	me-šè/da/ta/a		a-na ni-ya-šim AN.TA MURU$_4$.TA

MURU$_4$.TA KI.TA

NBGT I	65-70	u/a/i/en	ka-a-ta MURU$_4$.TA KI.TA
		ab	
		u$_8$	

AN.TA KI.TA

NBGT I	425	nu-da aš	a-di-ni AN.TA KI.TA
NBGT II	37-40	u/a/i/en-ga	ap-pu-na AN.TA KI.TA

AN.TA KI.TA MURU$_4$.TA

NBGT I	54-58	u/a/i/en	ya-a-ti AN.TA KI.TA MURU$_4$.TA
		mu	
NBGT II	61	[ ]	[ ].TA KI.TA[
NBGT II K.14991 obv.4'		[	] [AN].TA KI.T[A] (see *MSL* V pp.195ff.)

In our study of the structure and content of NBGT I and II we noted various apparent inaccuracies in the application of these terms. We suspected that they were applied haphazardly and without thoroughness, that is to say, that there were passages where the terms might have been expected to be present but were not; passages where one term was used where we should have expected another; and passages where a term was used where none was applicable. It is also apparently the case that where a term is used in a heading to describe the first of a succession of forms, it does not always apply to all the forms listed in that particular section. This would be a natural result of addition and compilation, and is in direct contrast to the practice with the Akkadian entries (as opposed to these grammatical comments): for we know of no instance where, when only one Akkadian entry is given, it does not apply also to all the other Sumerian forms listed in the lefthand column for that section (i.e until the next

105. Corrected by Thureau-Dangin in *RA* 32 (1935), p.106, on the basis of NBGT II 86-90 and NBGT II 23.

head). This suggests strongly that the grammatical terms were added at a later stage than that of the original composition of the texts.

To demonstrate in detail the haphazard application of the terms, we may consider the following collection of parallel passages (including certain examples from other texts) in which identical or similar Sumerian elements are listed with the Akkadian entry opposite them followed by a designation of one or more of the terms under discussion.

NBGT I	1-4	ù/a/i/e	a-na-ku ri-qu MURU$_4$.TA
	5-8	ù/a/i/e	at-ta ri-qu KI.TA
	9-12	ù/a/i/e	šu-ú ri-qu KI.TA
NBGT II	107-110	ù/a/i/e	šu-ú ša ri-i[q-ti] AN.TA MURU$_4$[.TA]
NBGT I	22-25	ù/a/i/e	šu-[a-t]i AN.TA MURU$_4$.TA
	42-45	[ù/a/]i/e	[m]a-ri-tum KI.TA
	47-53	u/a/i/en ab mu u$_8$	a-na-ku AN.TA MURU$_4$.TA
Aa III/4 30 (*MSL* XIV 340)		(mu-u) (MU)	ana-ku ri-qu AN.T[A]
NBGT I	59-64	u/a/i/en ab u$_8$	at-ta ma-lu-ú KI.TA
Aa II/6 ii 3 (*MSL* XIV 291)		(an) (AN)	ka-tú ha-am-ṭu KI
NBGT I	71-77	u/a/i/en ub/ab u$_8$	[šu-]ú ⌜ma-lu⌝-ú AN.TA MURU$_4$.TA
NBGT II	86-90	u/a/i/en ab	šu-ú šá e-li ti[u šu-ús-hur-ti ⌜e-li-ti⌝[AN.TA ù [MURU$_4$.TA]
NBGT I	78-84	u/a/i/en ub/ab/ib	šu-a-ti ma-lu-ú AN.TA MURU$_4$.TA
	85	ub	ana-ku šu-ús-hur-tim ma-li-tú MURU$_4$.tú
	86	ub	at-ta šu-ús-hur-tum <*malītu*> MURU$_4$.TA
	87	ub	šu-ú šu-ús-hur-ti ma-li-tú AN.TA MURU$_4$.TA
NBGT II	199	[[-tum]] e	at-ta ka-šam MURU$_4$.TA
K4808			
cols.iv & v	14	tum	at-ta NIGÍN SIG
cols.iv & v	18	tum	at-ta NIGÍN A[N]
Aa V/1 (*MSL* XIV 411)	155-57	bi-e BI	at-ta šu-a-tum ma-ru-u KI.TA at-ta NIGÍN KI.TA ù NU.NIGÍN (written in five lines)
S^a Voc F (*MSL* III 57)	9'-10'	[bi-e) (BI)]	at-ta šu-a-ti ma-ru-ú MURU$_4$-ú (written in two lines)
NBGT I	316	u$_4$-ta!	ap-piš AN.TA MURU$_4$.TA
NBGT II	23	u$_4$-ta	ap-piš AN.TA
NBGT IX	278	u$_4$-ta	ap-piš
NBGT II	188	me-a	ni-ya-ti AN.TA MURU$_4$.TA
	189-92	me-šè/da/ta/a	a-na ni-ya-šim AN.TA MURU$_4$.TA
NBGT I	141-45	e-ne e-ne-ne u/a/in-zé-en	at-tu-nu AN.TA
	46-47	e-ne e-ne-ne	at-tu-nu KI.TA
NBGT I	94-97	u/a/i/en-ga	(ri-a-tum AN.TA MURU$_4$.TA)
	448-51	u/a/i/en-ga	(ma-a KI.TA)
NBGT II	37-40	u/a/i/en-ga	ap-pu-na AN.TA KI.TA u šu-ú ma-a

NBGT I	310	ke_4-eš	aš-šum KI.TA
NBGT II	29	ke_4-eš	aš-šum KI.TA
NBGT I	460	giš-en	ma-an KI.TA
NBGT II	14	giš-en	ma-an KI.TA
NBGT I	461	e-še	mi-i KI.TA
NBGT II	13	e-še	mi-i KI.TA

The discrepancies in almost all but the last three pairs of passages quoted make us suspect error even before we begin to investigate the meanings of the terms. In an attempt to isolate the errors, we shall, however, assume that the majority of the entries are correct and attempt to explain them as they stand.

First the evidence supporting the assumption that AN.TA means 'prefix' will be examined. hé- (with variants conditioned by vowel harmony hu- and ha-) and ga- can only occur in Sumerian at the beginning of a verbal complex. en-na ('until') is a conjunction and therefore stands at the beginning of its clause, as in

en-na a-wi-il-la gal-zu-ukkin-na-mu di an-ne-en
'until you bring Awilla and my councillors to justice'[106]

mu- in its sense of 'because of, concerning' stands at the beginning of the phrase it qualifies, as in

mu-erén-lú-kúr-ra-ke_4 lugal ù-na-du_{11} šu mu-e-tag_4
'you sent a letter about the enemy troops to the king'[107]

The Akkadian equivalent of u_4-ta is the conjugation *appiš* meaning 'since, as', so we may conjecture that the Sumerian form had the same function, and, probably, position.[108]

nu-ub-da-, meaning 'not yet' or 'before', can be seen at the beginning of a verbal complex at *ana ittišu*, *MSL* I, p.33, 10:

nu-ub-da-me-a = la-a-am.

nu-uš- is a 'frustrative' verbal prefix,[109] as may be seen from

nu-uš-ma-ab-bé-en ku-li-mu nu-uš-ma-ab-bé-en
'if only I could tell you, my friend, if only I could tell you'[110]

Now so far it seems that an interpretation of AN.TA as designating an element occurring initially in a verbal complex *or* at the beginning of a clause makes good sense. It is interesting that the Babylonians should have grouped together the two features under one head. AN.TA thus denotes something a little wider than our 'prefix'.

The remaining occurrences of it, in NBGT I, are more difficult. DU (436; the reading is unknown in this context)[111] is impossible to classify. ù- and ši- (437-38) may be the verbal prefixes of previousness and assertion, in which case *mā* is probably the Akkadian exclamation used in introducing speech, 'now', 'I tell you', and not the enclitic *-ma* 'and'. If so, our interpretation of AN.TA holds good. -an!(text: da)-da- 'with him' (infixed) occurs towards the end of a long section (322-94) listing various dimensional expressions in combination with the singular pronouns, in which, exceptionally, it is the *only* entry to bear a grammatical designation as well as an Akkadian equivalent. Bearing this in mind, together with the fact that it is the final entry in a column and that the next entry, at the top of the next column, is

106. - F.A. Ali, *Sumerian Letters...*, A 2, 14.
107. *ibid.*, B 5, 4.
108. Sumerian u_4-bi-ta 'at that time, since that time', very frequent in royal inscriptions, may be compared.
109. According to Jacobsen in 'About the Sumerian verb', in *Toward the Image of Tammuz* p.249.
110. 'Gilgameš, Enkidu and the Nether World', line 247 (and cf. 172ff.).
111. It also apparently occurs on the tablet Rm 2, 429, line 4: [...]DU = ma-a (= *CT* 18, 47).

the verbal infix -an-ta- (also meaning 'with him'), we suggest that the appearance of AN.TA here is an error and should be discounted.

The remaining forms marked AN.TA, as also all those marked $MURU_4$.TA, are verbal infix forms, and as these present special problems, discussion of them is deferred until later.

The interpretation 'suffix' fits KI.TA well. -e-še is well known as a suffix that marks direct speech or the proverbial character of an utterance. -giš-en is found in OBGT Ia (rev. i 15) as a suffix marking the hypothetical nature of a phrase:

u_4-da-giš-en = šum-ma-ma-[an] 'if' (unreal).

-nu-me-a, 'except', 'without', is found suffixed at OBGT I 488ff:

⸢me-dè-da-nu-me⸣-a = i-na b[a-lu-ni] 'without us'.

-na-an-na, also meaning 'except', is suffixed at OBGT I 488ff.:

me-en-dè-na-an-na = ša la ni-a-ti 'except us'

-ke_4-eš and -ka-nam, meaning 'because', are familiar as suffixes. -ta is the ablative case ending, -mu the first person possessive suffix. -me-en-zé-en can occur as a suffixed form of the pronoun 'you' (plural), e.g. OBGT I 412:

in-ga-me-en-zé-en = at-tu-nu-ma 'it is you also',

and -u/a/i/en/b-zé-en are familiar as the incorporating suffixes for that person. The suffixes -um/àm/im, -dam, -da-àm, -nam, are various forms of the copula after verbal endings, -na-nam is a suffixed particle, and ì-me and ì-me-a are forms of the verb to be. ì-me-a, at least, is found at the end of a phrase at OBGT I 313, 330, 397, 879; whether it actually forms part of the complex which precedes it is difficult to say. -me (NBGT I 442) may possibly represent a form of me 'to be' in final position. ma (443) is more difficult to identify: there *is* a suffix -ma in Sumerian, presumably borrowed from Akkadian *-ma* 'and' (although we had so far supposed that the ma-a given as Akkadian equivalent here was not *-ma* but *mā*, 'I tell you', 'now'). It may be seen in:

inim-na-me ma-an-ne-eš-ma LUL-aš ba-húl-le
'they told me everything and I was very pleased'[112]

It is quite likely that the two ma's were confounded by the compiler.

u/a/i/en-ga and ab-ga are discussed below: they are probably labelled KI.TA here mistakenly. The KI.TA at 257 (ba = *gamartum*! KI.TA) is almost certainly a mistake. As is made clear by NBGT II 262-79, the term *gamartum* is associated with the verbal *pre*fix ba- (*pace* Jacobsen's claim to the contrary that -ba is here to be regarded as the suffixed 'in its...' denoting 'when such and such had taken place').[113] This line is already known to be corrupt (the text reads TA E TUM) and it seems justifiable to discount it in the present argument.

Discussion of the remaining occurrences of KI.TA, in connection with the verbal infixes, will be found below.

Of the combinations of terms occurring, by far the commonest is AN.TA $MURU_4$.TA and since it seems possible to identify it with a specific function, we incline to regard it as a unit with a proper meaning of its own, and not just as meaning 'AN.TA and/or $MURU_4$.TA'. It is probably to be read in Akkadian *elû qablû*, cf. the commentary (above, section 2.4), obv. 10:

SI.DUR : e-lu-u $MURU_4$-ú

— unless the correct reading here is *elû u qablû*. The latter is perhaps supported by NBGT II 88, AN.TA u [$MURU_4$.TA], if correctly restored on the basis of NBGT I 71-77. With the exception of three entries, all occurrences of AN.TA $MURU_4$.TA are with elements which can be immediately identified as occurring in Sumerian 'infixed at the front' of the verbal complex, i.e. infixed immediately before the verb itself. *We* should probably want to say 'infixed towards the front', to avoid the seeming contradiction. Thus there are the forms -ù/u_8-, -a-, -i-, -e-, -un-,

112. Ali, *Sumerian Letters...*, B 19, 3.
113. In 'Very Ancient Linguistics: Babylonian Grammatical Texts', p.57.

-an-, -in-, -en-, -ub-, -ab-, -íb-, -mu-, -me-a-, -me-šè-, -me-da, -me-ta-. The fact that some of these (-e-, -en-, -me-a-, -me-šè-, -me-da-, -me-ta-) *cannot* stand at the very front of the complex argues convincingly against taking AN.TA MURU$_4$.TA as 'prefix and/or infix'. It is true that some of the elements listed above can also appear as suffixes of the 1st or 2nd person singular (-u/a/i/en) or as forms of the suffix -e (-ù/u$_8$/a/i/e), but no other interpretation seems to make as good overall sense as the proposed 'infixed in the front part of the verbal complex'.

The three passages which do not so readily admit of explanation are NBGT I 90ff., 316 and 313. At 90ff. the forms um/àm/im me u/a/i/en-ga ma-ra/da/ta/da-ta are set against the entry *riātum* AN.TA MURU$_4$.TA The forms u/a/i/en-ga and ma-ra/da/ta/da-ta are clearly infixed before the verb, but it is difficult to identify the function of um/àm/im and me. It is argued (in section 3.4 below, where the term *riātum* is discussed) that these represent the element -m-, which is always 'infixed at the front', and our interpretation of AN.TA MURU$_4$.TA then holds good. The significance of me in 93 is still not clear. Possibly it is an attempt to represent the consonant -m-. The way in which, in sign lists, the final consonant of a gloss is clarified by writing it in with an insignificant support vowel may be compared, as for example i-li for íl.[114] At NBGT I 316 u$_4$-da = *appiš* AN.TA MURU$_4$.TA appears. This was corrected by Thureau-Dangin to u$_4$-ta.[115] The correct form appears at NBGT II 23 where it is described, as we should expect, as AN.TA 'occurring at the beginning of a clause'. Consequently MURU$_4$.TA is to be regarded as intrusive here. Finally mu...aš, set opposite *aššum* AN.TA MURU$_4$.TA in NBGT I 313, is a two-part expression meaning 'because' of which the first element stands at the front of a phrase, and the second, representing the terminative case-ending -(e)š(e) after the genitive -a(k)- (sometimes appearing as ak-eš), is of course suffixed. There seems therefore to be no accounting for AN.TA MURU$_4$.TA here.

A comparable instance of this last is NBGT I 425:

nu-da aš *adīni* ('not yet') AN.TA KI.TA.

As is made clear by

inim é-gal nu-ù-da-an-šub-ba-aš 'without his having relaxed the official claim on her'[116]

this, like mu...aš, is a two-part expression of which one element is prefixed and the other suffixed. The designation here is AN.TA KI.TA, which is thus easily interpreted 'prefixed and suffixed'. AN.TA KI.TA occurs again at NBGT II 37 to describe u/a/i/en-ga, which are also listed at NBGT I 94-97 (where they are in a list of elements of which the first has opposite it the designation AN.TA MURU$_4$.TA discussed above, pp. 85-6), 205-208, 395-98 and 448-52 (where, with ab-ga, they are in a list of forms which has at its head KI.TA). Now -nga- (of which -bga- must be a rare variant) is a verbal conjunction ('and...') which may only occur preceded by the neutral prefix ì- or by one of the preformatives hé-, ù-, ša- or narrative na-. According to our interpretation of the terms so far we should expect it to be designated AN.TA MURU$_4$.TA 'infixed at the front', as indeed it is at NBGT I 94ff. KI.TA at NBGT I 439 certainly seems inappropriate, and that passage is perhaps to be explained by assuming that KI.TA is not to be carried through, as *mā* is, as a ditto, down to 454, but applies to only some of the Sumerian elements listed: -dam, -da-àm, -nam, -na-nam, as well as the -um/àm/im (?me) at the beginning of the section. It will be recalled that difficulty was experienced in classing ì-me and ì-me-a, which follow the -nga- entries in 453-54, as 'suffixes' in the normal sense (above, p. 85). It is in any case argued below in section 3.4 that -nga- is mistakenly included in this entry owing to an erroneous identification of -um/àm/im (439ff.) with the -um-/-àm-/-im-, representing -m-, listed in 90ff. This hypothesis, however, will not account for the presence of AN.TA KI.TA at NBGT II 37, where we can only assume that it is a mistake for something like AN.TA MURU$_4$.TA.

---

114. *V.* S^b I 92 (*MSL* III 104).
115. In *RA* 32 (1935), p.106.
116. A. Falkenstein, *Die neusumerischen Gerichtsurkunden* (Munich, 1956-57), 43, line 5.

The remaining combinations of terms are MURU$_4$.TA KI.TA at NBGT I 65 and AN.TA KI.TA MURU$_4$.TA at I 54. These will now be discussed together with the remaining verbal infix forms marked AN.TA, MURU$_4$.TA or KI.TA. Thus the passages now under discussion are:

NBGT I	125-31	me me-en-dè me-en-dè-a u/a/i/en-dè-en	ni-nu AN.TA
	141-45	e-ne e-ne-ne u/a/i/en-zé-en	at-tu-nu AN.TA
	146-47	e-ne e-ne-ne	at-tu-nu KI.TA
	156-64	e-ne-šè u/a/i/en-ne-sè e-ne-da u/a/i/en-ne-da	a-na ku-nu-ti AN.TA
	185-201	e-ne-a e-ne-ne-a u/an-ne-ne-a e-ne-šè u/a/i/en-ne-šè/ta/da	šu-nu-ti AN.TA
	1-4	ù/a/i/e	a-na-ku ri-qu MURU$_4$.TA
	85	ub	ana-ku šu-ús-hur-tum ma-li-tú MURU$_4$-tú
	54-58	u/a/in mu	ya-a-ti AN.TA KI.TA MURU$_4$.TA
	86	ub	at-ta šu-ús-hur-tum <*malītu*> MURU$_4$.TA
NBGT II	199	[[-tum]] e	at-ta ka-šam MURU$_4$.TA
NBGT I	5-8	ù/a/i/e	at-ta ri-qu KI.TA
	59-64	u/a/i/en ab u$_8$	at-ta ma-lu-ú KI.TA
	65-70	u/a/i/en ab u$_8$	ka-a-ta MURU$_4$.TA KI.TA
	9-12	ù/a/i/e	šu-ú ri-qu KI.TA
	42-46	[ù/a/]i/e -ne	[m]a-ri-tum KI.TA

Certain entries in this list can probably be eliminated from the discussion. In the first passage cited (I 125-31), the second element listed is either a free form (me-en-dè) to which no designation of the type at present under consideration is applicable; or possibly a suffix (cf. OBGT I 410). In either case, this can be taken to indicate that AN.TA is only intended as a description of the first element (me). The necessity of attempting to explain how -u/a/i/en-dè-en could be described as AN.TA when it occurs only as a suffix is thereby removed. Concerning the whole passage NBGT I 141-201 we feel unable to comment, since, as was observed in section 2.2 above (p. 61), there is certainly some deep-rooted confusion at this point between the forms of 2nd and 3rd person plural, which it is impossible to disentangle. It is possible that the AN.TA which occurs four times in this passage (including 125) to describe what are apparently forms infixed 'at the front', i.e. before the verb itself, is to be regarded not as AN.TA 'prefix or introductory word', but as an abbreviation of or alternative form for AN.TA MURU$_4$.TA. This hypothesis is to some extent confirmed by the fact that the only examples of AN.TA susceptible of this interpretation occur in what was previously, on independent grounds, recognized as a single, unified section (141-201), suggesting that we have here a deviant usage copied into our text from the original from which this passage was collected or epitomized.

It has already been noted that the listing in the texts of the positions in which the elements may occur is by no means complete or exhaustive, and it is only by bearing this in mind that we can begin to explain the use of terms in the remaining passages. This illustrates well the point made in the introduction (above p. 7) that these texts are an analysis of written Sumerian. The writing en is not itself significant until one of the contexts in which it may appear is specified. Essentially these remaining forms must either be infixes before the verbal base or the verbal suffixes -e or -en coloured by various vowels. (NBGT I 46 -ne is presumably the plural suffix -e-ne). We propose that MURU$_4$.TA (or MURU$_4$-tú) be understood as designating the former circumstance, KI.TA as designating the latter. In this connection, the following passage may be compared:

(an) (AN) ka-tú ha-am-ṭu KI[117]

MURU$_4$.TA KI.TA (NBGT I 65) will then be taken as 'MURU$_4$.TA and/or KI.TA'. AN.TA KI.TA MURU$_4$.TA (NBGT I 54) must presumably mean much the same, although the rather odd order in which the terms are listed may indicate some sort of scribal mistake.[118]

The only problem then remaining is that mu (58), ab an u$_8$ (63-64 and 69-70) cannot occur in suffix position. It is true that, in the case of pre-verbal chains ending in -ab- or -u$_{(8)}$-, these elements may occur in final position when the pre-verbal chain is placed after the verb, in a second person imperative. But so far, in describing other elements, no attention seems to have been paid to this contingency. The explanation, instead, is probably to be sought in the tendency already noted in some cases for the grammatical term to apply more tenuously to entries towards the end of a list of which it stands at the head. mu-, -ab- and -u$_8$- all come at the end of their sections, and perhaps if the compiler were being more meticulous, he would only have described them as MURU$_4$.TA.

The conclusions to be drawn from the above investigation may be stated as follows:
The principal terms used by the Babylonian grammarians to identify the function of Sumerian 'bound forms' by describing the position in which they could occur, were:

1) AN.TA, designating an element or word occurring at the beginning of a complex or phrase or clause,

2) AN.TA MURU$_4$.TA (of which MURU$_4$.TA and (in the section NBGT I 125-201) AN.TA are variant forms), designating an element occurring infixed in a pre-verbal chain, i.e. at the front of a verbal complex, and

3) KI.TA, designating an element occurring at the end of a complex.

In addition mention may be made of MURU$_4$.TA KI.TA, which, if correct, designates elements of which some appear in the verbal suffix position and others in the infix position; and AN.TA KI.TA, which seems to designate expressions consisting of a prefixed element and a suffixed case-ending.

3.2 *Rīqu* and *malû*

We are concerned here with the terms represented by the following writings: ri-qu, ríq-tim, ša ri-i[q-ti], riq-ta-šu, NÌ.SUD, ša NÌ.S[UD], ma-lu-ú, ma-li-tú, and šá ma-li-ti.

It seems reasonable to conclude that these represent the adjectives *rīqu* and *riqtu*, *malû* and *malītu*, with logogram for the former pair NÌ.SUD. Akkadian *rīqu* means both 'empty' and 'distant', although here, in contrast to *malû* 'full', it is surely 'empty'. (NÌ.)SUD is properly a writing for *rīqu* (or *rūqu*) 'distant', but can also be used as a writing for the homophonous *rīqu* 'empty'.

117. Aa II/6 ii 3, *MSL* XIV, p.291.
118. We should expect here KI.TA alone.

The terms occur as follows:

NBGT I	1-4	ù/a/i/e		a-na-ku ri-qu MURU$_4$.TA
	5-8	ù/a/i/e		at-ta ri-qu KI.TA
	9-21	ù/a/i/e		šu-ú ri-qu KI.TA
		ul/al/il ša/ši na ba ab ta		
	23-34	ù/a/i/e		šu-a[-t]i AN.TA MURU$_4$.TA
		ul/al/il/ ša/ši na ba ab ta		
	35-41	?[un/an/in/en x x x]		[ha-am-ṭ]u$^?$ ma-l[u-]⌜ú⌝[119]
	47-53	un/an/in/en ab mu u$_8$		a-na-ku ma-lu-ú AN.TA MURU$_4$.TA
	59-64	un/an/in/en ab u$_8$		at-ta ma-lu-ú KI.TA
	71-77	un/an/in/en ub/ab u$_8$		[šu-]ú ⌜ma-lu-⌝ú AN.TA MURU$_4$.TA
	78-84	un/an/in/en ub/ab/íb		šu-a-ti ma-lu-ú AN.TA MURU$_4$.TA
	85	ub		ana-ku šu-ús-hur-tum ma-li-tú MURU$_4$-tú
	86	ub		at-ta šu-ús-hur-tum <*malītu*> MURU$_4$.TA
	87	ub		šu-ú šu-ús-hur-ti ma-li-tú AN.TA MURU$_4$.TA
	88-89	íb [[ta]]		šu-ús-hur-tú ríq-tim AN.TA MURU$_4$.TA
NBGT II	95-98	un/an/in/en		a-na-ku ya-ti šá [*malīti*]
	99-102	un/an/in/en		at-ta ka-a-ti ša ma-li-ti
	107-110	ù/a/i/e		šu-u ša ri-i[q-ti] AN.TA MURU$_4$.[TA]
NBGT IX	40	(HA)	(LI)	NÌ.SUD
	115	(...)	(...)	riq-ta-šu
	264			ša NÌ.S[UD] (collated)
Aa II/1 Commentary B rev.12	(*MSL* XIV 270)	né-e	NI	at-tú ri-qu KI.TA
Aa III/4 30	(*MSL* XIV 340)	(mu-u)	mu	a-na-ku ri-qu AN.T[A]
Ea fragment C 1'	(*MSL* XIV 518)	[...]-⌜ú⌝		ana-⌜ku ri$^?$⌝-[qu ma]-ru-u K[I .TA]
Sa Voc. F 11'	(*MSL* III 57)	(bé-e)	(BI)	at-ta ri-qu KI.TA
izi D iv 6	(*MSL* XIII 183)	e-ne in-ga-me-àm		šu-nu ri-qu-ma

It will have been gathered from earlier remarks that the position to be maintained on the interpretation of these terms is essentially that stated by Jacobsen (in 'Very Ancient Linguistics: Babylonian Grammatical Texts', p.59), viz. that *rīqu* and *riqtu* (literally 'empty') refer to the forms ù a i e and that *malû* and *malītu* (literally 'full') refer to un an in en ub ab íb (eb). This involves rejection of certain other entries as irrelevant or confused. Our position differs from that of Jacobsen, however, in that he assumes these forms to represent the personal infixes occurring directly before the verb *only*, whereas (as will have become clear in the preceding section) we include the various suffixed personal elements also.

First, we must consider the entries we propose to discount. In NBGT I 13-21 and 26-34 are listed elements which may indeed be equated with an Akkadian 3rd person pronoun but which were probably added from a different source and which disturb the balance of the section 1-34. It will be noted that none of the elements listed at 13-21 can occur in suffix position, as is, however, suggested by the head of the sub-section 9-21. It is therefore reasonable to assume that *rīqu* does not apply to 13-21, nor, for the same reasons, to 26-34.

If such was the structure of the first section listing *rīqu* forms, then it is fair to assume that the original content of the next section was 47-50, 54-57, 59-62, 71-74 and 78-81, i.e. un/an/in/en only for each person. This assumption is to some extent supported by the fact that e.g. ab and u$_8$ (63-64) cannot appear as suffixes (except in imperatives), yet such would appear to be entailed if the designation KI.TA were thought to apply to the entire entry.

We shall assume, then, that the significant content of the section 1-84 consists of the entries ù/a/i/e and un/an/in/en only.

It was argued earlier (above, section 2.2, p. 59 f.) that at NBGT I 88-89, íb was the entry

119. *V.* section 2.2 above, p. 57.

supposed to stand opposite *šushurtu riqtim* AN.TA MURU$_4$.TA, unless some greater compression had taken place. Compression is made more likely by the fact that (if *šushurtu riqtim* is correctly placed against íb) íb appears to be described as *riqtim*. The spelling of the word *riqtim* with the signs ríq-tim is unique, but quite clear on the tablet. It is probably better to exclude this passage from consideration, as being corrupt.

The entries in other lexical texts quoted in *MSL* IV present a number of difficulties. It is easy to see how the prefix mu- might be listed against *anāku*, and we can only assume that this entry has been excerpted from some list such as occurs at NBGT I 47ff. (only with the designation *rīqu*). However, the entry S^a Voc F 9-10 must be corrupt since be does not occur in suffix position. Conversely, at á-A II 1 -ni is correctly labelled KI.TA, but it is difficult to know how *rīqu* can be applied to what is an adjectival rather than a verbal form; the meaning of *ṣītu* is in any case not clear in this context. The remaining entry, Izi D IV 6, may be compared with OBGT I 415 e-ne-ne in-ga-me-a : šu-nu-ma 'it is they' or 'also they'. The meaning of *rīqu* in *šunu rīqūma* must, however, remain obscure. Certainly here it is not a grammatical term at all, but part of the Akkadian entry (as is suggested by the *-ma* occurring directly after it) and is perhaps to be rendered as something like 'it is just them' or 'only they'.

One further justified assumption seems to be that we may understand the presence of *rīqu* in NBGT I 22 and *malû* in 54 and 65. NBGT II 95-98 will then duplicate the content of NBGT I 47-50 and 54-57, and NBGT II 99-102 that of NBGT I 59-62 and 65-68. Similarly NBGT II 107-110 duplicates the content of NBGT I 9-12, with the difference that the former is designated AN.TA MURU$_4$.TA and the latter KI.TA.

Our exposition so far has been based on a large number of perhaps gratuitous — at least unprovable — assumptions. The excuse for this must be a growing body of evidence that the scribes responsible for introducing the grammatical terms into the grammatical analysis texts sometimes misunderstood their meaning (or misunderstood the texts into which they were introducing them). We can now summarize our evidence for the use of the terms *rīqu* and *malû*. The passages which we believe to be relevant are:

rīqu

NBGT I	1-4		á-na-ku ri-qu MURU$_4$.TA
	5-8		at-ta ri-qu KI.TA
	9-12	ù a i e	šu-ú ri-qu KI.TA
NBGT II	107-110		šu-ú ri-i[q-ti] AN.TA MURU$_4$.TA
NBGT I	22-25		šu-a-ti <*rīqu*> AN.TA MURU$_4$.TA

malû

NBGT I	47-50		a-na-ku ma-lu-ú AN.TA MURU$_4$.TA
	54-57	un an in en	ya-a-ti AN.TA KI.TA MURU$_4$.TA
NBGT II	95-98		a-na-ku ya-ti šá [*malīti*]
NBGT I	59-62		at-ta ma-lu-ú KI.TA
	65-68	un an in en	ka-a-ta MURU$_4$.TA KI.TA
NBGT II	99-102		at-ta ka-a-ti ša ma-li-ti
NBGT I	71-74	un an in en	[šu-]ú ⌜ma-lu⌝-ú AN.TA MURU$_4$.TA
	78-81		šu-a-ti ma-lu-ú AN.TA MURU$_4$.TA
NBGT I	85-87	ub	ana-ku šu-ús-hur-tum ma-li-tú MURU$_4$.tú
		ub	at-ta šu-ús-hur-tum <*malītu*> MURU$_4$.TA
		ub	šu-u šu-ús-hur-ti ma-li-tú AN.TA MURU$_4$.TA

The next task is to account for the usages of the terms AN.TA MURU$_4$.TA (= MURU$_4$.TA) and KI.TA in these passages. As has already been demonstrated, the first appears to mean 'infixed before the verb' and the second 'suffixed'. The view was expressed above that in the sections of the texts at present under consideration the application of these terms was haphazard and unthorough, and that consequently elements might not be marked as capable of standing in a position in which we know them to occur; and that if different entries appeared to assign an element to both positions, it was quite possible that both were correct, owing to the fact that e.g. en in itself is not an unambiguous description of a grammatical element, since it may be a writing for the -n- of hé-*en*-ši-du as well as for the -en of ba-gar-re-*en*.

Now we can probably ignore the distinction made between nominative and accusative cases of the Akkadian pronouns, since, as the Babylonian grammarians were well aware (it is evident from the verbal paradigms), whether a particular person appears in the (Sumerian) form as an infix or as a suffix depends as much on whether the so-called *hamṭu* or *marû* contructions are used as on the grammatical function of that person in the sentence. So, in the table which follows, the information is presented in a composite form, with nominative and accusative entries run together. When ù/a/i/e is described as a suffix, the reference must be to a form of the suffix -e (coloured by a preceding vowel in the cases of ù a and i) or else to a form of -en with final consonant amitted. When it is described as an infix, the reference is simply to the vowel colour of the previous element and to what is called a 'zero-form', i.e. no infix at all, or else (in the case of -e- alone) to the second person infix -e-. When un/an/in/en is a 'suffix', clearly the suffix -en (with vowel harmony if necessary) is meant; as 'infix', it is a description of the infix -n-.

	infix	suffix
rīqu (ù/a/i/e)		
1st person	x	-
2nd person	-	x
3rd person	x	x
malû (un/an/in/en)		
1st person	x	x
2nd person	x	x
3rd person	x	-

How does this summary of the evidence from the grammatical epitomes accord with what we already know of Sumerian verbal incorporation? It is well known that the 2nd person may be marked by an infixed vowel (-e-) and the first person by a suffixed form of -en. These can be added to the table. Most philologists, with the exception of A. Deimel,[120] would agree that the 3rd person singular is *not* expressed by a suffixed form of -en. On the other hand, it is surprising that these texts seem to maintain that the 1st and 2nd person singular, in addition to the 3rd, can be marked by the infix -n-. This may mean that we should not pay too much attention to the designation of position in these instances, which all occur close together in one text (NBGT I 50, 54, 65). In particular, AN.TA KI.TA MURU$_4$.TA, a unique marking, is probably corrupt.

It is particularly interesting that the Babylonian grammarians should have grouped the principal methods of marking personal incorporation in the following way: vowel infixes or 'zero-form' infixes and the suffixed -e (which may be an attenuated form of -en) as 'empty' forms, and infixed -n- and suffixed -en as 'full' forms. The class of empty forms is not always unambiguous as a description, and they do not appear to have found a way round that. Yet it is in precisely those cases that the Sumerian writing is itself ambiguous: is bí-gar bi+gar,

---

120. A. Deimel, *Das šumerische Verbum* (Rome, 1935), pp.22f.

bi+i+gar or bi+e+gar? and is mu-ak-ke$_4$ mu+ak+e or mu+ak+e(n)? The texts may thus be seen as an efficient analysis of written Sumerian.

Finally we must consider the section NBGT I 85-89, where ub is given as the full form of infix for all three persons, with the additional designation *šushurtum*. The last entry (88-89) seems to give íb as *šushurtu riqtim* AN.TA(MURU$_4$.TA, but this was excluded on grounds of probable corruption. The writing -ub- must represent the infix -b- preceded by (-)mu-, hu-, ù- or nu-. *Šushurtum*, it is hoped to demonstrate in the following section, characterizes the non-indicative forms, listed in the order 2nd, 1st, 3rd person in the verbal paradigms. It seems most likely, then, that what are here referred to are forms like:

OBGT VI	51	gar-mu-ub	*šuškinam*	
X	17	gub-mu-ub	*šuzizanni*	
NBGT VI	2	hu-ub-gub-[bu?]-dè-e[n		] (see p. 157)
	3	hu-ub-gub-bé-e[n		] (see p. 157)

These forms are unfortunately not very common; but in them -b- appears to mark the inert, rather than the agent cause, and so does not vary for the Akkadian persons.

3.3 *Šushurtum*

This term occurs several times in the grammatical epitomes, and in one or two other contexts also. The forms occurring are šu-ús-hur-tum (e.g. NBGT I 84), šu-ús-hur-tú (NBGT I 89), šu-ús-hur-ti (e.g. NBGT I 87) and šu-ús-hur-ta (Examination Text A, 16), suggesting that it is a (feminine) abstract noun. Note also šu-ús-hur-[K.14991 obv. 6 (part of NBGT II, see *MSL* V, pp.195 ff.). A line in the grammatical commentary implies that a Sumerian form was ÈM.KÚŠ:[121]

ú-nu a-na e-na i-na : ÈM.KÚŠ : šu-ús-hur-tum

This form also occurs at NBGT IX 39:

(HA) (LI) ÈM.KÚŠ

ÈM is the Eme-sal form of the prefix nì-, which serves in Sumerian to form abstract nouns, and the form NÌ.KÚŠ is also found, at K4808, (see section 5.2 below) line 16, cols. iv and v:

e NÌ.KÚŠ SIG-tu[m]

It may be supposed that *šushurtum* is derived from the root shr 'to turn', but no connection between that root and Sumerian kúš (which is usually equated with *nâhum* 'to be calm', or, read as súr, with *ezēzum* 'to rage') is known. This may mean that the scribe of the commentary was wrong and that there is no connection between *šushurtum* and NÌ.KÚS or that some other implication is here intended. Possibly NÌ.KÚŠ is another unexplained grammatical term. However, *sahārum* is sometimes written nigin (or nigín), and a writing nì-nigin (with variant nigin) is found corresponding to *šushurta* at Examination Text A, line 16. Possibly nì-nigin is to be read ^{nì}nigin. nì-gi (NBGT IX 46) may also be a syllabic writing for nigin. The sign read LAGAB by the editors of *MSL* IV is surely, then, to be read NIGÍN, i.e. *šushurtum*, and not *rīqu*, for which the Sumerian is, as might be expected, NÌ.SUD (see section 3.2 above), despite the passage S^a Voc F 11'-12' (*MSL* III 57, written in two lines), *atta rīqu* KI.TA *u* <?> (corresponding to Aa V/1 158f. (*MSL* XIV 411), *atta* NIGÍN KI.TA *u* NU.NIGÍN (written in two lines)). The S^a passage is probably erroneous since elsewhere the interpretation of NIGÍN as *rīqu*, given the apparently correct reading of *rīqu* as 'without final consonant explicit in writing', makes no sense. Finally, the writing ⌜NIGÍN⌝-tum (NBGT IX 274, collated) may be adduced.

We come now to consider the meaning and application of the term. The editors of *MSL* IV (in the index) link it with the term *riātum*, and take the former as denoting 'motion away from

121. Leichty *AfO* 24 (1973), p.79.

the speaker' and the latter as 'motion towards the speaker'. The same opinion was voiced later by Jacobsen, who set the terms up as opposites.[122] This is similar to the interpretation urged by Yoshikawa, who translated the terms as 'non-ventive' and 'ventive' respectively, borrowing a term from Akkadian grammar.[123] It is hoped to show that there is no evidence to support either of these interpretations of *šushurtum* or its connection with *riātum*. The only justification for linking it with *riātum* could be that *riātum* occurs directly after *šushurtum* in NBGT I 85-101. Against the assumed connection the following objection may be lodged. Presumably, following Yoshikawa's interpretation, all verbs must be either ventive or non-ventive, whatever that may mean in the context of Sumerian grammar, then all the verbs must be either *šushurtum* or *riātum* and must show this by their form. Assuming that the texts list all the possible ways of marking *šushurtum* and *riātum*, it follows that all verb forms must carry either one of the *šushurtum* elements or else one of those listed as *riātum*. In fact this is very far from being the case: many bear neither, and, what is more destructive of the theory, many bear both. It may be further objected that to describe a verb-form as non-ventive is not very informative, including as it does both all forms denoting motion in any direction but towards the speaker and also all forms not denoting movement at all. Against the interpretation of the editors of *MSL* IV it may be objected that if *šushurtum* denotes movement away from the speaker and *riātum* movement towards him, then the forms listed should only occur with verbs expressing movement either towards or away from the speaker, and again, should never co-occur. But this is not the case. More recently Yoshikawa has used the paired terms 'ventive' and 'ientive' and has qualified his earlier position by positing a metaphorical extension of the meaning to include 'emotional or mental movement'.[124] None the less his segmentation of the verbal forms in the verbal paradigms differs from ours, as he opposes im-ma- to ba- as 'ventive' and 'ientive', whereas the structure of the texts treats im-ma- as derived from ba- in combination with ì- and -m-.

Thureau-Dangin's original interpretation of *šushurtum* as 'tournure, forme'[125] has the advantage of giving a meaning for *šushurtum* which is obviously derived from the known meaning of its root shr 'to turn', and is to some extent supported by the fact that, at least whenever it occurs in NBGT I or II (with the possible exception of NBGT II 91), it is always followed immediately by what could be interpreted as a feminine adjective agreeing with it. Thus we should have:

šushurtum malītu qablītu	at NBGT I 85
šushurtum <*malītu*> *qablītu*	at NBGT I 86
šushurti malītu qablītu	at NBGT I 87
šushurti elīti[	at NBGT II 87

Elsewhere, however, *šushurtum* (or its equivalent) occurs on its own, which does not give a satisfactory sense. Also, there is something slightly too neat in the rendering by the French word *tournure*: it is inherently unlikely that French and Akkadian should use exactly the same metaphor in this respect.

Presumably *šushurtum* is correctly to be derived from the Š stem of *sahārum*, whose meaning is 'to turn round' (transitive), and should therefore mean something like 'that which is turned round'. Now, in what circumstances in Sumerian is something in the verb 'turned round'? One obvious possibility is the 2nd person imperative, in which the whole of the pre-verbal chain,

122. In 'Very Ancient Linguistics: Babylonian Grammatical Texts', schema on p.56.
123. Principally in *A Study of the Grammatical Terms Šushurtum and Riātum in Neo-Babylonian Grammatical Texts*, Hiroshima University Studies, Faculty of Letters, vol.33, Special Publications no.3 (March, 1974; in Japanese); more recently, he has used the terms 'ientive' and 'ventive', e.g. in 'Sumerian Ventive and Ientive', in *OrNS* 47 (1978), pp.461-82.
124. *V.* p.154, n.2 above.
125. In *RA* 32 (1935), p.102.

with the exception of the preformative, if there is one, is placed after the verb. This suggestion, among others, was made by van Dijk.[126] To test whether it will work, we must consider the passages where the term occurs. They are as follows:

NBGT I 85-89 (the transcription of this passage was defended above, section 2.2, p. 59 f.)

85	ub	*anāku šushurtum malītu qablītu*
86	ub	*atta šushurtum <malītu> qablītu*
87	ub	*šū šushurti malītu elītu qablītu*
88-89	íb	*šushurtu riqtim elītu qablītu*

NBGT II 86-94

86	un	*šu ša elīti*[
87	an	*u šushurti elīti*[
88	in	*elītu u*[
89	en	
90	ab	
91	ub	*šū ša šushurti* [
92	ab	
93	íb	
94	eb	*anāku* " [

There is damage all down the righthand edge of the obverse of the tablet, and only in line 88 is it certain that some signs are missing. The larger section of which the passage forms a part (for the bounds of which we may take the lacunae before 74 and after 117) was earlier recognized as condensed. This condensation is here apparent a) in the unequal distribution between the pronouns — 91-4 is probably condensed from:

u/a/i/eb	*šū ša šushurti*
u/a/i/eb	*atta ša šushurti*
u/a/i/eb	*anāku ša šushurti*

and b) in the Akkadian entry in 86ff., which is repetitive: *elītu* in this context certainly means the same as AN.TA *u* MURU$_4$.TA (the MURU$_4$.TA of which is tentatively restored on the basis of NBGT I 71), if indeed *qablītu* or some such is not broken away in 86 and 87; so we are told three times that these forms are 'infixed at the front', as well as that they are *u šushurti* 'also *šushurtum*'. These are the two significant passages in which *šushurtum* is mentioned. Summarizing their content, we can represent the information presented thus:

ub	eb	*anāku*
ub		*atta*
ub ab íb	un an in en	*šū*

— although this almost certainly is to be interpreted as u/a/i/eb for all three persons and u/a/i/en for *šu*. -n- and -b- are already listed elsewhere (e.g. NBGT I 47-84) as the 'full' forms of the infixed personal elements, and the only reason for listing them here can be that some extra circumstance is being taken into account. The difficulty with van Dijk's suggestion is that all three persons are mentioned in the passages where *šushurtum* occurs, whereas the imperative occurs only with the 2nd person. Instead the following interpretation is proposed.

In the verbal paradigms (OBGT VI, VII, VIII, IX and in one case V) a rigid principle of arrangement is observed according to which the verbal forms with prefixes i- a- bí- ba- mu- and ma- ('indicative' forms) are listed in the order 3rd, 1st, 2nd person; and 2nd person imperatives and forms with ga- and hé- ('non-indicative' forms) in the order 2nd, 1st, 3rd person. Thereby a distinction is made as if between two moods. This distinction is marked in

126. In 'La "confusion de langues"', in *OrNS* 39 (1970), pp.302-310, on p.309, no.1.

the texts solely by the fact of reversing the arrangement, and the reversal can only be intended to draw attention to the difference in character of the meaning of these forms. We propose that the term *šushurtum* 'turned round' relates to this distinction, and in particular distinguishes the 'non-indicative' forms. It will be found that in non-indicative forms in these texts the 3rd person element, if it is written, regularly occurs as -b-. There are only two exceptions:

OBGT VI	46	gar-mu-un	*šuknanni*
IX	55	sá du$_{11}$-ga-mu-un	*kušdanni*

and these, in the present context at any rate, are artificially selected forms designed to make a contrast with the forms set against Akkadian causatives:

OBGT VI	51	gar-mu-ub	*šuškinanni*
IX	58	sá du$_{11}$-ga-mu-ub	*šukšidanni* (text: *šutakšidanni*).[127]

The passage Aa V/1 158f. (*MSL* XIV 411) may be considered as well. It reads:

(bé-e)	(BI)	at-ta NIGÍN KI.TA
		ù NU.NIGÍN

(The *qadu* in the following line animadverts to the separate possibility of translating -bi as 'with'.) This entry would have to be interpreted as '2nd person singular, suffixed when 'turned round' (i.e. in the imperative); also 'not turned round' (i.e. indicative)'. It is excellently exemplified by two entries in OBGT VI:

56	gar-bi	*šukun*
105	bí-gar	(*taškun*)

The entry NÌ.KÚŠ SIG-tu[m] in K4808, line 16, column v, may be compared. The three other entries with NIGÍN on that tablet, as also the other occurrences of NIGÍN elsewhere, are unfortunately too confused or too brief to make any sense of:

K4808 (see section 5.2, p. 148 f. below)

	line 12, col.v			ana-ku NIGÍN AN
	14			at-ta NIGÍN SIG
	18			at-ta NIGÍN A[N]
NBGT V ii	6	[i-me-]⸢še⸣		ša i-na a-na ⸢NIGÍN⸣
NBGT IX	41	(HA)	(LI)	NIGÍN UL$_4$(i.e. *hamṭu*)
	274	(DAM)		⸢NIGÍN⸣-tum KI (collated)

(In K4808, *šushurtum* (NIGÍN) may be used, exceptionally, to refer to *Akkadian* non-indicatives, in this case 1st person volitives. See section 2.7, p. 74 above.)

3.4 *Gamartum* and *riātum*

These two terms will be considered together, not because they are supposed to be related in meaning, but because the unravelling of the meaning and use of each is to some extent bound up with that of the other.

First, *gamartum*. This term occurs as follows:

NBGT I	257	ba		*gamartum* (text: TA E TUM) AN.TA (text: KI.TA)
II	83	um		ga-mar-tu[
		àm		
		im		
IX	55	(HA)	(LI)	NÌ.TIL RI B[I?]
	118	(...)	(MU)	TIL-tum : ya-ši

127. Jacobsen (private communication) points out that imperatives in -(u)n do occur elsewhere, in literary texts, e.g. egir-mu ha-ha-za-mu-un 'hold on behind me' Kramer, *OrNS* 22 (1953), pl.42 Ni 9718:6'.

In Examination Text A, line 16, nì-til-la-a is translated as ga-mir-ti (var. ga-[mir]-ta). Finally there is the longer passage NBGT II 259-79, as follows:

262	ba-a	a-na-ku šu-a-ti TIL-ti
263	ba-e	at-ta šu-a-ti 〃
264	ba-an	šu-ú šu-a-ti 〃
271	ba-ni-ì	a-na-ku šu-a-ti šu-a-ti <TIL-ti>
272	ba-ni-e	
273	ba-ni-in	
277	[ba-na-ni-]ì	a-na-ku šu-a-ti šu-a-ti
278	[ba-an-ni-]e	a-na šu-a-šu u ga-mar-tum (see p. 157)
279	[ba-na-ni-]in	

These instances suggest an Akkadian noun *gamartum* or *gamirtu* with Sumerian nì-til(-la) and logogram TIL, with literal meaning of 'completed', 'completion' (*gamārum* 'to finish').

In the forms listed in the passage NBGT II 256-79, the long vowel, -e- and -n- represent respectively the 1st, 2nd and 3rd person singular pronouns. From the analysis above (section 1.2.2) it will be clear that -ni- corresponds to the Akkadian Š theme, denoted here by the phrase *šuāti šuāti* (while *šuāti* on its own denotes the G theme), and that -na- corresponds to the Akkadian *ana šuāšu*. This leads to the conclusion that it is the feature ba- that is identified by the term *gamartum*. It was shown that in the verbal paradigms Akkadian -t- themes are regularly set against these forms, except in cases where ba- is used in its stative sense.

From this it seemed reasonable to restore AN.TA for KI.TA in NBGT I 257, since obviously the prefix ba- is meant. The other feature listed as *gamartum* is um/àm/im (NBGT II 83ff.) and this will be dealt with later.

The term *riātum* (*riyātum*) occurs as follows:

NBGT I	90ff.	um	ri-a-tum AN.TA MURU$_4$.TA
		àm	
		im	
		me	
		u/a/i/en-ga	
		[ma-]ra	
		ma[-]da	
		⌜ma⌝-ta	
		ma-da-ta	

Other occurrences are less informative. They are:

K4808 (see section 5.2 below)				
	line 4	cols. iv and v	um	ri-a-[tum]
	line 28		um	ṛi-ya-a-tum

izi A iii 23			
(*MSL* XIII 175)	a]n-ga		ma-ši-iš-tum
	a]n-ga		ap-pu-na
	a]n-ga		ma-a
	a]n-ga		ri-a-tum
	an-g]a-àm-ma-⌜x-x⌝		[ ]-ma
Aa III/4 32			
(*MSL* XIV 340)	(mu-u)	(MU	ri-[[ŠÁ]]-⌜a⌝-[tum]

Concerning the word itself, no satisfactory etymology has been proposed, and no logographic writing is known. The form of the word is strange, suggesting a frozen Old Babylonian writing, since the type of vowel cluster *-iā-*, in verbs at least, was contracted to *-â-*

after the Old Babylonian period. The variant spelling ri-ya-a-tum confirms the reading of the word.

It is important to point out that there is no evidence to link the term *riātum* with the term *šushurtum*, as has been done by the editors of *MSL* IV (index *s. vv.*). The mere fact that the section NBGT I 90ff., where *riātum* appears, directly follows a section devoted to *šushurtum* forms (85-89) is not sufficient in this respect.

The situation is complicated by the occurrence elsewhere in the epitomes, with different Akkadian designations, of almost all the elements listed above as *riātum*. Thus:

u/a/i/en-ga-	occur at NBGT I	205-208	as *u*,
	I	395-98	as *appūna*
	and at NBGT II	37-40	as *appūna* AN.TA MURU$_4$.TA, *u šū*, *mā*
-u/a/i/em, me/a	occur at NBGT I	439-43	as *mā* KI.TA
u/a/i/en-ga-		448-51	
u/a/i/em-, mi/mu-	occur at NBGT II	74-78	as *ana yâši*
u/a/i/em-, mu/a/i-	occur at NBGT I	241-46	as x y z-[y]a-a (?*ana yâšim*)[128] and
u/a/im-ma-		254-56	
u/a/i/em-	occur at NBGT II	83-85	as *gamartu*.

Cf. also
NBGT IX 118 (MU) TIL-tum : *yâši* (collated)

Now it is already sufficiently well known that -nga- is an infixed verbal element occurring only after the prefixes ì- or a- or the prefomatives ù-, ša-, hé- or narrative na-, meaning 'moreover', 'in addition', i.e. *appūna, u šū* or *mā*. (There may be some confusion here between *mā* 'indeed' and *-ma* 'and'.) How does it come to be listed here as *riātum* together with u/a/im and me, and ma-ra, ma-da and ma-da-ta? Of the last three forms it is reasonable to assume that the reason why they are so listed together is because of their common feature ma, and that it is this which is designated by the term *riātum*. Our earlier investigation showed that the compilers of our texts regarded -m- and its by-forms ma- and mu- as susceptible of being equated with the Akkadian ventive, and it now seems likely that it is precisely this feature which is intended by the term *riātum*. This interpretation is maintained, though not worked out in detail, by the editors of *MSL* IV (index *s.v.*) and by Yoshikawa.[129] In the passages cited, -m- is presented preceded by the prefixes ì- or a-, the preformative ù- or other preformatives ending in a vowel. The writing me cannot be the infix -me- (which is connected with the 1st person plural). In early texts -me- is written for -mi- in the verbal prefix chain im-mi-. Since it was argued above (section 1.2.1.2, p. 24) that im-mi-, like im-ma-, contains the element -m-, which is equated with (among other things) the Akkadian ventive, *riātum*, it is possible that -me- is included here for that reason.

Now u/a/i/en-ga also occur with um/àm/im me and ma in the entry NBGT I 439-51, where they are glossed *mā* KI.TA. It is probable, in the light of the succeeding entries -dam, -da-àm, -nam, -na-nam, that -um/àm/im are here forms of the suffixed copula, meaning 'indeed', 'it is...'. However, in order to explain the presence of u/a/i/en-ga alongside um/àm/im in this section *and* at I 90ff., we must posit a sequence of assumptions from which a false conclusion has been drawn in the mind of some compiler or redactor of the text:

a) u/a/i/en-ga may be set against *mā* (possibly the result of confusion between *mā* and *-ma*),
b) -um/-àm/-im may also;
c) um/àm/im- contain the element -m-, which is *riātum*, therefore
d) u/a/i/en-ga is *riātum* too,

128. But this does not seem to accord with the traces.

129. In *A Study of the Grammatical Terms Šushurtum and Riātum...* and more recently (in English) in 'Sumerian Ventive and Ientive', in *OrNS* 47 (1978), pp.461-82.

which of course is false. He has confused the *suffixes* written u/a/im with the pre-verbal chains um/àm/im-. We may now return to consider one of the other passages where u/a/i/em is listed as *gamartu*, viz. NBGT II 83-85. This is surely a false inference from u/a/im-ma (NBGT I 25-56), which according to our argument will be both *gamartum* (because of ba-) and *riātum* (because of -m-). The unfortunate epitomator has chosen the wrong part of the prefix chain to list as *gamartum*.

Finally the evidence for the meaning of *gamartum* and *riātum* may be drawn together. Of *gamartum* we may say:

a) Its literal meaning is 'completed', 'completion'.

b) It designates Sumerian forms with ba-/-ma- (NBGT I 257, II 83ff., 262ff.), regularly set against Akkadian -t- infix themes in their separative sense (OBGT VI-X). The superficially attractive equation of *gamartum* and perfect tense made by von Soden[130] and the editors of *MSL* IV (index *s.v.*) cannot stand.

c) Various exceptions to this exemplify quite a different, 'stative', use of ba-. It is unlikely that *gamartum* refers to this second sense of ba-, since *gamartum* evidently includes ba- in the form -ma-, and the stative sense of ba- rarely, if ever, appears in this form; also the long prefix chains at NBGT II 271ff. and 277ff. are expressly designated *gamartum*. 'Stative' ba- is usually a sole prefix.

Concerning *riātum* we may say:

a) It is set against the Sumerian element -m-/ma-/mu- (NBGT I 90ff.)

b) This element -m-/ma-/mu- is elsewhere set against *ana yâši* (NBGT II 75-78, ? I 241-45) or *yâši* (NBGT IX 118) and, in the verbal paradigms OBGT VI-X, is regularly set against the Akkadian ventive.

3.5 Other grammatical terms

Certain other grammatical terms occur in the extant texts. They are:

lû(m).

That this word is a noun, and not merely the particle *lū*, is confirmed by an entry in the sign-list and vocabulary Ea (IV 25ff.)[131]

25	[ga-a	GA M]IN	lu-ú-um
26	[ge] - ⌜e⌝		2
27	[gu] - ⌜ú⌝		3

It is clear from passages like NBGT II 42-45, where it is given against ga- and hu/ha/hé-, that it refers not only to *lū* as in *lū akšud* or *lū balṭāta*, but also to e.g. *luprus* (or *liprus*), so we may translate it 'a *lu*- form'.

mû

Closely analogous to the foregoing is *mû* at NBGT I 403:

lú mu-u

The reference here is apparently to the use of Akkadian '*mu*- words', i.e. participles (many of which begin with *mu*-), as a translation of Sumerian phrases with lú, meaning 'he who...'

130. In 'Das akkadische t-Perfekt in Haupt- und Nebensätzen und sumerische Verbalformen mit den Präfixen ba-, imma- und u-', in *AS* 16 (1965), pp.103-110.

131. *MSL* XIV, p.356.

eterrubum
An interpretation was earlier proposed (v. section 2.3, p. 64 f. above) for the entry NBGT II 53 according to which it should be translated '-ta when it is used in the sense of -a'. This suggests a technical use of the Gtn theme of *erēbum* to mean the regular occurrence of a grammatical form. Shaffer's interpretation of it to mean 'to be infixed' cannot stand.

uhhurtum, watartum
These two words are clearly grammatical terms from the context in which they make their sole appearance: Examination Text A, line 16. However, there is no evidence for their meaning. *Uhhurum* is literally 'to be late'; its derivatives *ahrâtu* 'future time' and *ahrâtaš* 'in the future' may suggest a meaning of sorts.

šuāti and *šuāti šuāti*
These expressions occur in the section NBGT II 256-79, which was analysed above, p. 68 f. From the context it is evident that *šuāti* is used to designate Akkadian forms of what we would call the G theme, to which is opposed *šuāti šuāti* for forms of the Š theme. The use of the accusative form of the third person pronoun in this way is presumably derived from the observation that a G theme form will usually have one direct object and a Š theme form two, as for example:

karānam ašti	'I drank the wine'
karānam ušaštišu	'I made him drink the wine'

3.6 DIŠ, MEŠ, hamṭu and marû

These terms are treated together because they appear together and because the categories denoted by the two pairs (respectively DIŠ and MEŠ, and *hamṭu* and *marû*) clearly overlap.

The principal passage where DIŠ and MEŠ occur is NBGT II 1-12. The following passages, however, may also be cited:

Aa I/5 15	(*MSL* XIV 223)	[me-e]š	ME	m[a-a'-du]-⌜tum⌝
Aa II/4 179	(*MSL* XIV 284)	e - eš	EŠ	ma-a'-du-ti
Aa VII/1 110	(*MSL* XIV 460)	(de-e)	(DÉ)	ma-du-tum
NBGT IX 114		[(...)]	(...)	ma-a'-du-tum

NBGT II 1-12 may be transcribed as follows:

[gen	*al]āku hamṭu ša* DIŠ
du	" *ša* DIŠ[ ]x
re_7	*alāk* MEŠ *hamṭu*
su_8-bé	" *marû*
gub	*uzuz* DIŠ *hamṭu*
súg	*uzuz* MEŠ *marû*
de_6	*babālum hamṭu*
túm	" MEŠ *marû*
du_{11}	*qabû hamṭu*
e	*qabû marû*
tuš	*ašāb* DIŠ *hamṭu*
dúr-ru-un	" MEŠ *hamṭu u marû*

Collation of the printed text with the tablet revealed that in line 2, after DIŠ, there is not room for [ma-ru]-⌜ú⌝ and also that the trace is not of ú. Possibilities consonant with what remains would be et or at.

The problem is to know how to transcribe DIŠ and MEŠ. The occurrence of *mādūtum, mādūti* in other lexical contexts may suggest that MEŠ should be so read here, presumably to be understood as the masculine plural of the adjective *mādum* 'many'. As a reading of DIŠ the editors of *MSL* IV suggest *ištēn* (index, *s.v.* ištēn) and that is the obvious reading. At this point it may be instructive to consider the forms taken by the grammatical terms so far investigated, with a view to determining whether they tend to be nouns or adjectives, masculine or feminine. The forms of *hamṭu* and *marû* are also included.

elû	*elīti*	*ša elīti*
rīqu	*riqtašu*	*ša riqti*
malû	*malīti*	*ša malīti*
	šushurtum/i/a	*ša šushurti*
qablû	*qablītu/a*	
marû	*marītum*	
šaplû[?]	*šaplītum*[?] (SIG-tum)	
	riyātum	
hamṭu		
mādūtum/i		

There are a number of masculine adjectives (*elû, rīqu, malû, qablû, marû, šaplû*[?], *hamṭu*) and a number of (grammatically feminine) forms with -t- affix which might be nouns or adjectives. A noun *elītum* is attested by the dictionaries, sometimes written AN.TA-*tum*, meaning 'upper part'; *malītu* occurs once as a noun, meaning 'full amount'. The forms with *ša* (*ša elīti, ša riqti, ša malīti*) and the writing NÌ.SUD, if that does represent *rīqu*, might also suggest that these forms are nouns. But Sumerian forms with nì- can occur as adjectives;[132] and the form *riqtu* is clearly in fact a feminine adjective (as a noun *riqūtum* exists separately), so we can almost certainly infer that *malītu* is an adjective here as well. Probably *elītu, qablītu* and *šaplītu*[?](SIG-*tum*), and also *marītum*, can be so construed. The construction with the genitive can then be compared to forms like *šum damiqti, amat damiqti.*[133] The distinction between the feminine form of the adjective and the abstract noun is not always very clear — *lemuttu* for instance functions as both, so do *damiqtu* and *šapiltu*. There seems to be no particular explanation for the distribution of the various forms, although it may be noted that NBGT I uses only the forms *rīqu, malû* and *marītum*, while NBGT II has only *elīti, ša elīti, ša riqti, ša malīti* and *marû*. The other forms occur in other texts. It has generally been assumed that *šushurtum, gamartum* and *riyātum* are (feminine, abstract) nouns, and there is no reason to doubt this. No masculine adjectival forms of them occur. On the other hand, *mādūtum*, as has been said, is a masculine plural adjective, 'many (people)'.

Can we draw any conclusions from these writings of other grammatical terms? The analogy of *mādūtum* might suggest that DIŠ is to be read *ištēn*, 'one (person)'. However, the fact that the words standing immediately before it (*alāk, uzuz* and *ašāb*) are all in the construct implies that it is to be read as a genitive. The reading of the text in the first two lines is far from clear, but it seems from them that the form *ša* DIŠ is also possible. In this case, the parallel with *elīti, ša elīti* etc. may suggest that a feminine form is to be read, i.e. *ištêt* or *ištiāt*. Thus the possibility of reading the last sign of line 2 as et or at (i.e. 1^{et} or 1^{at}) should be considered.

The interpretation of DIŠ and MEŠ is discussed below. Next, *hamṭu* and *marû*, which occur in the following places:

NBGT I	42	[ù] [a] i	[...m]a-ri-tum KI.TA

132. As for example kaš nì-du$_{10}$-ga 'good beer' in 'Lahar and Ashnan', lines 65ff.

133. Examples of these forms may be found in *AHw s.v. damqu.*

		e	
		ne	
	171	e-ne	šu-nu ma-ri-tum
		e-ne-ne	
		un-ne	
		an-ne	
		in-ne	
		en-ne	
		un-n[e-ne]	
		a[n-ne-ne]	
		[in-ne-ne]	
	411	ù	lu ma-a u ma-ri-tum (see pp. f.)
		a	li ma-a u ma-ri-tum
		e	
		ul	
	455	ù	ma-a u ma-ri-tum
		a	
		i	
		e	

NBGT II 1-12 (cited above, p. 99)
NBGT IX 41 (HA) (LI) NIGÍN UL_4(= *hamṭu*)

Eme-sal vocabulary III (see section 2.5 above)

1	ma	DU	*alāku*
2	de-de	du	KI.MIN *marû*
3	de	gen	KI.MIN *hamṭu*
4	ga-ga	túm-ma	*babālu marû*
5	ga	de_6	KI.MIN *hamṭu*
6	er	de_6	KI.MIN KI.MIN
7	er	de_6	*tabālu* KI.MIN
8	er	de_6	*leqû* KI.MIN
9	er	de_6	*šūlû ša titāpī* KI.MIN
10	er-er	túm-túm	KI.MIN *ša titāpī marû*
11	sag er-er	sag túm-túm	*qullulu marû*
12	múš ga	múš túm	*naparkû marû*
13	múš nam-ba-an-ga-ga	múš nam-ba-an-túm-ma	*ai ipparkû*
76	ma-ma	ga-ga	*šakānu marû*
77	ma-al	gál	*šakānu marû*
78	mar	gar	*šakānu hamṭu*

Other passages outside grammatical texts are:

Aa V/1 152-53	(*MSL* XIV 411)	bé-e	BÉ	qa-bu-u ma-ru-u (written in two lines)
155-57	(*MSL* XIV 411)	("	")	at-ta šu-a-tum ma-ru-u KI.TA (written in three lines)
cf. Sª Voc. F 9'-10'	(*MSL* III 57)	("	")	at-ta šu-a-ti ma-ru-ú $MURU_4$-ú (written in two lines)
Aa V/2 259-60	(*MSL* XIV 420)	(mu-ur)	(MUR)	šu-a-ti ma-ru-u ka-tú ma-ru-u
Aa VII/1 111-13	(*MSL* XIV 460)	(de-e)	(DÉ)	i-na a-na ma-ri-tum K[I.TA]

Ea fragment C:1' (*MSL* XIV 518) [...]-⌜ú⌝ ana-⌜ku ri?⌝-[qu ma]-ru-u K[I.TA]

Nabnītu I	16	[tu]-ud	MIN(= ba-nu-u šá a-la-di) ha-am-ṭu
	17	[ù-tu-(ud)]	MIN(= ba-nu-u šá a-la-di) ma-ru-ú
Nabnītu I	99	si-mul	ge-e-šu
	100	si-mul dug$_4$-ga	MIN ha-am-ṭ[u]
	101	si-mul di	MIN ma-ru-[u]
	102	si-mul ak-a	MIN
Nabnītu V	1	ár ak-a	te-e-lum
	2	ár dug$_4$-ga	MIN ha-an-ṭu
	3	⌜ár⌝ ad ak-a	MIN ma-ru-ú
	4	⌜ár di⌝	MIN
	5	ár	te-el-tum
	6	⌜i-bi⌝-i-lu	MIN
	7	[i-bi]-⌜i-lu⌝ dug$_4$-ga	MIN ha-an-ṭu
	8	[i-bi]-i-lu di	MIN ma-ru-ú
Aa II/6 ii 3 (*MSL* XIV 291)		(an) (AN)	ka-tú ha-am-ṭu KI <.TA>

Examination Text A
line 16 [ŠE ul$_4$-]lá [x x (x) nu-tu]ku
ma-ra-a ha-an-ṭa šá [x x]-a? la i-šu-u

The excerpts from lexical series cited above may be misleading and are difficult to interpret. It is possible, for instance, that the entry Aa VII/1 111ff. conceals a reference to the infix -ed-, as in ha-lam-e-dè (which might be rendered in Akkadian as *ana nābutim*). No doubt numerous other instances will be found of grammatical terms in other lexical lists. On the whole, these are to be regarded as secondary to the occurrences in grammatical texts, from which they are probably derived. They seem often to be confused or incomplete, and no concerted attempt has been made to analyze them.

From the above passages it is clear that the forms are *hamṭu* (UL$_4$), *marû* and *marītum* (ŠE).[134] The modern literature on the subject of *hamṭu* and *marû* has been considerable and must now be reviewed. Concerning DIŠ and MEŠ, there is no reason to disagree with the general assumption that they refer to singular and plural. It is hoped, however, to show that a further general assumption, viz. that both DIŠ and MEŠ and *hamṭu* and *marû* are concerned with the Sumerian verb, is unjustified. It is none the less germane to our present purpose to elucidate which Sumerian forms are involved in the entries in our texts, and to this end the theories of Yoshikawa and Edzard will be examined in some detail.

3.6.1 Interpretations of hamṭu and marû

Zimmern noted the occurrence of *hamṭu* and *marû* as terms of Akkadian native grammar as early as 1885[135] and was of the opinion that they served to contrast i) the full pronunciation of Sumerian words with that in which the final consonant was dropped, and ii) the fuller, reduplicated pronunciation with the simple, non-reduplicated. He maintained that they were thus relative, not absolute terms. Muss-Arnolt followed Zimmern's interpretation in his dictionary,[136] describing the terms as in opposition to one another. He defined *marû* (*s.v.* *marû* 3) as a 'fuller, more complete form, as compared with a shorter, reduced, without respect to its position in the first (neo-Sumerian) or second (early-Sumerian) column' (*sic*). Clearly this refers to the text now called the Eme-sal Vocabulary.

134. For the writing ŠE, see the Eme-sal vocabulary, section 2.5 above.
135. In *Babylonische Busspsalmen* (Leipzig, 1885), pl.84, n.1.
136. *A Concise Dictionary of the Assyrian Language* (Berlin, 1899-1905).

Sayce's suggestion[137] that the terms were used in a grammatical sense as 'male' and 'female', or as we should say 'masculine' and 'feminine'', was criticized by Delitzsch,[138] who proposed instead that *marû* signified the intensification expressed in Sumerian by reduplication, and this definition also appeared in his *Sumerisches Glossar*.[139] Haupt combined this with Zimmern's original interpretation and attempted to produce an etymology.[140] *Marû* means literally *fett* ('fat') and *hamṭu* schnell ('fast'), but these were then used, he suggested, in ancient grammatical theory, to mean *stark* ('strong') or *schwer* ('heavy') and *leicht* ('light') or *schwach* ('weak'). Sumerian gál, with final consonant, was *stark*, and gá, without, was *schwach*; gá was also *leicht* compared with the reduplicated gá-gá, which was *stark*, i.e. *intensiv* ('intensive'). Bezold followed this interpretation in his *Assyro-Babylonisches Glossar*,[141] where *marû* is defined as *gesteigert, intensiv* '(grammatically) increased, intensive'.

When the H volume of the *Chicago Assyrian Dictionary* appeared in 1956, it was able to cite as evidence for the meaning of the verbs *hamāṭum* and *marûm* a passage from a letter of the Old Babylonian period found at Ur,[142] in which these verbs are used in such a way that the meaning is clear: (lines 6-11)

ina Maškan-šabir kiam aqbikum: umma anākuma, ana Ešnunna pānūa šaknū, ahammuṭam u amarriam ūla īde.

The *CAD* translates: 'It is my intention to go to Ešnunna (but) I might come early or I might be late — I do not know (yet)'. Landsberger[143] translates the same passage: 'I intend to go to Eshnunna; (but) I don't know whether I shall move slowly (and arrive late) or move quickly (and arrive soon)'. These translations may be criticized: the first for its use of 'come early' suggesting both that the writer has some Estimated Time of Arrival in mind, which is not clear from the context, and that the addressee is himself in Eshnunna, which, as is evident from the preceding phrase and the provenance of the letter, he is not; and the second for its suggestion that the writer thinks of himself as a sort of tortoise: it surely does not make sense to say that Sîn-šamuh, the writer, *doesn't yet know* whether he is going to *hurry or dawdle*. What he wants to say is that he doesn't know how long the trip is going to take and therefore wants his colleague Sîn-ašarēd to look after some business for him in the meantime. The passage means: 'What I said to you at Maškan-šabir was, "I intend to go to Ešnunna. I may have a quick journey and I may not — I don't yet know"'. It was inferred from this passage that the grammatical terms *hamṭu* and *marû* were to be regarded as verbal adjectives of *hamāṭum* A 'to be quick' and *marûm* 'to be slow'. (It will be noted that ŠE [= the homophonous *marûm* 'fat, of cattle'] is none the less used as a logographic writing for *marû* in a grammatical context.) *sub voce hamṭu* A (2) we find: 'preterit, lit.: quick (pronunciation) as contrasted with *marû*, "present", lit.: slow (pronunciation) as grammatical terms for Sumerian verbs, which use different stems for present and preterit'.[144] This interpretation is novel in four respects. First, it is suggested explicitly for the first time that the terms are confined principally to verbs. A further note in the entry raises the possibility that *hamṭu* may be used of pronouns, quoting a line of the list Aa II/6 ii 3 (*MSL* XIV 291):

an AN ka-tú ha-am-ṭu KI<.TA>

137. In *ZA* 4 (1889), p.393.
138. In *Grundzüge der sumerischen Grammatik* (Leipzig, 1914), p.21, n.2.
139. (Leipzig, 1914), *s.v.* nitáĝ = *marû*.
140. In *ZA* 33 (1921), pp.66-67.
141. (Heidelberg, 1926).
142. Published in *UET* V (1953), 78.
143. In *MSL* IV, p.21*, n.1.
144. See also Landsberger, *MSL* IV, p.21*, n.1.

that is, 'an = you (accusative singular), *hamṭu*, suffixed form'. There is an inconsistency here, since -an is not a pronoun in Sumerian. I take this to be an oversight for Sumerian 'pronominal elements'. Second, the etymological meanings 'quick' and 'slow' are suggested and (most curiously) assumed to refer to the pronunciation. What is this supposed to mean? Siedl,[145] explaining the *CAD*'s interpretation, quotes in this context (facetiously, I assume) a sentence from a medical text[146] which characterizes a man whose speech is rapid: *dabābašu ihmuṭ* ! Third, for the first time the equations *hamṭu* = preterite and *marû* = present, referring, as is clear from what follows, to *Sumerian* verbs, are introduced. Finally, fourth, all previous interpretations had represented *hamṭu* as a normal, 'unmarked' form and *marû* as a 'marked' form used in special circumstances. Now an interpretation is offered in which both forms are represented as of equal importance. Von Soden's *Akkadisches Handwörterbuch*[147] gives definitions which fuse the *CAD*'s reference to tense and 'pronouns' with Zimmern's and Muss-Arnolt's idea that the length of the forms was somehow involved. *Hamṭu* is listed on pp.381b f. as '6) *gramm. v. Kurzformen* a) *sum.*: *Prt.* b) *sonst in LL: v. Pron.*', that is 'grammatical, of short forms: a) Sumerian preterite, b) elsewhere in lexical lists, of pronouns'. *Marû* is listed (on p.616b) as '3) *jB gramm. v. Langformen* (*Ggs. s. hamṭu 6*) a) *sum. Wurzelreduplikation* b) *v bestimmten Wurzelformen usw* c) *v sum PrSuff. usw.*', that is 'neo-Babylonian, grammatical, of long forms (opposite of *hamṭu*, q.v.): a) Sumerian reduplication of root, b) of particular forms of root etc., c) of Sumerian pronominal suffixes etc.', with reference to á = A = *nâqu*. It is not clear whether it is here being suggested that pronouns and pronominal elements might have short or long forms too.

The idea that Sumerian verbs have forms which may be classified as present and preterite has been taken over from the grammatical theory current at the time. As we shall see, the analysis of the meaning of *hamṭu* and *marû* is inextricably bound up with the way in which we classify the occurring forms of Sumerian verbs. Two of the earliest grammars,[148] Langdon (1911) and Delitzsch (1914), divided Sumerian verbs into two tenses, Langdon a present-and-future and past, and Delitzsch a present and preterite. Poebel's grammar (1923) was heavily influenced by his knowledge of Akkadian; it was also the first to be based extensively on the ancient paradigms as well as on other texts. He wrote of the themes of the verb[149] and divided the forms into three: preterite, present-future and intransitive preterite, called permansive, exactly as in Akkadian (as it was at that time described). The influence that knowledge of a Semitic language could have on a writer's description of Sumerian grammar was again exemplified by the grammars of Gadd and Deimel, which appeared independently of each other in the following year (1924). Gadd wrote of 'states' of perfect and imperfect, recalling the current terminology for Hebrew. Deimel, while disagreeing with Poebel, mentioned the supposed Hebrew parallel explicitly.[150] He too called the forms perfect and imperfect, while adding that they could generally be translated as preterite and present or future, respectively. He also mentioned aspect (*Aktionsart*) as a possible consideration (p.288), but regarded the question as unsusceptible of a solution with the state of knowledge at the time. The grammars of Falkenstein[151] follow the analysis of form of Poebel, retaining the terminology present-future and preterite and replacing permansive by 'standard forms of the intransitive and

145. In *Gedanken zum Tempussystem im Hebräischen und Akkadischen* (Wiesbaden, 1971), p.37.
146. Kraus, *Texte zur babylonischen Physiognomatik, AfO* Beiheft 3 (Berlin, 1939), no.23, rev.3.
147. (Wiesbaden, 1965-81).
148. The works referred to in the following pages are all described in full in the bibliography at the beginning of this volume. An extended bibliography of works on Sumerian grammar can be found in Sollberger's *Système verbal...*, pp.3-13.
149. Elsewhere called by him tenses, e.g. in *AJSL* 50 (1934), pp.143-70.
150. In *Šumerische Grammatik der archaistischen Texte* (Rome, 1924), p.302.
151. *Grammatik der Sprache Gudeas von Lagasch* (1949-50), and *Das Sumerische* (1959).

passive verb'. Present-future and preterite, as in Poebel's system, are confined to the transitive verb. Both the Akkadian preterite, described as 'punctual', and (sometimes) the stative may be thought of as corresponding to the preterite of Sumerian.[152]

If an unnecessarily complicated attempt to discover how categories familiar from Semitic and Indo-European languages found their expression in Sumerian may be described as the principal drawback to Poebel's and Falkenstein's grammars, the works of Jestin,[153] while containing much of interest, may be described as an equally extreme attempt to avoid categorization of any sort, permeated with a sort of institutionalized chaos. '...D'un autre côté, le jeu des préfixes peut, grâce à la façon dont il situe les propositions l'une à l'égard de l'autre à un point de vue souvent très général et où le spatial n'exclut pas le temporel, devenir un moyen de localisation relative dans le temps sans qu'il faille bien entendu attacher une valeur spécifiquement temporelle à quelque préfixe que ce soit.'[154] Jestin recognized a twofold distinction which he called at first by the terms *inachevé* and *achevé.*[155] Later in his grammar (1951) and in the supplement to *Le verbe sumérien* (1954) these were changed to, respectively, *actualisé* and *non-actualisé.* His use of these terms suggests that they are to be understood as meaning something like immediate and non-immediate. It depends on whether actions *frappent encore l'esprit.*[156] He was, however, also prepared to use the terms present-future and preterite.

The first work on Sumerian grammar to employ systematically the method of modern linguistics, in particular those of Saussure, was that of E. Sollberger.[157] His analysis, formally similar to Falkenstein's and Poebel's, employs his own terminology. It may be summarized as follows. Within the indicative mood three groups of forms are identifiable: *factif* (which can be translated as a past tense, marking the statement of a fact), *adventif* (to which the future generally corresponds, marking the announcement in advance of an event, with suffix -e) and *achronique* (extra-temporal, with neutral temporal value). I.T. Kaneva regards it as "now sufficiently proved that the Sumerian finite transitive (but not the intransitive) verb differentiated two aspects, perfective and imperfective", and refers to a study by Diakonov but without further elucidation of these terms.

The effects of modern linguistic work can be seen in a different way in the system of Jacobsen, in an increasing sensitivity to the subtle and unfamiliar distinctions to be found in non-Indo-European, non-Semitic languages. (One thinks in particular of the American Indian languages in Boas' handbook.)[159] We are concerned here with the theoretical aspects of the 'Introduction to the Chicago Grammatical Texts'[160] and the essay 'On the Sumerian Verb' which expanded the theory.[161] Jacobsen distinguished in the Sumerian verb[162] 1) aspects or modes of awareness (the features u-, a- and i/e-, respectively 'outwardly present, manifest fact', 'imperfective aspect' and 'aorist aspect'), 2) *marû* and *hamṭu* character root and 3) differentiation between unfinished action (root + e) and finished action (plain root). The modes of awareness are degrees of awareness. The facts may be 1) central in the awareness i.e. present — usually outward present — manifest fact (u-) or 2) linger in the awareness

152. *V. GSGL* II, pp.155ff.
153. *Le verbe sumérien* I (1943) and II (1946), and *Abrégé de grammaire sumérienne* (1951).
154. *Le verbe sumérien* I, pp.203f.
155. *Le verbe sumérien* I, p.209.
156. *Abrégé de grammaire sumérienne* p.73.
157. *Le système verbal dans les inscriptions "royales" présargoniques de Lagaš* (Geneva, 1952).
158. See I.T. Kaneva in *MIO* 16 (1970), p.549; I.M. Diakonov, '*O rabote s šumerskimi istoričeskimi istočnikami* [Work with Sumerian historical sources]', in *Vestnik Drevnei Istorii* 2 (1958), p. 52.
159. F. Boas, *Handbook of American Indian Languages* (Washington, 1911-).
160. In *MSL* IV (Rome, 1956), pp.1*-50*.
161. First published in *AS* 16 (Chicago, 1965), pp.71-102, and later in *Toward the Image of Tammuz* (Harvard, 1970), pp.254-70.
162. *V.* 'Introduction...', p.5*.

(imperfective a-) or 3) merely touch briefly at the periphery of the awareness (aorist e/i-) (p.20*). The distinction between the *marû* root, e.g. e, and the *hamṭu* root, e.g. du_{11}, may, he wrote, be tentatively described as one of process and event (p.13*). Against these are set, in the grammatical paradigms, the Akkadian aspects of durative (= present and permansive [stative] and punctive (= preterite and perfect). Of importance for our investigations here is the implicit attitude of Jacobsen concerning the composition of the grammatical texts. There are two points: 1) it is clear that he thinks of the texts as composed from an Akkadian-speaker's point of view, with a view to rendering the distinctions of Akkadian 'as far as possible in Sumerian'; cf. p.20*, the choice of particular Sumerian forms 'may have been dictated by a desire to obtain the best possible correspondence to' Akkadian forms and 2) *hamṭu* and *marû* are assumed from the outset (p.5*) to be grammatical terms analytically descriptive of features of the Sumerian language; cf. p.21*, 'for practical purposes *marû*, as a grammatical term, may be translated as 'Present' and *hamṭu* Preterit'. The distinction is frequently parallel, though not exactly equal'. We shall aim to show that both these assumptions are unfounded.

The phraseology and terminology used by Jacobsen raise a host of philosophical questions concerned with, among other things, the nature of perception. We cannot go into these here. But at this point some word needs to be said about the terms used by Jacobsen and other writers. Aspect in linguistic terminology is a name given originally to an explict feature of the grammar of Slavonic languages (as translation of Russian *vid*), where it is usually explained as the distinction between action viewed as completed or finished (perfective aspect) and action viewed as incomplete or unfinished (imperfective aspect). This distinction is supernumerary to the distinction of tense; Bulgarian, for instance, has present, future, aorist and imperfect tenses *as well.* (Note that in Jacobsen's system unfinished action and imperfective aspect are two separate categories. He also has an aorist aspect; yet aorist is the name customarily given to the simple past tense of Ancient Greek and to the punctive imperative, infinitive, subjunctive and optative moods formed from the same stem.) Presumably because of a supposed similarity the term aspect was subsequently extended to the essentially binary division within the verbal system of Arabic, and since then to many other languages. An excellent account of distinctions between tense and aspect is to be found in Denz' account of a modern Arabic dialect.[163] While this is a good theoretical description, it will be found that aspect in, for instance, Bulgarian, works *practically* along different lines. This is due to the unsatisfactory nature of the term. To my mind, Comrie's book *Aspect*[164] fails in this respect as it seeks to find a general explanation of aspect so broad that it will fit every language from Georgian to Lithuanian. This general meaning of aspect is a mare's nest: the term has no *Grundbedeutung*. It is helpful only to talk of aspect *as used* of Arabic or Russian or Chinese.

Aktionsart was formerly used by some German writers as the German for aspect. Now it is used by most linguists to describe a variety of different characters of actions, states or processes as e.g. durative, punctive, ingressive, iterative etc. These characters lie entirely in the actions, states or processes themselves and in no way depend on the construction put upon them or attitude adopted by the observer. They are thus completely different from what is generally understood by aspect, although regarded by some writers as subsumed under the heading of aspect. There is, however, considerable disagreement among linguists over the exact definition of the terms.[165]

---

163. A. Denz, *Die Verbalsyntax des neuarabischen Dialektes von Kwayriš (Irak)* (Wiesbaden, 1971). But see, for a different approach, K.G. Prasse, *Manuel de grammaire touarègue (tăhăggart)*, vol. 3 (Copenhagen, 1973). pp. 29-44.
164. B. Comrie, *Aspect* (Cambridge, 1976), with extensive bibliography.
165. See, for instance, Lyons, *Language and Linguistics: an introduction*, pp. 314-15; Comrie, *op.cit.*, esp. pp. 3, 5, 41, 127; Palmer, *Descriptive and comparative linguistics: a critical introduction*, p. 116; Kuryłowicz, in *OrNS* 42 (1973), pp. 114, 116; — and note: "I do not give the following system as representing various 'aspects' or 'aktionsarten' of the verb, but expressly say that the different phenomena which others have brought together under this one class (or these two classes) should not from a purely notional point of view be classed together" (O. Jespersen, *The philosophy of grammar* (1924), p. 287).

Tense may be defined as the distinction in verbal forms which marks the position of an action, state or process in time by locating it directly, or relatively, with respect to the present moment (clearly explained by Denz).

A distinction must be drawn, however, between the possible uses of all these words as terms in a theoretical system, and their historical use in the practical grammars of various languages. Tense, for example, is the name generally given to the verbal forms of Indo-European languages, even though we might wish to call the Ancient Greek perfect tense an aspect (in Denz' sense) or formulate one of the distinctions between the English simple present (I go) and present continuous (I am going) tenses as one of *Aktionsart*.

The introduction into the description of Sumerian grammar of such terms as those discussed above deserves to be given more thought than it has so far inspired. The bandying about of terms such as 'imperfective', 'perfective', 'durative', 'punctive' and so on, without any attempt to define their meaning precisely, represents no advance in the descriptive grammar of Sumerian on the older usage of 'preterite' and 'present-future', itself largely based on a misreading of the grammatical texts.[166]

The stage is now set for a consideration in detail of the writings of two recent commentators on the terms *hamṭu* and *marû*, Yoshikawa and Edzard. However, mention may first be made of the contentions expounded by Siedl.[167] Siedl, whose primary interest is in the verbal system of Hebrew and Akkadian, argues from the fact that *rīqu* and *malû* and AN.TA, MURU_4.TA and KI.TA clearly refer to and describe the Sumerian forms and not the Akkadian, to the conclusion that so also do *hamṭu* and *marû*, even though they are Akkadian words. His argument after this point is not very clear to me (pp.33f.) but I think it is that because Akkadian clearly has a means (preterite and present-future) of expressing a notion corresponding sufficiently closely to the difference between the Sumerian forms to be able to act as a translation of them, then the concept of the difference must actually exist in an Akkadian-speaker's mind and therefore must exist in the natural distinction within the Akkadian verb. This is of course nonsense. Some of the forms marked *marû*, he continues, are longer words than those marked *hamṭu*, especially, of course, if they happen to be reduplicated. Probably, he suggests, the terms were coined as phonetic descriptions and once the functions were identified the terms could be extended to those forms which did not conform to the original principle. The function, it is then argued, of these longer, reduplicated forms is to express plurality of subject or object, or 'plurality' in the verb, i.e. repeated or lasting action or a lasting state or a greater intensity of action or state. This is in effect a durative *Aktionsart* and so, the author concludes, the distinction between tenses in Sumerian (and hence, on his argument, in Akkadian and also Hebrew [because it is related to Akkadian]) is to be replaced with a system of *Aktionsarten*, with durative, iterative and intensive on the one hand and punctive on the other.

It is not necessary to expose in detail the fallacies of this argumentation. However, it will be convenient to remove once and for all the question of 'short' and 'long' words. First, *hamṭu* and *marû* do not etymologically mean 'short' and 'long' (or 'fat') but 'quick' and 'slow' and the notion that short words take less time to pronounce than long words is hardly seriously to be entertained. In any case the etymological meaning of the word alone is no guide to their application, as the use of words can change beyond recognition in even a short time. Second, the notion that they might refer to short and long words has little basis in evidence, being a traditional interpretation of dictionary compilers dating from Zimmern's suggestion in 1885,

---

166. Thus P. Michalowski, in *JCS* 32 (1980), p. 90: "The verb distinguishes two aspects, perfect and imperfect", then (n. 15): "The use of the terms 'perfect' and 'imperfect' is quite arbitrary; perhaps 'punctive' and 'durative' could have equally been utilised".

167. S.H. Siedl, *Gedanken zum Tempussystem im Hebräischen und Akkadischen* (Wiesbaden, 1971).

which was based on a certain limited few passages where the forms marked *marû* all happened to be longer than those marked *hamṭu*. Subsequent evidence has shown this interpretation to be false (e.g. *hamṭu* du_{11}, gen compared with *marû* e, du).

Yoshikawa, whose theories we shall examine next, follows the lead taken by Jacobsen in referring without further explanation to the *hamṭu* and *marû* roots and writes of the supposed affix -e- as having *'marû* function'.

3.6.1.1 Yoshikawa

'On the grammatical function of -e- of the Sumerian verbal suffix -e-dè-/-e-da(m)'.[168]

The segmentation of this suffix by Falkenstein is into -ed- and -e/-a/-am, of which -ed- is an extension of the verb and -a a mark of the infinitive; or of the participle in intransitive and passive transitive verbs. -e is a later form of this ending and -am represents the suffixed copula.[169] The avowed purpose of Yoshikawa's paper is to prove that the -e- contained in this suffix has a meaning of its own and that the suffix proper is therefore -dè/-da/-dam. It is stated that -e-dè and -dè are commonly regarded as forms of the suffix post-consonantally and post-vocalically respectively. There are, however, cases where -dè is written after a consonant. In these cases it is generally assumed that the sound of a vowel is included in the writing of the verb itself; or that a reading of the verb involving final consonantal amission is required. Thus TAG_4-TAG_4-dè may be read tag_4-tag_4(e)-dè or ta_{12}-ta_{12}-dè.

Yoshikawa aims to show that the -e-, where it occurs in the writing, is significant. Now to do this he will have to show a) that its proposed meaning, or the conditions requiring its presence, are present when it is present, and b) that its proposed meaning, or the conditions for its presence, are absent when it is absent (unless marked in some other way); and also perhaps c) that -e- does not co-occur with other means of marking what it is supposed to mark.

The proof involves the division of verbs into three groups:

1) *The reduplication group.* These verbs reduplicate themselves before adding -dè, -da or -dam. Of the ten verbs examined, the precise readings of two are not known (nos. 7 and 8). Of the remaining eight, four end in a vowel in the reduplicated form. This leaves tag-tag, tag_4-tag_4, $tur_{5/x}$-$tur_{5/x}$ and šám-šám. Of these, tag_4 seems better read as ta_{12} (cf. the verbal paradigms from Ur), and šám is read by Falkenstein as sa_{10}. A number of other verbs are listed also: nag-nag, sug-sug, kin-kin, tuk-tuk, kúš-kúš, zig-zig, íl-íl, all of which except kin-kin and kúš-kúš have possible readings ending in a vowel.

On the basis of the above evidence it cannot really be claimed that -e- is absent in most cases for any other reason than that the verbs end in a vowel. The argument offered on p. 256 (from the behaviour of pà(d)) does not help: it merely shows that pàd does not lose its final consonant.

2) *The alternation group.* This is Yoshikawa's third group, but is here treated as second for convenience of argument. The group uses alternating pairs of verbs. In fact tùm ('always, though with a few exceptions' used before -dè, -da or -dam) is found both followed directly by -dè, -da or -dam, and written out as túm-mu-dè, túm-mu-da, i.e. with the -e- (changed to -u- by vocalic assimilation) explicitly marked. No examples are given of the form taken by šu...ti/ti-gá[170] or du_{11}/e before the suffixed -dè or -da. For gen/du, only two examples are

168. In *JNES* 27 (1968), pp.251-61. See now, in much greater detail, G. Steiner, 'The vocalisation of the Sumerian verbal morpheme /-ED/ and its significance', in *JNES* 40 (1981), pp.21-41, who is especially concerned with the phonetic form of of the affix, and also incorporates a summary and comparison of Yoshikawa's and Edzard's work. My sections 3.6.1.1 and 3.6.1.2 run parallel to some of Steiner's article but with certain differences of emphasis, so I have left them unaltered.

169. Falkenstein, *Das Sumerische*, p.43, §25.

170. To be read ti-ge_x, *v.* Edzard in *ZA* 66 (1976), p.51, n.203.

given, and they conflict: Gudea, Cyl. B iii 25 DU-da and xv 22 gen-na-da. In one -e- is absent, in the other (as -a-) it is present.

3) *The affixation group.* It is postulated by Yoshikawa that these verbs affix -e- before -dè/-da/-dam (sometimes coloured by vowel harmony of the verb; also sometimes coloured by -da to -a-). The affixation of -e- is not, however, universal, since some of the verbs occur with the suffix tacked straight onto them. It is unusually absent in the case of verbs ending in a vowel (p.259, nos. 24-6). Some verbs where it is written in are also reduplicated (pp.258-9, nos. 22-3).

By far the most important conclusion to be drawn from the evidence here assembled is that Sumerian verbs may be divided into three classes according to the form they assume in certain circumstances. Whether these circumstances are conditioned semantically or merely grammatically will depend on what significance is assigned to the circumstances in question. What is clear is that some verbs reduplicate in circumstances where others alternate with a different verb, although the evidence so far presented for this latter group is scanty; and that there are some verbs (possibly, in fact, most verbs) which fall into neither of these classes. It is not, however, proven beyond doubt that the mark of this third class is the tendency to affix -e- in those circumstances, since a) -e- is sometimes found directly after the verb and before the syllables -dè, -da and -dam in both the other classes as well, and b) -e- is not absolutely regularly written in the same circumstances in those verbs which neither reduplicate nor alternate.

The problem is perhaps better solved if we assume that the third class of verbs remains *unaltered* before the suffixes in question and that the suffixes are -e-da, -e-dè and -e-dam. Let a further assumption be that the pronunciation of all these forms was with the stress on the verb itself, and with a short -e-, viz. *['dugĕda] not *[du'gēda]. From this it will be easy to see how after a verb ending in a consonant, and especially in a reduplicated form in which it was probably the first element that was stressed,[171] i.e. *['dugdug] rather than *[dug'dug], an unstressed -e- might be omitted in a writing which only needed to identify the form of suffix being used, not necessarily to spell it out.

The question of 'aspect or *Aktionsart*' is mentioned on p.259, and the terms *hamṭu* and *marû* are mentioned a number of times a) as a designation of the so-called alternating 'roots' of Yoshikawa's third group of verbs and b) as a designation of the presumed grammatical function marked by alternation in that group and, by analogy, by reduplication and alleged affixation in the other two groups. Thus on p.261 reduplication and affixation are said to represent, in their groups, the '*marû* function'. This is supported by the glossing in ancient texts of the reduplicated forms of gá-gá (Eme-sal vocabulary III 76) and túm-túm (*ibid.*, I 1-13) as *marû*. The idea was developed in the author's next paper:

'The marû and hamṭu aspects in the Sumerian verbal system'[172]

In a footnote on the first page, the possibility that the terms *hamṭu* and *marû* have a semantic range covering 'what are usually called aspectual differences of completion, incompletion, momentariness and continuation' is suggested. I return to this later.

The principal aim of this paper is to attempt to demonstrate the identity of the postulated affix -e-, said to occur before the suffixes -dè, -da and -dam, with the suffix -e conventionally described as the marker of the third person singular in the present-future tense of transitive active verbs, i.e. the suffixed means of marking a third person singular agent or cause. Yoshikawa suggests that the -e- of -e-ne, the corresponding third person plural suffix, is also to be identified with these, but says that as the data on this are not sufficiently numerous it will be treated only by occasional references. To prove his contention, it will be necessary to show that -e occurs in complementary distribution with reduplication and alternation, i.e. that it does not co-occur with them, and that it occurs regularly after verbs that neither reduplicate

171. Cf. Falkenstein, *Das Sumerische*, pp.42f., §24 b 2.
172. In *OrNS* 37 (1968), pp.401-416.

nor alternate in the particular set of circumstances chosen for this paper, viz. when the optative preformative hé- is present. (The unspoken assumption here is that hé- has the same effect on verbs as -dè, -da, -dam.)

1) *The reduplication group.* The verbs exemplified here are gá-gá-, gi$_4$-gi$_4$, ra-ra, tur$_{5/x}$-tur$_{5/x}$ (now read ku$_4$) and zi-zi. It is demonstrated that hé- exerts the same grammatical constraint as -(e)-da, -dè, -dam, viz. that with verbs that reduplicate, the reduplicated form is required. Without exception the reduplicated forms listed end in a vowel. Verbs 6-10 (p.406) amount to very little evidence. No examples are brought forward which are not consonant with the more conventional explanation that the expected third person marker -e has been absorbed into the final vowel of the verb; similarly with -e-ne.

2) *The alternation group.* (Here again Yoshikawa's third group is treated second for convenience' sake.) The verbs du$_{11}$/e, túm/tùm, ti/ti-ge$_x$ and gen/du are exemplified. It is shown that with verbs that alternate, the verb labelled *marû* is usually required after the preformative hé-. (The paradigms OBGT VIII and IX contain exceptions to this rule. The unreduplicated forms of gar after hé- in OBGT VI may be compared. But these are on the whole completely at variance both with textual usage and with the general principles operating in other paradigms and in the paradigmatic sections of, e.g., *ana ittišu*.) With forms of gen/du it is of course impossible to know the correct reading, since both verbs are written with the same sign. The verb ti appears in all three possible forms, as ti-ti, ti-ge$_x$ and plain ti; even once as ti-e. It is impossible to tell whether the suffix -e is (notionally) present here or not (except with ti-e). This leaves túm/tùm. It is shown that TÙM is at least usual, although not universal, after hé-, and this is the only example of a verb whose *marû* form appears to end in a consonant. Thus it appears to uphold Yoshikawa's position, as it is not followed by suffixed -e. However, I think we should follow Poebel, Falkenstein and Sollberger in generally adopting the reading tùmu for this sign in these cases. It will be noted that although assigned by Yoshikawa to the alternation group, the verb TÙM is not listed in any grammatical text as the pair of túm, although túm itself is listed as both *hamṭu* (Eme-sal vocabulary III 5) and *marû* (NBGT II 8). TÙM is the only (apparently) monosyllabic verb to be regularly followed by -da, -dè, -dam, *except* when it is written out as túm-mu-da, túm-mu-dè, using a different sign. I have been able to find only one exception to this: tùmu^{mu}-dam.[173] Similarly TÙM is usual after hé-, but is occasionally written with a suffix, as in Yoshikawa's example on p.413, ha-ba-túm-mu (where, again, a different sign is used). The manuscript variants at Wilcke *Lugalbandaepos* 101, may be compared:

mu-un-túm-en
mu-un-túm-me } i.e. tum + e(n)
mu-un-tùmu

Thus tùmu is simply an alternative spelling for túm-mu (= tum + e),[174] and the verb is not properly one that alternates, but should be placed in the remaining class, called by Yoshikawa

3) *The affixation group.* A good deal of evidence is produced here to show that verbs which neither reduplicate nor alternate and which end in a consonant, habitually take the suffix -e after hé-. The -e is also written in after kú and dé (p.411). The presence of this -e is, it should be said, perfectly explicable according to the traditional interpretation of it as a marker of a third person singular agent or cause, see for instance Poebel, *GSG* section 450. Certain of the examples listed none the less weigh against the author's contentions. These fall into two classes:

173. *V.* T. Fish, *Catalogue...*, no.534, 6.

174. This does not apply to early texts, in which tùmu appears to have had a different meaning from túm: túm 'to bring, carry', tùmu 'to carry away'. But cf. later remarks on the likelihood that unsuffixed (standard) forms of this verb should be read de$_6$, below p. 128.

a) Those where the suffix -e occurs in addition to reduplication; hu-mu-ra-an-bal-bal-e, na-an-dím-dím-e (p.409).[175] In these cases it may be possible to explain the reduplication as semantic i.e. denoting plurality, iteration, etc. This idea is suggested by Yoshikawa[176] and has been developed at length by Edzard.[177]
b) Those examples where the suffix -e does not occur after hé- in verbs ending in a consonant and belonging to the so-called affixation class. The most notable cases are the verbs gub (pp.410-11) and gál (examples on p.415, n.1). These verbs are regularly constructed after hé-, without -e, yet they neither reduplicate nor alternate. This is the most serious blow to Yoshikawa's contention of the existence of an affixation group since these very forms are easily explicable according to traditional theory, for (with the exception of zal, for which no hé-forms are listed) gub and gál are the only two 'intransitive' verbs exemplified, and it is precisely these which we should not expect to be marked for a 3rd person agent.

It cannot thus be granted that the conclusion stated on p.415 has been proved. The suffix -e is not to be regarded as identical with the -e- of the suffixes written -e-dé, -e-da, -e-dam. Nor is that -e- to be regarded as significant in itself; rather the traditional segmentation of the suffixes as -ed-a/-ed-a and -ed-am is to be retained. On the other hand, we should be grateful to Yoshikawa for demonstrating the extremely useful principle that hé- operates the same stricture as the affix -ed- with certain verbs, causing some to reduplicate and others to alternate. There are certain exceptions to this, it is true, but the principle holds many more times than not. But the existence of an 'affixation' group cannot be accepted. There are instead many verbs which are not affected by hé- or -ed- in this way.

'The marû conjugation in the Sumerian verbal system'[178]
Yoshikawa's third paper on this subject did not appear until 1974, after the first two parts of Edzard's '*Hamṭu, marû* und freie Reduplikation...', but it was not much influenced by these and can be dealt with here. The aim of the paper is to show that the suffixes of the 1st and 2nd persons singular and plural, -en, -enden and -enzen, are to be analyzed into two elements, the -e-, which is the mark of what he calls the *marû* form in verbs which neither reduplicate nor alternate, and the personal elements -n, -nden and -nzen. This will involve showing a) that -e- is always present in verbs of the alleged affixation group when the *marû* form is used, and absent when the *hamṭu* form is used; b) that the only suffixes used after reduplicated verbs or *marû* 'roots' are -n, -nden, -nzen. It will be noted that in order to demonstrate the first of these requirements, it ought first to be necessary to identify *marû* forms by some criterion independent of the presence or absence of -e- (as was done by the presence of suffixed -(e)-dè/da/dam or prefixed hé- in the two earlier papers) so as to avoid a *circulus vitiosus*.

Yoshikawa also admits what he calls the B conjugation, of which the form is ultimately derived from the exceptions in the last paper (*ibid.* p.416). Thus the B conjugation of reduplicating verbs uses the unreduplicated verb, with the addition of the "*marû*" element -e- before suffixes. (This is actually different from the divergent conjugation noted on p.416, which is without the -e-.) The B *marû* conjugation of alternating verbs is said to use the *hamṭu* root with "*marû*" element before the suffixes.

First, certain points concerning orthography are made (on p.17):
1) In reduplicating and alternating verbs, the suffix of the 1st and 2nd person singular generally occurs only as -en (rather than as -un/an/in or -n) only when the verb itself ends in -e, whereas in the alleged affixing verbs the suffix always appears as -e(n).

175. It is assumed, but nowhere stated, that na-, the 'negative optative', i.e. vetitive preformative, exerts the same influence as hé- in determining the form of the verb. Cf. also the note (2) on p.404. To these may be added Wilcke, *Das Lugalbandaepos* 27 hé-em-mi-ib-sè-sè-ge.

176. In 'On... -e-dè/-e-da(m)', p.258, n.13.

177. In '*Hamṭu, marû* und freie Reduplikation...'; *v.* 3.6.1.2 below.

178. In *OrNS* 43 (1974), pp.17-39.

2) The forms of the suffix occurring with reduplicating and alternating verbs, said to be conditioned by vocalic assimilation, -un, -an, -in (and -en) never appear with amission of -n, whereas -en may occur as -e with verbs of the affixation group. This is said to show that the -u-, -a-, -i-, -e- of the former forms are merely indicators of the immediatly preceding vowels.
3) In verbs of the affixation group, the -e- affixed before -n does not generally undergo assimilation.
4) The extended writing -e-en is almost exclusively attested for the affixation group.

Concerning the first point, it may be noted that all the verbs of which the reduplicated forms with suffix -n are listed, end in a vowel. Thus we should not expect the suffix to occur as anything but -n. Of the alternating verbs 1) túm/tùmu has been treated above; it should not be assigned to this group, and 2) šu...ti/te/ti-ge$_x$/te-ge$_x$ is only represented in Yoshikawa's paper by one *marû* example, nam-ba-te-ge$_x$-dè, which does have the ending -e(n) and not -n. '*Marû*' forms of this verb always seem to have the affix -ed-. The forms at OBGT V 4-6 may be compared. The other forms cited by Yoshikawa from this text (*sub* 2.a) are set against Akkadian preterites (i-ṭè-hi-šum and e-ṭè-hi-šum in 7 and 8 are errors for *ittehišum* and *ettehišum*) and are thus not to be regarded as *marû*. It is certainly no argument for their being *marû* that they have the suffix -(e)-en. 3) The *marû* verb du ends in a vowel. Thus du-un is expected and du-ù explicable. 4) The *marû* verb meaning to say consists of the vowel e. Thus e-en (or -bẹ́(-en)) is expected.

Of the verbs of the affixation class which are listed, nos. 4, 7-21 and 22a, b, d, e, f, i all end in a *consonant* (še-ga is really šeg-). 22c is the verb gíd/gíd-i which, as is clear from the Ur verbal paradigms, belongs to the alternation group. That leaves only 22g, sa$_4$-sa$_4$ (presumably reduplicating) and 22h, lá; and the verbs dù, kú, si...sá, du$_8$ and ha-za. Some forms of these, e.g. an-na-ha-za-an, na-an-kú-un-zé-en and the uncited Gudea, Cyl. A ix 7-8, ma-dù-na (ma+du+(e)n+a), show that these verbs can take the suffix without -e-, absorbing the vowel into themselves. The few remaining take the forms -e, -en, -e-en.

Concerning the second point, as has been said, virtually all the verbs exemplified end in a vowel and therefore would only be expected to show the suffix in the form -n. The point here is surely that if a form *gá-gá + (e)n is written with assimilation, it is spelt gá-gá-an; and if it is written with assimilation of the vowel *and* amission of final -n (*gá-gá + a(n)) it is spelt gá-gá. A number of forms of this sort may be found among Yoshikawa's examples, e.g. p.19, no. 1(a), p.20, no. 1(f) line 127 (variants), line 195 (variants) etc.

The third point is not supported by the evidence. The verb túm almost always affects suffixed -e, -en etc. to become -u, -un etc.; gub has the same effect in i-gub-bu-nam.[179] The verb sum regularly occurs with the suffixes sum-mu-un, sum-mu-un-zé-en etc. It is in any case not clear what would be proved by showing that -e(n) was not affected by vocalic assimilation in verbs of the affixation group, since the affix -e occurring after hé (which is claimed to be identical with the -e- of -en) is commonly so affected, as may be seen from the examples in 'The *marû* and *hamṭu* aspects...', pp.407-408 (sum) and p.410 (ur$_x$).

The occurrence of the extended writing -e-en may perhaps be thought to be quite good evidence for the independent significance of -e-, but, as Yoshikawa himself admits, it is not confined to the affixation group; cf. p.21, 1(j) gá-gá-e-en with variants gá-gá-e and gá-gá-an; p.28, 2(b) line 14 (variants), lines 111, 124 and 125 (with variants). The spellings in the Ur grammatical texts may also be compared:

UET VII 102, iii 8 ta$_{12}$-a-ab-[zé-]en
10 mu-ni-ib-ta$_{12}$-ta$_{12}$-a-[an-]zé-en
(cf. 11, 12).

The occurrence of this writing with -e-en is on the whole confined to verbs ending in a vowel. Exceptions to this among Yoshikawa's examples are:

179. Kramer, 'Schooldays', 12, cited by Yoshikawa, p.31.

p.30 7(b)	ba-ab-ús-e-en
p.33 15(a)	a-ra-ab-taḫ-e-en-dè-en
p.34 19	ab-ta-ab-bal-e-en
p.34 22(e)	na-ab-ta-ab-ḫa-lam-e-en-zé-en (and cf. variants)

It seems quite possible, therefore, that in most cases the -e- is an attempt to represent a glide in pronunciation from the final vowel of the verb to the vowel of the ending -en. But if so, it is impossible to explain the above exceptions.

Finally the question must be raised whether all the forms listed under the heading of verbs of the affixation group are in fact *marû* forms. Most of them are what would be called in the traditional terminology the first or second singular or plural of the present-future tense of active transitive verbs. Yoshikawa has already suggested that this tense is to be renamed '*marû* aspect' (and the preterite '*hamṭu* aspect') and this, presumably, is the basis for his selection of forms with the personal elements suffixed. 'Preterite' forms (which for him would be '*hamṭu*') have their personal elements mainly infixed before the verb. This selection does not allow for forms which in the traditional description would be called intransitive, i.e. where a suffixed personal element marks not an agent but an 'inert' (a noun which stands in the unmarked case). Some of the examples are of this type, viz.;

p.31 8(c)	i-gub-bu-nam
10(a)	hé-em-ši-dal-dal-en
10(b)	ba-dal-en
p.33 17	ši-im-diri-ge-e̜n
p.34 20	nu-ub-še-ge-en
p.35 22(i)	nu-mu-un-til-le-en

If these are *marû*, then all 'intransitive' forms must be *marû*. Is this an acceptable conclusion? One would have thought not. If we consider verbs of the alternating class, we find throughout OBGT VII and UET VII 101 etc. (the paradigms gen etc. = *alākum*) that *marû* forms of the verbs 'to go' appear as du-un, su_8-bé-en-dè-en and su_8-bé-en-zè-en and *hamṭu* forms (set against Akkadian preterites and imperatives) as gen-en, re_7-en-dè-en and re_7-en-zè-en. Now according to Yoshikawa's theory these latter forms (which would presumably be analyzed by him as *hamṭu* verb + affix -e- + endings -n, -nden, -nzen) should be forms of the 'B *marû* conjugation'. The *marû* forms proper would then presumably be *du-n, *sub-nden, *sub-nzen. But these two latter forms will be found nowhere in Sumerian literature; nor will the impossible *tum-n proposed on p.35.

It cannot be granted that it has been satisfactorily demonstrated that the -e- of the suffixes -en, -en-dè-en, -en-zé-en is especially significant of the *marû* form since a) there is not sufficient evidence to show a clearcut distinction in writing between forms with -e- and forms without it; b) it can only be by virtue of the presence of the suffixes in question that the forms can be identified as *marû*; c) these suffixes also occur in 'intransitive' forms (and to mark what in traditional terminology would be called the objects of transitive active verbs); and d) this very identification itself is based on an unsubstantiated equation of *marû* and 'present-future tense' which is later claimed as part of the conclusion on p.39.

It seems preferable to retain the traditional description of the 1st and 2nd person suffixes as -en, -en-dè-en, -en-zè-en for all verbs, with the proviso that the -e- may be absorbed into a preceding vowel in some cases; and to conclude that there is so far no evidence that verbs which do not reduplicate or alternate are affected by the distinction of forms to which Yoshikawa and other modern writers have applied the ancient terms *hamṭu* and *marû*.

3.6.1.2 Edzard

'Hamṭu, marû und frẹie Reduplikation beim sumerischen Verbum' [180]

The content of this important study is summarized in what follows.[181] The author's own paragraph numbering is preserved.

01. Various earlier attempts to explain the terms are noted. Biggs and Civil, in *RA* 60 (1966), p.16, regarded them as applicable to all Sumerian verbs. The 'decisive breakthrough' came with Yoshikawa's isolation (in the first of the three papers summarized above, section 3.6.1.1) of the -e of -e-dè, -e-da, and -e-dam as a marker of *marû* forms. In this paper he made a division of Sumerian verbs into three groups. In a subsequent paper[182] he used the presence of the preformative hé- (precative) (and also the prohibitive or vetitive na-) as a test for *marû* forms. Yoshikawa, like Biggs and Civil, assumes that the terms are applicable to all Sumerian verbs. Edzard himself is inclined to avoid the equation of *marû* with Sumerian present and of *hamṭu* with preterite.

02. Contrary to Jacobsen, and following Yoshikawa, he excludes from his study the verbal paradigms, as they can be demonstrated to contain erroneous forms which are a confusion of precative and assertoric (under Akkadian influence). In part I (§§1-11) he will investigate forms constructed with a preformative of modal meaning (except for §10, on 'free reduplication'). In part II (§§12-20) he will consider non-finite forms from the point of view of *hamṭu* and *marû*. In part III (for which the plan was subsequently revised) he will consider the relation of *hamṭu* and *marû* to the Sumerian present-future and preterite. So as not to anticipate the conclusion, the examples will be chosen as far as possible from reduplicating and alternating verbs, and the preterite and present-future terminology will also be retained. (It is clear in any case that *hamṭu* and *marû* could not be fully equated with Sumerian present-future and preterite, if *hamṭu* and *marû* are assumed to be applicable to all Sumerian verbs: since the categories present-future and preterite are only applicable to the so-called transitive verbs.)

1. hé- in its precative or optative sense. Yoshikawa showed that this use of hé- requires the *marû* form in 'transitive' verbs. Of Edzard's examples, some of the apparent exceptions to this principle are intransitive verbs, and so he tentatively formulates the rule that with intransitive verbs hé- requires the *hamṭu* form. Is the evidence for this sufficient? Of the exceptions, only two are from verbs that either reduplicate or alternate to form their *marû* equivalents (so as to be indubitably one or the other), and of those, one is from Statue B of Gudea, a text which can be demonstrated to contain a large number of irregular 'short' forms of verbs and which therefore should really be excluded from consideration; the remaining examples are from unvarying verbs and permit no such conclusion. A more reasonable conclusion is that hé- virtually always requires the *marû* form.

2. Other forms in which hé- appears are assertoric. Whether this is a borrowing from Akkadian (*lū aprus*) or *vice versa* is not clear.[183] The conclusion here is that assertoric hé- probably requires the *hamṭu* form.

3. ba-ra- as promissory negative or as vetitive (1st or 2nd person). The examples here point to the use of the *marû* form.

4. ba-ra- as assertoric negative regularly takes the *hamṭu* form.

---

180. In *ZA* 61 (1971), pp.208-32, 62 (1972), pp.1-34 and 66 (1976), pp.45-61.

181. The recent detailed article of B. Kienast, 'Probleme der sumerischen Grammatik. 4-6', in *ZA* 70 (1981), pp. 1-35, is likewise a midrash on Edzard's work. Since Kienast's position is by no means identical with my own, it was felt desirable to retain the following section. Kienast accepts without demur the terms 'perfective' and 'imperfective' (*loc.cit.*, p. 8) and maintains the distinction between (Sumerian) transitive and 'intransitive-passive' verbs. He also insists (pp. 7f.) on a distinction '*marû*'/'*hamṭu*' in 'intransitive-passive' verbs even though in the vast majority of cases there can be no perceptible difference in form.

182. In *OrNS* 37 (1968), the second paper summarized in section 3.6.1.1 above.

183. Edzard later assumed, in his paper on the *Sprachbund* (*v. infra*, p.217) that the Akkadian *lū aprus* was conditioned by the Sumerian hé-dím.

5. na- as prohibitive or vetitive. If the verb is transitive, *marû* is obligatory. No examples of intransitive forms are listed, but there is no reason to suppose that they would behave differently.

6. Narrative na- appears to take *hamṭu* or *marû*, i.e. is not prescriptive. Just as assertoric hé- is favoured in declarative statements, by themselves or others, of rulers' achievements, so narrative na- is favoured in the introduction of a narrative ('now...').

7. ša- seems similarly not to be prescriptive of either *hamṭu* or *marû*.

8. ga- occurs only with the 1st person (as volitive or, in plural, cohortative) and usually requires a *hamṭu* verbal form. Reduplication (probably pluralic) is sometimes found in plural forms.

9. In the second person imperative the *hamṭu* form is required; but in the plural it seems that reduplication (probably pluralic) is also possible.

Table to show the prescriptive preformatives, with form of verb required and persons used.

	hamṭu	*marû*
imperative	2.	—
ga-	1. volitive/cohortative	—
hé-	1,3. assertoric	2,3. precative
ba-ra-	1,3. assertoric negative	{ 1. promissory negative 2. vetitive
na-	—	2,3. prohibitive, vetitive
ù-	1,2,3. anticipatory	—
nuš-	(?) 1,2,3. frustrative	

ša/ši-, -nga- and narrative na- do not seem to be prescriptive.

Edzard does not discuss ù-, -nga-, nu- or nuš-. Falkenstein had already stated that in Gudea's writings ù- is followed by the preterite in transitive verbs,[184] and Yoshikawa affirms that the *hamṭu* form is general after ù-.[185] To demonstrate this rule the following examples may be considered:

ELA[186]	526	ù-mu-e-du$_{11}$ 'when you have told me'
LE[187]	12	um-ma-ni-in-dúr-ru-un 'when I have seated them'
LFG[188]	121	ne un-kú 'when he has eaten this'
LE	14	um-ma-da-an-ri 'when he has fetched her'
LE	44	un-gíd 'when it stretches itself'
LE	45,70	si$_x$ un-gi$_4$ 'when it cries out'
LE	104	ù-bi-du$_{11}$ 'when I say'
LE	181,198	um-mi-dím...um-mi-gub 'when I have had them set up... when you stand'
LE	241	ù-mu-nag 'when I have drunk'
LE	404	ù-ba-ra-è-a...ù-ba-ra-an-dab$_5$ 'when he has fetched it and caught it'
LE	411	um-ma-an-di-ni-ib-gar-gar 'when he brings all these away'

10. Free reduplication. This is sometimes distinguishable by spelling, e.g. gar-gar as opposed to gá-gá (*marû* reduplication). The examples show that free reduplication is used to mark a)

184. In *GSGL* I, p.273, §76b.
185. In 'The *marû* and *hamṭu* aspects...', p.404, n.2.
186. Sol Cohen, *Enmerkar and the Lord of Aratta* (University Microfilms, 1973).
187. C. Wilcke, *Das Lugalbandaepos* (Wiesbaden, 1969).
188. Cited *ibid.*, p.56.

various forms of plurality, or distribution, and b) importance, size, long duration or great efficacy of subject or object or action. It can also be lexicalized as in (inim) gi_4 -gi_4 'to answer, reply'.

11. Resume of parts 01-10. The working hypothesis has been used that with transitive verbs the *hamṭu* base is used with the preterite conjugation; and the *marû* base with the present-future conjugation.[189] With intransitive verbs there is only one form of conjugation, the so-called standard form (*Normalform*), but there can be an opposition of bases.

12(a). Edzard now considers the various non-finite forms of the verb. du_{11}-ga and di are the nominal forms ('participles') corresponding respectively to du_{11} and e. di occurs in various phrases, such as gù-nun di 'making a loud noise'. When followed by the copula -am̃, di always appears as di-dam (i.e. di+(d)+am) as do many non-finite forms, e.g. gá-gá-dam. From this the author concludes that the *marû* participle ends in -d, i.e. has the affix or extension -/ED/.

This conclusion is important. It is in direct contrast to that of Yoshikawa, whose explanation of the data is that when -/ED/ is added to a non-finite form, the *marû* form of the verb is required. The difference in these two approaches consists in whether we regard -/ED/ as the meaningful element and the *marû* form as a grammatically conditioned result of its presence; or regard *hamṭu* and *marû* as having inherent meanings of their own and -/ED/ as being a semantically empty, grammatically conditioned marker of the presence of a *marû* form. It will not, I think, be possible to settle this question by any example, since while it might be thought that Yoshikawa's view entailed the possibility of a *marû* form without the element -/ED/, a) such a form would be indistinguishable from the form *with* suffixed -/ED/, as the -d would drop and the -e- might assimilate to a preceding vowel, and b) the only other excuse for a *marû* form (if *marû* is a grammatically conditioned category) would be the presence of one of several preformatives, which (with the exception of nu-) are of course absent from non-finite forms. But the advantages of regarding -/ED/ as the conditioner and *marû* as the grammatically conditioned result would be a) that -/ED/ has already always been thought to have a specific semantic 'future' or 'probleptic' meaning of its own (see p. 119, below), and b) that not all *marû* forms are followed by -/ED/, whereas all forms with -/ED/ *are* preceded by a *marû* verb, whether finite or non-finite. The implications of this will be developed at some length below. The best way to draw a conclusion here will be a slight adaptation of Edzard's viz. that the non-finite forms of the verb are four in number:

a) the (*hamṭu*) base on its own: húl, kúr, du_{11}, gar, gen,

b) the base with suffix -a (in which case the *hamṭu* base must be used): húl-la, kúr-ra, du_{11}-ga, gar-ra, gen-na,

c) the base with suffix -ed (in which case the *marû* base must be used): húl-le^d, kúr-ru^d, gá-$gá^d$ (the -d falls away and the -e- may assimilate),

d) the root with suffix -ed+a or +am (-ed+a sometimes written -e-dè) in which case the *marû* base must be used): húl-le-da/dè/dam, kúr-ru-da, di-da, gá-gá-da, du-da. Of course only reduplicating and alternating verbs have a distinctive *marû* base.

12(b). Different from the phrases of the type mah-di etc. are those like dub-sar, constructed with the *hamṭu* base and without -ed.

13. Phrases of the type kur gul-gul use the *hamṭu* base in free reduplication.

14. The type sá-du_{11} is formally indistinguishable from the type dub-sar. Whether these should be construed as transitive or intransitive does not matter, as this is not a productive construction. Edzard calls it a fossil (p.9).

15(a). -a may be added only to the *hamṭu* base, or to the *marû* base with *suffix* -ed. (This was discussed above under paragraph 12a.)

189. The use of the word 'base' rather than the inappropriate 'root' is due to Edzard.

15(b). Similarly the Mes-an-né-pà-da construction always uses the *hamṭu* base.

16(a). In the so-called pronominal 'conjugation', the nominalized form of the verb with suffix -a (added to the *hamṭu* base, or, if -/ED/ is present, the *marû* base) appears with one of the 3rd person (possessive) suffixes, -(a-)ni, -bi or -(a-)ne-ne.

16(b). The form DU-ni, occurring in messenger tablets, is probably irregular and to be read du-ni in place of the expected *gen-na-ni or *du-da-ni. It seems to me possible[190] that DU-ni is to be regarded as a common abbreviated writing (indicating a form of the verb 'to go' with a 3rd person suffix) for gen-na-ni, just as lugal-NI is written for lugal-a-ni.

16(c). Certain examples in Gudea are difficult to explain.

17. Forms of the type nigín-na-mu/zu-dè seem to complement the 3rd person forms of paragraph 16.

Edzard suggests that there may be an aspectual difference between ku_4-ra-mu-dè and ku_4-ku_4-da-mu-dè. The difference in meaning surely lies in the absence and presence of -/ED/ rather than in the form of the verb used. If the difference of aspect were present in the simple alternation between *hamṭu* and *marû*, it would be difficult to explain the presence of -/ED/; also one would expect the *same* difference in aspect to exist between e.g. (ki-bi) hé-bí-gi_4 'I restored' and hé-em-gi_4-gi_4 'you are to send'. It is difficult to see how this could be so.[191] (This is discussed below.)

18. The author next presents a revised statement of his view of the meaning and function of -/ED/.[192] The revised view is that -ada is added to *hamṭu* bases and -eda to *marû* bases.

Does the evidence support this revised view? Surely -ada is simply -eda with vowel harmony. Sometimes -uda is found also. Proof of this lies in the fact that -a-dè will nowhere be found.[193] The -a- of -a-da is -e- assimilated to the -a of -da.[194] Conversely the -u- of -u-da is -e- assimilated to the -u- of e.g. sum-, so that sum-mu-dè may be found. The substance of the evidence listed is the five forms du_{11}-ga-da, gar-ra-da, gen-na-da, zi-ga-da and gi_4-a-da (all except the last of which come from Gudea's Cylinder B), in which known *hamṭu* bases are followed by -a-da. But the interpretation suggested is in conflict with the whole body of evidence amassed in paragraphs 12-17 of the present study, the burden of which is to suggest that (p.17) 'bei *marû* -/ED/ obligatorisch ist, während es bei *hamṭu* nicht stehen darf', although I would rephrase this as: 'with -/ED/ *marû* is obligatory; but -/ED/ never occurs with *hamṭu*'. The five forms above must be regarded as exceptions.

19. An explanation of the development from Old Sumerian -am_6 to neo-Sumerian -àm is offered.

20 and 20(a) list various problem cases and summarize paragraphs 19-21.

21. Edzard next ties up a number of loose ends and criticizes Yoshikawa. The distribution of *hamṭu* and *marû* in the various conjugation patterns (preterite, present-future, present-future with -/ED/, 'standard form', 'standard form' with -/ED/) is more complicated than was originally supposed in paragraph 11 when the pattern was assumed to be:

preterite or 'standard form' + *hamṭu*
present-future or 'standard form' + *marû*

It is not possible to replace preterite and present-future by *hamṭu* and *marû*, nor to talk of a '*marû* conjugation'.

More information is needed on the plural verbs, e.g. e is *marû* of du_{11}, but plural also of du_{11}, whether *marû* or *hamṭu*.

---

190. Though it was regarded by Edzard as very unlikely (in conversation).

191. Aside from the fact that it is not at all clear *exactly* what might be meant by aspect when used of Sumerian.

192. Earlier expounded in 'Das sumerische Verbalmorphem /ed/ in den alt- und neusumerischen Texten', in Edzard, ed., *Heidelberger Studien zum alten Orient* (Wiesbaden, 1967), pp.44-47.

193. -dè is supposed by Falkenstein *Das Sumerische*, p.43, §25 c 2 a, to be a later variant of -da.

194. Yoshikawa has gone into this more recently in 'Aspectual morpheme /a/ in Sumerian', in *ZA* 69 (1980), pp.161-75. He regards -a- as a mark of a third 'aspect' distinct from the '*hamṭu*' and '*marû*' aspects.

Edzard thinks Yoshikawa is wrong to posit an affixation group, since the -e- is really a 'constituent part' (p.48) of the subject marker, and the verbs in that class are invariable. There are really two classes in Yoshikawa's alternation group: i) verbs like te/teĝ whose base varies (another example of which, as is clear from the verbal paradigms from Ur, is gíd/gíd-i) and ii) true complementary pairs such as gen/du. Reduplicating and invariable verbs and those whose bases vary are to be designated 'regular' and all others 'irregular'. Among 'irregular' verbs he would also list $dug_8/dug_8{}^r$ and perhaps also $ku_5/ku_5{}^{d/r}$.

Excursus (p.50). Concerning invariable verbs, it is difficult to argue either way, owing to the danger of circular argument. To show that the suffix -e has nothing to do with *marû* and that verbs like sum, sikil, lá etc. are invariable, one can only resort to verbs a) whose *marû* reduplicated forms end in a consonant (of which none are known!) or b) whose alternating *marû* forms end in a consonant. An example is (šu)...ti/teĝ, tiĝ. The spelling te-gá (= te-g + e) is to be read te-ge_x and the frequent te-gá-e as te-$ge_x{}^e$ or te-ge_x-e, where -e serves as a clarification. (The same is surely true for hun-gá-e.) Yoshikawa's statement of the *marû* form of this verb as te-gá is self-contradictory; the 'present-future' te-gá-e should not occur, as te-gá would already be *marû*. This is in Edzard's opinion the strongest argument for a *marû* stem teĝ and for the definition of -e as a 3rd person singular marker.

22. Finally we come to the attempt to define *hamṭu* and *marû*. The Sumerian verb has 'stems' (*Stämme*) which occur in various morphological contexts, such that we can speak of verbal 'classes'. These are:

regular:	1) invariable
	2) reduplicating
	3) verbs whose stem alters
irregular:	4) complementary pairs (alternating verbs)
	5) verbs like dug_8 (of irregular distribution)

The *hamṭu* stem is used for the preterite, and in non-finite forms followed by -a; the *marû* for present-future and wherever the morpheme -/ED/ is present.

Edzard's view is that the *hamṭu* and *marû* have no function in their isolated forms (i.e. no meaning of their own); but that in the context of a verbal complex they have a function. He wants to retain the traditional terminology of preterite, present and 'standard form'. The precise 'temporal or aspectual principal and secondary functions' of the various conjugated or non-finite forms are not discusssed by him. Of the pronominal conjugation, it may, he says, be surmised (*vermutet*) that ku_4-ku_4-da-ni 'when he enters' is imperfective in aspect and that ku_4-ra-ni 'when he had entered' is perfective. This direction of research (pursued by Diakonoff and Kaneva)[195] is doubtless worthwhile; maybe the connection with Akkadian must be further considered.

This study is extremely interesting and contains a large number of useful results. The most important conclusion to be drawn from it can be stated as follows:

We may in a sense regard the '*hamṭu*' form of the verb (in those verbs which make a distinction of form in that respect) as the basic form. The occasions on which the '*marû*' form is used can then be quite simply summarized in a set of rules:

1) In any verbal form, whether finite or non-finite, in which the morpheme -/ED/ is present, the *marû* form is used. The most complete account of -/ED/ is Edzard's own work, 'Das sumerische Verbalmorphem /ed/...'[196] Its reference seems to be to future events, although its use in descriptive passages suggests a connotation of vividness. More important, it marks an action as *not yet begun at the moment of observation* (which can be a moment in the past). This

195. Diakonoff's work was not available to me.

196. In *Heidelberger Studien zum alten Orient*, pp.44-47.

I would call a relative tense, in the sense in which the phrase is used by Denz,[197] as it is concerned with reference to a moment of observation rather than to the moment of utterance (which would make it a simple tense). Forms without -/ED/ are not 'marked', and therefore not necessarily *not* (*not yet begun at the moment of observation*). If we had to give a name to this affix, we could call it 'prospective';[198] or better 'probleptic'.[199]

2) In finite forms of the verb, the *marû* form must be used

a) after the precative hé- of the 2nd or 3rd person,

b) after the preformative ba-ra- (promissory negative of the 1st person, vetitive of the 2nd person), and

c) after the prohibitive na- of the 2nd or 3rd person.

This leaves verbal forms constructed with the preformatives ša-, nu-, narrative na-, forms of -nga-, and the prefixes ì-, a-, mu-, ba- and bí-. The alternation of *hamṭu* and *marû* in these forms is yet to be accounted for.

197. *Die Verbalsyntax des neuarabischen Dialektes von Kwayriš*, especially pp.22-47.

198. If it were not that 'prospective' is already used for the preformative ù-.

199. Steiner (*JNES* 40 (1981), pp.21-41) goes into much more detail on this whole question, but the position maintained here is essentially the same as I take his to be, which would support Edzard's earlier interpretation of -/ED/, where the variation in vocalisation of the affix is due to morphological phenomena, and is independent of any functional variation (Steiner, *loc.cit.*, p.30 2b.1, p.33 2c.4). However, as I understand him, Steiner takes the evidence of du_{11}-ga-da, gar-ra-da, gen-na-da, zi-ga-da and gi_4-a-da (see above, p.117) to show that -/ED/ is also compatible with '*hamṭu*' bases (*loc.cit.* p. 28 2a.4).

4 *Conclusions*

4. CONCLUSIONS

In this section an attempt is made to draw together the evidence so far presented with a view to establishing the significance of the terms *hamṭu* and *marû*, in the light of a general survey of the working of the grammatical texts and a theory of the way in which the choice of verbal forms operates in Sumerian. In the preceding analysis we have so far for convenience' sake used the terms *hamṭu* and *marû* in the sense in which the various modern scholars have used them, viz. to refer to the two systems of marking person in Sumerian, one with the cause infixed and one with it suffixed, and to the variable bases associated with these systems in certain verbs. Since the drift of our argument will be to suggest that this identification is incorrect, we propose from this point on to distinguish between the Sumerian systems of incorporation with their variable bases and what we regard as the correct denotation of the terms *hamṭu* and *marû*. To this end some new terms are called for and the reader's indulgence in this is requested. The French term *structure* (used by Marr and Brière in their *La langue géorgienne* to describe something rather similar) would seem quite appropriate.[201] English 'structure' sounds too passive as a translation of it and so 'construction' is proposed. The traditional Sumerian 'preterite' together with the intransitive conjugation I call then the *standard construction*. 'Standard' has already been used as a translation of Falkenstein's *Normalform* and it is intended precisely to suggest that it is the regular or simple form. For the traditional 'present-future of the transitive verb' *secondary construction* will be used. 'Inverted' is not used as it does not strictly apply to verbs with an inert but no agent, since there is in these cases only one person to incorporate and it is always suffixed. The terms chosen describe merely the form of the construction and avoid any suggestion of function.

In the foregoing study we have tried to show that the grammatical texts, of which there are three sorts, are if anything more complicated and highly organized than has hitherto been assumed. The nature of the list literature is such that the theoretical presuppositions on which it is based are revealed to a large extent only by the order in which the material is presented. The first sort of grammatical text examined was the verbal paradigm, in which a list of verbal forms is arranged in such a way as to demonstrate paradigmatically the function of certain elements. In these texts singular forms predominate among the verbs. A twofold distinction is found between Sumerian forms with prefix ga- or hé- or with imperative (Akkadian *lu*-, *li*-

---

200. It is not always clear whether those who use the terms in these senses include standard-form one-participant ('intransitive') verbs under the category *marû* or *hamṭu*. For instance, forms with the person marked by suffix are labelled *marû* by Foxvog in *OrNS* 44 (1975), examples on p.401; others seem to regard such forms as capable of being either *marû* or *hamṭu*.

201. N. Marr and M. Brière, *La langue géorgienne* (Paris, 1931).

or imperative), in which the order second, first, third person is regularly observed, and Sumerian forms with prefixes ì-, mu/mi-, mu/ma-, a-, bí- or ba- (Akkadian stative, present or preterite), in which the order 3rd, 1st, 2nd person is regularly observed. It is important to notice that this does not correspond to a formal distinction in *either* language, i.e. it is a genuinely theoretical division based on meaning. A second major division is betweeen forms with and without Sumerian mu/ma-/-m- (corresponding exactly to the forms in Akkadian with and without ventive). Here there is no need to assume more than an overlap of meaning; what is more important for us is the way in which the equivalence affects the structuring of the texts. It would in fact be naive to read into this opposition any more than we read into an equation ta = *ištu*, which means 'there are occasions when ta should be translated as *ištu*'. The actual details of the overlap are less important here than the need to illustrate the structure of many verbal forms containing the element in question and the guises under which it may occur.

We can distinguish in the compilation a twofold approach. As far as the overall arrangement of forms is concerned, Akkadian is the dominant determinant. This may be due to the uses to which the texts were put, or it may be due to the agglutinative nature of Sumerian, which means that an almost indefinitely large number of forms is possible. The forms of the Akkadian verb can at least be numbered finitely. Within this arrangement Sumerian is sometimes the determining factor. The internal consistency of the texts sometimes throws up forms which cannot have had much naturalness in the languages and which in certain cases can be shown to be extraordinary. Such forms are familiar from grammars of all languages. In order to fill out a paradigm in two languages, it is usually necessary to invent some forms in one of them. Among these are, in Sumerian, some of the causative forms. Among the Akkadian entries we noted *-am ana ṣērīya* (corresponding in the scheme to *-akkum* and *-aššum*) concocted to bring out the fact that Sumerian has two distinct elements, one elsewhere set against the dative, the other set against the ventive. Since in the 1st person singular these coincide formally in Akkadian, *ana ṣērīya*, while perfectly good Akkadian for 'to me' (perhaps in a slightly emphatic sense), is thus in the present context specifically a periphrasis for the dative suffix of the 1st person singular as contrasted with the ventive. The N theme of *uzuzzum* and the Nt of *šakānum* appear to have been specifically invented for the occasion. Again verbal suffixes in Akkadian are of three types: dative, accusative and ventive. Most of the possible combinations of these occur in the texts and are equated with various forms of the Sumerian infixes for dative and locative-terminative and with -še- and -da-. However, the ablative infix -ta-, common in Sumerian, is wholly absent, probably because no convenient Akkadian form exists to convey its sense. The reverse process can be observed in regard to themes. The Akkadian verbal themes represented in our texts are G, Gt, D, Dt (very rare), Š, Št, N, Nt, i.e. the iterative -tan- themes are entirely absent. In this case it is probably because no suitable Sumerian equivalent exists. (Free reduplication is already equated in the texts with intensive or lexicalized senses of the D and Dt themes.) The element -ed-, also common in Sumerian, is hardly represented, perhaps because Akkadian lacked a means to distinguish between the present and future sense of its own present tense (which was already used as an equivalent of certain secondary construction forms).

The correspondence between Sumerian forms and the Akkadian tenses may be summarized as follows:

standard construction

ga-	set against	e.g.		*luprus*
a-, sometimes ba-	"	"	"	*paris*
imperative	"	"	"	*purus*
ì-, mu/mi-, mu/ma-, ba-, bí-	"	"	"	*iprus*

secondary construction

i-, mu/mi-, mu/ma-, ba-, bi-	„	„	„	*iparras*
a-	„	„	„	*iparras*
hé-	„	„	„	*liprus*
na-	„	„	„	*lā taparras*

From this it must be clear that an identification of standard construction with English preterite or of secondary construction with present is both logically impossible and unlikely. The same must also be true of interpretations along the lines of 'imperfective'/'perfective' or 'durative'/'punctive', however those terms are understood. Does it make sense to say that all 1st person optatives are perfective or punctive while all 3rd person optatives are imperfective or durative? Or that a- with a punctive form could be translated by the Akkadian stative? There is no reason why 1st person optatives should be more perfective than imperfective; and if both are possible, why does only the form with the standard construction occur?

These objections are methodological, and must be insisted upon. Clearly the standard and secondary constructions each have more than one function; but there is no *Hauptbedeutung*. The notion that they should have more than one function is of course no odder than the idea, now established, that reduplication fulfils more than one function: a) it is used intensively, b) it is a sign of the plural and c) it is one of the marks of the secondary construction.

The third sort of grammatical text investigated was the grammatical analysis (in epitomized form), in which the principles exemplified in the verbal paradigms and grammatical vocabularies are abstracted and presented in a more elemental version. In these texts it is usually necessary to identify Sumerian elements out of context, and, as no examples are given, it is also necessary to refer to Akkadian forms in a systematic way. For this purpose various grammatical terms were used. Numerous passages suggest that the grammatical terms were added in the text, sometimes incompetently, at a later stage than the original composition of the epitomes (although they may have accompanied the oral exposition) and also that the Sumerian sections were sometimes extended with extra entries to which the grammatical terms did not apply. A version of the principle detected by Cavigneaux[202] in sign-lists operates, viz. that entries towards the end of a section may even be included as contrary examples or approaches to synonyms, or are simply associatively suggested by the earlier entries. The same alternation between Sumerian and Akkadian as organizing principle may be expected in these analysis texts as well. It would certainly be an oversimplification to maintain that they were texts for the use of Babylonians and therefore organized entirely from the Babylonian point of view. We cannot predict in any given case which way round the text will be organized but must examine each individual passage.

As a sample passage to illustrate the above points we may take NBGT I 1-84 (omitting the broken section 35-46). AN.TA, MURU$_4$.TA and KI.TA clearly refer to the *position in which the Sumerian elements occur*. *Rīqu* and *malû* describe the *written form of the Sumerian elements*, whether with final consonant or not. From the point of view of these terms, then, the passage is oriented towards the Sumerian. But the division of the individual sections is *anāku/yâti, atta/kâta, šū/šuāti* (47-84) i.e. nominative/accusative. Here the arrangement is determined by an Akkadian category.

If we look at some of the other terms, we can see for instance that *šushurtum*, if our interpretation is correct, distinguishes non-indicative forms from indicative. This distinction, as was said before, is not conditioned by formal features of either language. *Gamartum* was found to be a term occurring in cases where ba- was listed in its separative sense, equated in the grammatical vocabularies with the Akkadian *t-themes*, i.e. it indicates a sense or meaning as well as a formal feature of Akkadian. The question is whether *gamartum* 'means' 'separative

202. In *Die sumerisch-akkadischen Zeichenliste: Überlieferungsprobleme* (Munich, 1976).

ba-' or whether it means '*t-theme*'. We need to think here a little about what is meant by the words 'means' and 'refers to', since our argument to some extent depends on the difference between them. I think we must say that the term *gamartum* refers to or describes the separative function of ba- by virtue of being set opposite it in a list, but that the word actually *means* '*t-theme*'. The purpose of AN.TA, MURU$_4$.TA and KI.TA, and *rīqu* and *malû* is to identify the Sumerian elements concerned more precisely, and to distinguish them from similar elements, by describing them. The purpose of *gamartum*, however, is to explain the connotation of Sumerian ba-. It *defines* ba- in Akkadian terms, rather than merely explaining more about the behaviour of ba-. That this is so appears to be settled by the fact that *gamartum* occurs in the Akkadian column *on its own* as the equivalent of ba- (and of -m-, erroneously for (-m)-ma-, as argued *supra* p. 97 f.). That is to say, merely to put '*gamartum*' is enough to tell the reader what Akkadian forms are meant. *Gamartum* is not added as an extra, descriptive term. For this reason we say that *gamartum* "means '*t-theme*'". This is never the case with AN.TA, MURU$_4$.TA, KI.TA, *rīqu* or *malû*. *Gamartum* is to be thought of, then, as the Akkadian for '*t-theme*', or rather, strictly speaking, for 'Ğt and Št themes in their separative senses'. Precisely the same argument applies to *riyātum*, which we may say is the Akkadian for 'ventive' (by which of course the Akkadian ventive is meant). *Riyātum* occurs on its own, unambiguously, at NBGT I 90. The AN.TA MURU$_4$.TA which follows is just to help identify *which* Sumerian um/àm/im etc. is meant. Similarly the term *lûm* must mean Akkadian forms beginning with *lu-* or *li-*, i.e. precative or optative, as equivalents of Sumerian forms with ga- or hé-; and *mû* means Akkadian participles, many of which begin with *mu-*, as equivalents of Sumerian forms beginning with lú. These terms actually describe the Akkadian forms to be used as translations of the Sumerian forms to which they (the terms) refer.

We propose to argue by analogy from the above conclusions concerning *gamartum* and *riātum*, that DIŠ and MEŠ are to be understood in the same way, viz. as meaning the singular and plural forms of the Akkadian verb by which the Sumerian verbs e.g. gen and re$_7$, or tuš and dúr-ru-un, are to be translated. This interpretation is supported by occasional occurrences of *mādūtum* on its own. We propose also that *hamṭu* and *marû* be understood in the same way as meaning *Akkadian* 'preterite' and 'present', ways in which certain Sumerian forms are to be translated, and not as gratuitous descriptions of *Sumerian* verbal bases.[203] The latter interpretation ignores the primarily practical nature of these texts and is essentially anachronistic, imputing to the Babylonians the methods of our own modern speculative or descriptive linguistics. If *hamtu* and *marû* merely informed us about the behaviour of already identified Sumerian forms, it would be difficult to explain why they appeared in the Akkadian column at all and what practical purpose they served. This argument would collapse if the Sumerian and Akkadian categories coincided exactly in function, but it is because they can be demonstrated to overlap only partially that it makes sense, i.e. there are uses of Akkadian present where Sumerian secondary construction would not do, and uses of the secondary construction where Akkadian present would not do.

Our interpretation is supported by various occurrences of *marû* in contexts where *no* Sumerian verbal base is given, where, for example, merely the Sumerian 3rd person cause suffix -e (-ù, -a, -i) or the 3rd person plural -e-en is given. Thus NBGT I 171ff. is to be interpreted: -e-ne = they, i.e. 3rd person plural, (Akkadian) present The remaining entries in this section are other sorts of 3rd person plural forms; that the grammatical term should apply only to the first word in the entry is quite in accordance with what we have already seen. NBGT I 455ff.

---

203. Exactly this position is convincingly argued for in an important contribution by G. Steiner, '*Hamṭu* und *marû* als verbale Kategorien im Sumerischen und im Akkadischen', in *RA* 75 (1981), pp.1-14. Steiner's conclusions were reached independently of mine. His point (p.11) about the entry dúr-ru-un = *ašāb mādūti hamṭu u marû* (NBGT II 12) is particularly telling: the Akkadian note *hamṭu u marû* can only make sense if it is the Akkadian forms which are referred to.

lists various forms of a suffix which seems to be taken both as the abbreviated copula (hence *mā*, cf. NBGT I 411ff., 439ff. and commentary on those passages) and as the 3rd person singular cause suffix (hence *marītum*). Both suffixes, singular and plural, appear in the passage NBGT I 42ff. It is unlikely that a verb was given in the lacuna; *šū* is a possibility. It is further to be noted that these non-verbal occurrences are always of elements labelled *marû*, not *hamṭu*. The significance of this lies in the character of the Sumerian secondary construction as a special, non-standard form.

We may adduce as further proof an *argumentum ex silentio*. Against the supposition that *hamṭu* and *marû* mean the standard and secondary constructions of the Sumerian verb in whatever contexts they occur (which is the position entailed by most current views), it may be pointed out that neither *hamṭu* nor *marû* ever occurs where the prefixes ga- or hé- are listed, even though ga regularly occurs with the standard, and hé- with the secondary, construction. In this context the passage NBGT I 405-413 is particularly instructive. (I take the ul of 414 as an irrelevant *scriptio praecox* for the Akkadian *ul* of the next entry.) The passage may be transcribed as follows:

ga- hu/ha/hé- ša/ši-	*lû* (i.e. optative form, see section 3.5 above)
-ù/a/e	*lu* (*lu*-), *li*-, *mā u marītum*

Note that *marītum* does not occur opposite the entry with hu/ha/hé-. (It seems that there is some confusion on the part of the compiler here. Either he has taken the lu of 405 as *lū* (indeed) and therefore added the preformative ša/ši- to the section, or the Akkadian of line 411 is contaminated but really belongs with ša/ši-. The reading *lu*-, i.e. 1st person optative, in 405, is also possible, but would then be incorrect, since forms with ga- do not take the ending -u/a/e.)[204] But what is crucial here is the remainder of the entry: *li*-, *mā u marītum*: '3rd person optative, emphatic ('indeed') *—and also present tense*'. This makes it clear that the term *marû* does not refer to all uses of the secondary construction.

We can now turn to the passages Eme-sal Vocabulary III 1-13 and NBGT II 1-12. How are we to 'read' them? The passage from the Eme-sal Vocabulary may be paraphrased as follows. ma (Eme-gi DU) may be equated with *alāku*. As *alāku* there also occur de-de (Eme-gi DU, probably du), which can be equated with the present, and de (Eme-gi DU, probably gen), which can be equated with the preterite. ga-ga[205] (Eme-gi túm-ma) may also be equated with the present of *babālu*, ga (Eme-gi túm) with its preterite. Also occurring in the same sense is er (Eme-gi also túm), but this can as well be equated with the preterite of *tabālu*, *leqû*, or of *šūlû* said of *titāpū*. In this latter case the form er-er (Eme-gi túm-túm) can be equated with the present. er-er (Eme-gi túm-túm) also occurs in combination with sag, in which case it is to be equated with the present of *qullulu*. ga (Eme-gi túm) further occurs with múš, when it is to be equated with the preterite (text, erroneously: present) of *naparkû*. The form múš nam-ba-an-ga-ga (Eme-gi múš nam-ba-an-túm-ma) would then be rendered *ai ipparkû* (text D erroneously adds a ditto). (Probably unsuffixed túm should be read as de_6 here.)

---

204. Jacobsen's interpretation of this passage is different. He takes the ù/a/e of 411-13, and likewise ul in 414, as referring to the preformative usually cited as u-, "which becomes a or i before ba- or bí- and is written ul when preceding the prefix -l-" (private communication), and the *lu-/li- ma u marītum* of 411f. as "1st or 3rd person Akkadian optative with suffix *-ma*, followed by a second verb in the present-future". I do not think this accounts for the e (413) of ù/a/e; but it is certainly possible that the ul of 414 refers to prefix chains such as Falkenstein, *NSGU* no. 215 l.3 ù-ul-gíd, which might well be set against an Akkadian 3rd person optative. However, this would not explain the presence of ul here.

205. Inspection of the tablet shows that the scribe probably wrote ga, but from l. 13 it is clear that he intended ga-ga.

The passage NBGT II 1-12 is rather different. It consists of six independent sections concerned with the Sumerian finite bases equivalent to the Akkadian verbs *alākum, uzuzzum, babālum, qabûm* and *wašābum*. However we read the Akkadian of lines 1-2, the content of the section is clear: the distinctions preterite singular, present singular, preterite plural and present plural were made. For the other verbs the situation is more complicated. We should remember that in this text a number of abbreviated passages were earlier identified. It is likely that a two-line section like 5f.:

gub   *uzuz* DIŠ *hamṭu*
súg   *uzuz* MEŠ *marû*

is to be regarded as such an abbreviated section, shortened from an earlier four-line section in which all the possibilities were given as with *alākum*. That is to say that we should not necessarily assume that the text is telling us that the Sumerian verbs only distinguished between what in Akkadian would be preterite singular and present plural. It may actually be reminding the reader of a more complicated section which he would have been expected to know by heart. What we know of the verbs gub and súg suggests that the original section might have read:

gub   *uzuz* DIŠ *hamṭu*
gub   *uzuz* DIŠ *marû*
súg   *uzuz* MEŠ *hamṭu*
súg   *uzuz* MEŠ *marû*

i.e. that it had been abbreviated by quoting the first and last lines. The same may be assumed to have happened with the verbs 'to bring'. On the basis of what we already know, we might have expected:

de$_6$ *babālum hamṭu* <*ša* DIŠ>
lah$_4$ *babāl* MEŠ *hamṭu*
túm   *babāl* DIŠ *marû*
túm   *babāl* MEŠ *marû*.

(I have already suggested that by the Ur III period tùmu was used merely as a writing for túm-mu (túm + e), even though it originally had a separate meaning.)[206] It seems certain that non-suffixed forms of this verb should be read de$_6$, as implied by the gloss in this text, and not túm, as they usually are. For the verbs 'to say', what we already know[207] suggests that here there was only a three-line section originally. In line 9, as in line 7, the epitomator has again omitted the designation 'singular':

du$_{11}$ *qabû hamṭu* <*ša* DIŠ>
e   *qabi* MEŠ *hamṭu*
e   *qabû marû*

The last section was also clearly only of three lines:

tuš   *ašāb* DIŠ *hamṭu*
?   *ašāb* DIŠ *marû*
dúr-ru-un   *ašāb* MEŠ *hamṭu u marû*

— but what the Sumerian form that is missing is, is not clear.

The interpretation of these terms proposed is in direct contrast to what has been assumed by every writer on the subject of *hamṭu* and *marû* since Zimmern in 1885. (It is only since Jacobsen [1956] that the terms have regularly been used in the general discussion of Sumerian grammar.) The conclusion we draw allows us to assume no more than that the Babylonian

206. On lah$_4$ see P. Steinkeller, 'Notes on Sumerian Plural Verbs', in *OrNS* 48 (1979), pp.54-67.
207. *V.* especially Edzard in *ZA* 66 (1976), 46f., cf. OBGT IV iii 8'-9' (above, p. 42).

grammarians had formulated the equivalences 'standard construction in certain circumstances = preterite' and 'secondary construction in certain circumstances = present'. We do not know how much to trust the theoretical basis of these texts. For instance the rule ba- = -t- theme appears to make sense, from what we can deduce of the meaning of Sumerian forms in contexts apart from Akkadian equivalents, in cases where a verb of motion is used in the separative sense of 'away'. How much further the area of common meaning extends is not clear. Stative ba- clearly could not be rendered by a -t- theme. There are uses of a- with the standard construction in Sumerian contracts of Old Akkadian date which clearly refer to states now no longer existent resulting from events in the fairly distant past.[208] Could these have been translated by the Akkadian stative? Are we to assume that the uses of -m- and of the Akkadian ventive exactly coincided? In this context, the mutual influence of the two languages needs to be considered. This idea has recently been developed by Edzard in his theory of the 'linguistic area' (*Sprachbund*).[209] To bring together our results and the theory of the *Sprachbund*, we might say: the Babylonians were not interested in accurately 'translating' in our modern sense. How well they spoke Sumerian we shall never know. Instead they tried to produce *calques*, faithful 'tracings', of the Sumerian texts they rendered, and an effect of this may have been that the *calque* translations had to acquire a meaning in the language into which they were put (just as through the Authorized Version of the Bible Hebrew idioms passed into English) and thus idioms were received from the other tongue.

The principle of the naming of grammatical forms in Classical theory may be considered. The *casus dativus* is so called because it occurs *par excellence* after the verb *dare* to give. Many of its functions have nothing to do with giving. Somewhat analogously, if ba- in its separative sense could be construed as a verb of motion in its -t- themes, then this equivalence can be formulated as a sort of rule of thumb which could be extended to all other cases. We know that the Babylonians themselves realized that this was not always the case from the alternative equation of ba- forms with statives. That reflects a quite different function of ba-. An entry like sá ha-ba-na-ni-ib-du_{11} = *lištakšissum* should not be interpreted so much as 'the Sumerian form sá ha-ba-na-ni-ib-du_{11} may be translated as *lištakšissum*' as 'the sequence of elements present in sá ha-ba-na-ni-ib-du_{11} can be analyzed as

ha	=	*li-*
ba	=	-t-
na	=	*-šum*
ni	=	š
sá -b-du_{11}	=	*kašādum*

and embodied in a form like *lištakšissum*'. This is to argue that the compilers were conscious of the artificially constructed nature of the forms in their texts. From what we have already seen, and from clear examples where they have tried to concoct forms and not succeeded, I think this is so. The concocted forms, then, although consciously artificial, were none the less useful because they were paradigmatic. It is thus to some extent even irrelevant whether sá ha-ba-na-ni-ib-du_{11} or *lištakšissum* have any idiomatic existence in Sumerian or Akkadian, because of this paradigmatic function. The grammatical texts are the embodiment of a traditional theory of Sumerian grammar which must once have had its origins in a sound knowledge of real Sumerian but as here represented is purely theoretical, although still practical in intent.

---

208. Cf. Edzard, *Sumerische Rechtsurkunden*...(Munich, 1968), p.51, no.21: ll. 2,5 an-ši-sa_{10} 'had been bought', 10 an-ne-sum 'had been given to them'.

209. This theory was outlined in an unpublished paper delivered in Paris in January 1978, entitled *Le sumérien et l'akkadien - aire linguistique*'.

The questions which follow from this discussion and which we must now ask are:
1) What are the functions of the two constructions, standard and secondary? (I take it that the smallest linguistic unit in connection with which we can talk about meaning is the word. Of the morphemes of which words are made up, we can usefully say only that they have a function. Of some words, it makes little sense to talk of meaning, only of function; but no morpheme has a meaning.) We should not be misled into looking for the 'original function', but we may legitimately ask whether the various usages have anything in common.
2) What were the usages that led the Babylonians to identify certain standard construction forms with their own preterite and certain secondary construction forms with their own present?
3) (Not quite the same question) What are the particular circumstances in which preterite and present *are* appropriate translations?

We may begin by trying to answer the easiest question, (3), by a process of elimination. From the grammatical texts we know that when the prefixes ga-, hé- amd na- are present, Akkadian forms other than the simple present and preterite are called for. The Sumerian imperative regularly uses the standard construction and is translated of course by the Akkadian imperative. a- with the standard construction is set against the Akkadian stative; only with the secondary construction is it set against the present. The work of Edzard and others has shown that the prefix ba-ra- has special meanings when used with one construction or another, that ù- is regularly used with the standard construction but does not usually refer to the past, that -ed- normally requires the secondary construction, and that the non-finite affix -a requires the standard base. (Clearly present and preterite are irrelevant in this last case.) We are left with finite forms with the prefixes ì-, mu/mi-, ma/mu-, ba-, bí-, nu-, narrative na-, and perhaps ša/ši-, although Falkenstein's work on the last showed that a majority of forms with ša/ši- took the secondary construction.[210] There may be further formal or syntactic constraints even in these cases, such as the tendency to use the secondary construction after question words or in introducing direct speech.[211] The standard construction seems to be used after tukumbi. In the case of paired actions, the second may often be put in the secondary construction. All these possibilities need to be investigated. Within the group of forms left to us, however, it seems that standard construction forms would normally have been translated by Babylonian scholars as preterite, and secondary as present. Why? The many functions of the constructions suggest that they carry no particular connotations of tense, aspect or *Aktionsart in themselves*.

What follows is tentative, but may offer a solution to (1) above, and go some way as well to explaining why the particular constraints operated by the preformatives ga-, hé-, ba-ra-, na- and ù- operate as they do.

The standard account of the conjugation, or rather incorporation, of the Sumerian verb is set out by Falkenstein.[212] Intransitive verbs take the following suffixes:

sg.	1	-en	pl.	1	-enden
	2	-en		2	-enzen
	3	-		3	-eš

210. A. Falkenstein, 'Untersuchungen zur sumerischen Grammatik. 4. Das affirmative Präformativ ši/ša-', in *ZA* 48 (1944), 69-118. The prefixes bí-, nu- and na- occur only rarely in grammatical texts, ša/ši- not at all.

211. As for example with the particle i-ri: i-ri in-ga-am-me 'and then he said as follows'. (i-ri is not a preformative.) In the epic of Lugalbanda (ed. C. Wilcke), the secondary construction occurs immediately before direct speech at 97/8, 132-34 (= 161, 184), 167, 209, 226 (= 234), 238, 284, 353 and 357/8.

212. A. Falkenstein, *Das Sumerische* (Leiden, 1959), pp.44-45 and 47.

Transitive verbs in the preterite tense incorporate as follows:

sg.	1	-?-	pl.	1	-me?-
	2	-e-		2	-e-...-ane?[213]
	3	-n/b-		3	-n-...eš

If they have an object, the object may be marked as follows:

sg.	1	-en	pl.	1	-enden
	2	-en		2	-enzen
	3	-n/b-		3	-eš

In an attempt to get away from the transitive/intransitive, subject/object terminology, I have used the terms *inert* and *cause*.[214] Inert describes a noun which stands in the unmarked case (i.e. in translation the subject of an intransitive verb or the object of a transitive verb), and cause a noun which stands in the agentive (i.e. in translation normally the subject of a transitive verb). The distinction transitive/intransitive thereby disappears and the above paradigms may be rewritten as follows:

inert is incorporated by:

sg.	1	-en	pl.	1	-enden
	2	-en		2	-enzen
	3	-		3	-eš

cause is incorporated by:

sg.	1	-?long vowel-	pl.	1	-me?-
	2	-e-		2	?
	3	-n/b-		3	-n-...eš

The forms for 1st and 2nd person plural cause are very poorly attested, and it may be that what we are dealing with here are elements which do not vary for number but where number can be marked if desired by a plural suffix, i.e. the infixes are used with the optional suffixes 1st person -enden, 2nd person -enzen and 3rd person -eš. This feature can be compared with the subject markers in the objective construction of Georgian, which do not vary for number, but can be marked with a plural suffix if desired:

1	m-	} (plural -th)
2	g-	
3	h-/s-	

The plural -th is also used to mark the plural of the object suffixes, with a resulting possibility of ambiguity.

The forms set out above (for inert and cause) represent, then, the basic or standard form of the incorporation in Sumerian. The only real alteration in our re-writing of the paradigms is the reinterpretation of the 3rd person singular 'object' infix -n/b- as a cause infix. The 3rd person inert is not marked in the verb (or 'is marked by a zero suffix'). Clearly the two -n/b- infixes could not co-exist: that is a fault of Falkenstein's system already pointed out by Edzard.[215]

The above system is simple enough but presents certain problems. It is impossible to mark a 3rd person plural inert *and* a 3rd person plural cause unambiguously, and impossible to distinguish between a 3rd person plural inert with a 3rd person singular cause and a 3rd person plural cause (with inert not marked). The cause infixes for 1st and 2nd person singular are liable to confusion and could well be lost altogether (presumably by assimilation to a

213. This is certainly incorrect.

214. Jacobsen's definition of his own term 'carrier' ('Introduction to the Chicago Grammatical Texts', p.*31) is confusing. It includes the agent of present or future actions and the object of preterites. In 'he struck the dog' the 'striking' is no more 'in' the dog than it is in 'he' in 'he strikes the dog'.

215. In *ZDMG* 109 (1959), pp. 234-52.

preceding vowel). We must suppose (taking into account the optional nature of Sumerian verbal incorporation, which is not true conjugation) that at a prehistoric stage of the language it was felt necessary in certain cases to mark the *person of the cause* in a less ambiguous manner, and that to this end the inert suffixes were taken over, with additions, as cause markers:

sg.	1	-en	pl.	1	-enden
	2	-en		2	-enzen
	3	-e		3	-ene (or -eš)

Such evidence as there is suggests that the infix -n/b- was then used to mark the inert. Only this 3rd person -n/b- is really attested (Falkenstein's object infix).[216] The above arrangement corresponds to Falkenstein's 'present-future tense of the transitive verb'. This inversion of the personal elements may again be compared to Georgian, which has two systems, the so-called subjective and objective constructions. Some verbs conjugate according to one, some according to the other, and many verbs can occur in both. The verbs conjugated in the objective construction tend to be verbs concerned with the sensations, but this is not absolutely regularly so. In the objective construction the subject is marked by a prefix and the object by a suffix, as: *m*rtsam*s* 'I believe him', where m- is 'I' and -s 'him'; in the subjective construction more or less the same affixes serve to mark the object (prefix) and the subject (suffix), as *m*iklav*s* 'he kills me'. It is not always possible to deduce which construction is in use from a given form, unless the behaviour of the verb in question is known.

It may be that this inversion, in Sumerian, has the effect of emphasizing the cause in some way, or focussing on it. It seems that a parallel development was that the inversion of the form of incorporation should in some cases be signalled in the verb itself. Some verbs therefore reduplicated and others which must at one time have been separate verbs with separate meanings (cf. English go/went) amalgamated to become alternating pairs of bases. This was presumably a parallel development: it is impossible to know the extent to which one was dependent on the other. Yet it is not surprising that the distribution between standard and secondary bases and other factors, e.g. singular and plural, is, as for example in du_{11}/e, irregular.[217] Some verbs extended their simple forms (or perhaps used their full forms), as te/teĝ, gid/gidi. It is to be hoped that studies of individual verbs will reveal more details about this.

It is this desire to mark the cause less ambiguously or perhaps to focus on it which is, I submit, the principle behind the alternation of forms in the Sumerian verbs. In this respect alone it may be compared with the alternation of active and passive in the Indo-European languages. Now if the main purpose of the inversion is to mark the *person* of the cause clearly, it will not be necessary to use that alternative form when the person is made sufficiently clear by the preformative or other features. ga- is used only with the 1st person, so that no further clarification is necessary. The imperative occurs only in the 2nd person, so the same applies. With a preformative like ù-, there will often be a second verb following with the same cause and it is therefore perhaps not important to make it absolutely clear, or at least not important to emphasize it, in the first verb. Alternatively it is used as a polite imperative and so is clearly 2nd person. All these forms are, in consequence, constructed using the standard construction.

With prohibitive na-, which is used both for the 2nd and 3rd person (and possibly also for the first), the necessity of distinguishing cause is greater. So the cause is marked by a suffix and as a result the secondary base, where one exists, is used.

---

216. But cf. OBGT IX 103-104.

217. As Kienast has shown (*ZA* 70 (1981), pp.22-28), the distribution of bases in the forms of this verb may be much more irregular than was previously thought.

This leaves, of what we may call the prescriptive preformatives,[218] hé- and its negative ba-ra-. The alternation of constructions and forms here serves to distinguish between the two senses of each preformative. Falkenstein[219] regarded the assertoric sense of hé- as its primary function. This declarative sense (and possibly the negative sense of ba-ra-) are used, on the whole, where the person of the agent is clear from the context, such as rulers' accounts of their own achievements (or statements about them), e.g.

ki-bi hé-bí-gi$_4$ 'I restored it'; igi hu-mu-un-du$_8$-uš-àm 'they looked at me';
lugal-na-me alan ba-ra-ni-in-ku$_4$ 'no king brought in a statue';
lú á-lá lú á-dah ba-ra-bí-tuku 'I allowed no-one to receive too little or too much wages'[220]

So it is only with the precative sense of hé- and the promissory negative and vetitive senses of ba-ra- that the alternative base, if there is one, and the secondary construction are employed. In connection with the possibility suggested earlier that the secondary construction is regular after interrogative words, it is interesting to consider the suggestion of C. Wilcke that the vetitive sense of ba-ra- is derived from an original requisitory question: 'you are not to do that' from 'you won't do that, will you?'

The uses of the secondary construction which remain unaccounted for are three: 1) those in which it is used because of the presence of -ed-, 2) those which have no cause, only an inert (and would be translated as intransitives) in forms where the use of the standard or secondary construction is not conditioned by a prescriptive preformative, but where (through reduplication or alternation) it is possible to distinguish between standard and secondary bases, and 3) those which carry any of the prefixes ba- bí- i- mu- ša- nu- or narrative na-.

In the case of -ed-, one can see that it is often necessary for some incorporating element to be suffixed if the presence of -ed- is to be apparent: for if followed by no suffix, the -d would drop and the -e- might assimilate to a preceding word. It is possible that in cases where the -e- does not assimilate (i.e. where the verb ends in a consonant), the secondary form is used because of the similarity to other secondary construction forms with suffixed -e (3rd person cause marker), thus:

*...-base-e^d becomes *...-secondary base-e^d
because of *...-secondary base-e

From the use of the secondary construction in finite forms, the extension of it to all occurrences of -ed-, in non-finite forms as well, is easy to envisage. Note that in the case of the verbs 'to say', the base di is always used before -(e)d-, never e.

The only verbs which I can find which fall under the second case are the group of verbs gen, re$_7$, du, su$_8$-b, to go. With the non-finite forms gen-na and du-da there is no difficulty. In finite forms without suffix (3rd person singular) it is not possible to know whether gen or du is to be read. (In these cases it is probably better to read the standard gen, unless there is some particular reason not to.) The problematic cases are then the 1st and 2nd persons singular and all the plurals. Thus we have to account for the following sets of forms:

ì-	
mu/mi-	
ma/mu-	-gen-en/-du-un
ba-	-re$_7$-en-dè-en/-su$_8$-be-en-dè-en
bí-	-re$_7$-en-zé-en/-su$_8$-be-en-zé-en
ša/ši-	-re$_7$-eš/-su$_8$-be-eš
nu-	
narrative na-	

218. Because they prescribe the construction to be used.
219. *Das Sumerische*, p.50.
220. These and other examples may be found in Edzard *ZA* 61 (1971), pp.214ff. and 218ff.

These forms, which are unfortunately infrequent in texts,[221] remain at present unexplained.

The third group consists of all finite forms where there is no prescriptive preformative. Until the use of these forms is further codified, we shall assume either that the secondary construction is used to focus on the cause or that one of the other constraints operates, such as the presence of a question word of the immediate succession of direct speech.

Finally the second question posed on p. 130 remains: what led the Babyonian scholars to identify certain standard construction forms with preterite and certain secondary construction forms with present-future? Clearly they needed a means of identifying the two constructions in the verbal paradigms, in which technical terms are not used. It will have become clear from our argument that the use of preterite and present-future in grammatical texts as metalinguistic indicators to *distinguish* the Sumerian forms does not imply an overall equation of function or meaning. In the same way, *ana*, set against Sumerian dimensional cases, does not just mean 'to' but is used metalinguistically to mark all oblique cases. The use of actual words as metalinguistic indicators in the work of Pāṇini may be compared.[222] The use of the preterite was probably originally suggested by the fact that e.g. *lū aprus* and *lū iprus* (preterite in Akkadian) may be used to translate affirmative hé-ku$_5$ (standard construction in Sumerian). Vetitive or promissory negative ba-ra- refers to actions in the future by its very nature, and so might be rendered by a present-future. So does prohibitive na-, the Akkadian equivalent of which is actually constructed with a present-future: nam-mu-ni-ib-ta$_{12}$-ta$_{12}$-ne = *lā izzibū*. These various modal uses, as also the fact that -ed-, which of course always has the secondary construction, generally refers to events in the relative future, may have led the ancient scholars to set up the equivalences as distinctive general rules, which were then applied throughout to produce (as they thought) a faithful *calque* of the texts they were translating. These rules were doubtless the basis on which the interlinear Akkadian translations were made for literary texts in later centuries. These translations and the grammatical texts can alone be the source of the notion held by modern grammarians that Sumerian has a tense system parallel to that envisaged for Akkadian.

---

221. In fact the only substantial evidence for them is the paradigm gen etc. = *alākum* (OBGT VII etc.). It may be that the opposition ba-gen-en / ba-du-un (where the form of incorporation is the same but the base varies) is a false one thrown up by the paradigm. If not, it would tend to suggest that alternation of base can operate independently of alternation of form of incorporation. Form of incorporation (construction) can only vary where both a cause and an inert are present; in the paradigm gen etc. = *alākum* it is the base which varies after a prescriptive preformative like hé-, not the construction. Probably these verbs behave in this way because other alternating verbs do. It is precisely on this point that the theory of a split ergative system, proposed by P. Michalowski ('Sumerian as an ergative language', in *JCS* 32 (1980), pp. 86-103, esp. p. 92) founders, in my opinion. It is already generally agreed that in verbal forms with two participants in the "perfect aspect", infix (called by Michalowski "prefix") marks agent, and suffix marks inert, i.e. agreement is ergative. In the "imperfect aspect" it is agreed that in forms with two participants, infix marks 3rd person inert and suffix marks agent (i.e. subject of "transitive active" verbs). Michalowski's pattern is only completed if it is granted further that *in the "imperfect aspect"* suffix marks the subject of "intransitive" verbs as well and that *in the "perfect aspect"* suffix likewise marks the subject of intransitive verbs. But it was just because there is no perceptible difference in "aspect" (or as Falkenstein called it, "tense"), that the latter called the forms of one-participant (i.e. "intransitive") verbs, which have their associated nominal element ("subject") always *suffixed*, the 'standard form' (*Normalform*) of the "intransitive" verb. In other words, how do we know that exx. 10 and 11 (Michalowski, *loc.cit.*, p. 92) *are "perfect aspect"*, and exx. 14 and 15 (ibid.) *"imperfect aspect"*? The only possible criterion could be the presence of the reduplicated or suppletive base which marks the "imperfect aspect" (my 'secondary construction') in some verbs. In the examples given, the transliterations tuš and dúr represent the same sign. Until such evidence can be produced from vernacular texts (and not grammatical texts), the ergative system is *not* split, since (according to my view in which any form not explicitly marked as being in the secondary construction will be described as being in the standard construction) inerts will always be suffixed and agents infixed *except* in secondary construction forms, where agents are suffixed (and inerts may be infixed). So far as I can see (and in accordance with the tentative reasoning offered for the development of the secondary construction, viz., the foregrounding of the agent), secondary construction forms will only be found with two-participant predications.

222. See for instance L. Renou, *La grammaire de Pāṇini* (Paris, 1966).

5 *Appendices*

5.1 Text of the verbal paradigms from Ur

No information seems to be preserved about the archaeological context of the discovery of these paradigms from Ur, with the exception of Burrows' statement in *Antiquaries' Journal* 7 (1927), p.404, that 'Sumerian-Akkadian tables of verbs' were found in the same level as business documents dated to late Kassite kings, Kadašman-Ellil to Marduk-apla-iddina (13th–12th centuries BC). This must surely suggest that the tablets were found in a secondary deposit.

5.1.1 gen etc. = *alākum* (*UET* VII 97, 98, 100 and 101)

This version of the paradigm survives in three mss., as follows:

SIGLA

A = *UET* VII 101 (basic text) col.	i =	sections	1-12	(lines 1-49)
	ii =		13-38	(lines 50-100)
	iii =		38(contd.)-55	(lines 101-45)
	iv =		55-69 +	(lines 146-89)
			catchline of 70	(line 190)
B = *UET* VII 100	obv. =	sections	1-18	(lines 1-41)
	rev. =		19-25	(lines 42-80)
	left edge =		32-33	(lines 81-86)
C = *UET* VII 97 + 98	97 obv. =	sections	65-67	(lines 171-76)
	98 obv. =		67(contd.)	(lines 178-81)
	98 rev. =		68	(lines 182-85)
	97 rev. =		69 +	(lines 186-89)
			catchline of 70	(line 190)
	(omitting the total in line 177)			

The line numbers above are those of A. These will be found down the righthand side of the text below. Down the lefthand side is a numeration of A by columns. The sections are always numbered according to the Nippur versions (OBGT VII). The line count after line 86 in A (which falls at the end of the singular section in the middle of a column) demonstrates that A must have been copied from an archetype of the same format as B, if not from B itself. B varies from A in only a couple of places: 16, possibly 21, with errors at 41, 45, 46, 66, 69, 73 and 74. C, which is almost certainly a small excerpt tablet, has errors or omissions at 172, probably 173, 175, 181, 184, 185, 189 and 190. The line count '86 lines' at line 177 in A is correct although there are actually 89 lines between it and the previous total at 86, because the scribe inadvertently wrote section 38 (lines 100-105) twice before realizing his mistake. Note the use of gána to mean 'section' in A at line 87.

col.i	1	gen - à[m]	1	[al] - kam	1
	2	ga-àm-gen		[lu - ul] - li - kam	2
	3	hé-em-du		[li]-⌜il⌝ - li - kam	3
	4	gen-àm-še	2	al-⌜ka⌝-aš-šum	4
	5	ga-àm-ši-gen		lu-⌜ul-li⌝-ka-aš-šum	5
	6	hé-em-ši-du		li-⌜li⌝-[ka-aš]-šum	6
	7	gen-àm-mu-še	3	al-⌜kam⌝ [a-na ṣe-ri-y]a	7
	8	ga-mu-e-ši-gen		lu-⌜ul⌝-[li-ka-ak-kum]	8
	9	hé-mu-e-ši-du		li-[li-ka-ak-kum]	9
	10	gen-àm-⌜ma⌝	4	at-[la-kam]	10
	11	ga-àm-ma-gen		[lu-ut-ta]-⌜al-kam⌝	11
	12	hé-em-ma-du		[li-it]-⌜ta⌝-al-kam	12
	13	⌜gen-àm-ma⌝-[še	5	at] - x - ka-aš-šum	13
	14	[ga-àm-ma-ši-gen		lu] -⌜ut⌝-ta-al-ka-aš-šum	14
	15	⌜hé⌝-[em-ma-ši]-⌜du		li⌝-it-ta-al-ka-aš-šum	15
	16	⌜gen-àm-mu⌝-še	6	at-la-kam a-na ṣe-ri-ya	16
	17	ga-àm-mu-e-ši-gen		lu-ut-ta-al-ka-ak-kum	17
	18	hé-em-mu-e-ši-du		li-it-ta-al-ka-ak-kum	18
	19	gen-ì	7	a - [[li]]erased-lik	19
	20	ga - gen		lu - ul - lik	20
	21	hé - du		li - il - lik	21
	22	[gen]-⌜en-ši⌝	8	a-[[li]]erased-lik-⌜šum⌝	22
	23	⌜ga-en-ši-gen⌝		⌜lu⌝-ul-lik-[šum]	23
	24	hé-en-ši-⌜du		li-il-lik-šum⌝	24
	25	gen - ba	9	at-⌜la⌝-[ak]	25
	26	ga-ba-gen		lu-ut-ta-⌜la⌝-[ak]	26
	27	ha-ba-du		li-it-ta-la-⌜ak⌝	27
	28	gen-ba-ši	10	at-la-ak-šum	28
	29	ga-ba-ši-gen		lu-ut-ta-la-ak-šum	29
	30	ha-ba-ši-du		li-it-ta-la-ak-šum	30
	31	àm - du	16	i - la - kam	31
	32	àm-du-un		a-al-la-kam	32
	33	àm-du-un		ta-al-la-kam	33
	34	àm-ši-du	17	i-il-la-ka-aš-šum	34

1 (a) B : gen-àm

13 (b) x = 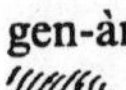 (? tal); B (erroneously): -la-

16 (a) B : gen-am-ma-mu-še

21 (a) B : hé-en-du

	35	àm-ši-du-un		a-la-ka-aš-šum	35
	36	àm-ši-du-un		ta-al-la-ka-aš-šum	36
	37	mu-e-ši-du	21	i-la-ka-ak-kum	37
	38	mu-e-ši-du-un		a-la-ka-ak-kum	38
	39	àm-ma-du	18	it-ta-al-la-kam	39
	40	àm-ma-du-un		at-ta-la-kam	40
	41	àm-ma-du-un		ta-at-ta-al-la-kam	41
	42	àm-ma-ši-du	19	it-ta-al-la-ka-aš-šum	42
	43	àm-ma-ši-du-un		at-ta-al-la-ka-aš-šum	43
	44	àm-ma-ši-du-un		ta-at-ta-la-ka-aš-šum	44
	45	àm-mu-e-ši-du	20	it-ta-al-la-ka-ak-kum	45
	46	àm-mu-e-ši-du-un		at-ta-al-la-ka-ak-kum	46
	47	ì - du	12	i - la - ak	47
	48	ì - du - un		a - la - ak	48
	49	i- du - un		⌜ta⌝ - la - ak	49
col.ii	1	in-ši-du	13	⌜i⌝-[la-ak-šum]	50
	2	in-ši-du-un		a-⌜la⌝-[ak-šum]	51
	3	in-ši-du-un		ta-⌜la⌝-[ak-šum]	52
	4	ba - du	22	it-ta-[al-la-ak]	53
	5	ba - du - un		at-[ta-al-la-ak]	54
	6	ba - du - un		ta-[at-ta-al-la-ak]	55
	7	[ba-ši]-⌜du⌝	23	⌜it⌝-[ta-al-la-ak-šum]	56
	8	[ba-ši-du-un]		[at-ta-al-la-ak-šum]	57
	9	[ba]-⌜ši-du-un⌝		⌜ta⌝-[at-ta-al-la-ak-šum]	58
	10	i-im-gen	26	il-li-[kam]	59
	11	i-im-gen-en		al-li-[kam]	60
	12	i-im-gen-en		ta-al-li-⌜kam⌝	61
	13	i-im-ši-gen	27	il-li-ka-aš-šum	62
	14	i-im-ši-gen-en		al-li-⌜ka⌝-aš-šum	63
	15	i-im-ši-gen-en		ta-al-[li]-⌜ka⌝-aš-šum	64
	16	mu-e-ši-gen	31	il-⌜li⌝-[ka]-ak-kum	65
	17	mu-e-ši-gen-[en]		[al]-⌜li⌝-ka-ak-kum	66

41 (b) B : ta-at-al-la-kam
45 (b) B : it-ta-al-la-ka-aš-šum
46 (b) B : ta-at-ta-la-ka-aš-šum
66 (b) B : mu-e-ši-du-un

18	im-ma-[gen]	28	[it]-ta-al-kam	67
19	im-⌈ma⌉-[gen-en]		[at]-⌈ta⌉-al-kam	68
20	im-[ma-gen-en]		[ta-at]-ta-al-kam	69
21	⌈im-ma⌉-[ši-gen]	29	[it]-⌈ta⌉-al-ka-aš-šum	70
22	⌈im⌉-ma-ši-⌈gen⌉-[en]		[at]-⌈ta⌉-al-ka-aš-šum	71
23	⌈im⌉-ma-ši-⌈gen⌉-[en]		[ta]-⌈at⌉-ta-al-ka-aš-šum	72
24	im-mu-e-⌈ši⌉-[gen]	30	[it]-⌈ta⌉-al-ka-ak-kum	73
25	⌈im-mu-e⌉-ši-⌈gen⌉-[en]		at-ta-al-ka-ak-kum	74
26	[ì] - gen	24	il - ⌈lik⌉	75
27	[ì - gen] - en		al - [lik]	76
28	⌈ì⌉- [gen] - en		⌈ta⌉- [al] - lik	77
29	in-ši-⌈gen⌉	25	⌈il⌉-lik-šum	78
30	in-ši-gen-en		al-lik-šum	79
31	in-ši-gen-en		ta-al-lik-šum	80
32	ba - gen	32	it-ta-la-ak	81
33	ba - gen - en		at-ta-la-ak	82
34	ba - gen - en		ta-at-ta-la-ak	83
35	ba - ⌈ši-gen⌉	33	⌈it⌉-[ta]-⌈la⌉-ak-šum	84
36	ba-ši-gen-[en]		[at-ta]-⌈la⌉-ak-šum	85
37	ba-ši-gen-[en]		[ta-at]-⌈ta⌉-la-ak-šum	86
38	ŠU.NIGÍN 1.20.⌈6⌉[		MU.BI.IM]GÁNA 30	87
39	gen-àm-zé-en	34	[al]-⌈ka-nim⌉	88
40	ga-àm-re$_7$-en-dé-en		i ni-li-kam	89
41	hé-em-su$_8$-bé-eš		li-li-ku(text: ka)-nim	90
42	gen-àm-ši-zé-en	35	⌈al⌉-ka-ni-iš-šum	91
43	ga-àm-ši-re$_7$-en-dè-en		i ni-li-ka-aš-šum	92
44	hé-em-ši-su$_8$-bé-eš		li-li-ku-ni-iš-šum	93
45	gen-mu-še-en-zé-en	36	al-ka-nim- a-na ṣe-⌈ri⌉-ya	94
46	ga-mu-e-ši-re$_7$ -en-dè-en		i ⌈ni⌉-li-ka-ak-kum	95
47	hé-mu-e-ši-su$_8$ -bé-eš		li-li-ku-ni-kum	96
48	gen-àm-ma-zé-en	37	⌈at-la⌉-ka-nim	97
49	ga-àm-ma-re$_7$-en-dè-en		i ni-it-ta-al-kam	98
50	hé-em-ma-su$_8$-bé-eš		li-it-ta-al-ku-nim	99
51	gen-àm-ma(text: an)-ši-en-zé-en	38	⌈at-la-ka⌉-ni-⌈iš⌉-šum	100

69 (b) B : at-at-ta-al-kam
73 (b) B : it-ta-al-ka-ak-šum
74 (b) B : at-ta-al-ka-ak-šum
77 ruling after this line only in B
87 B : ŠU.NIGÍN 1.20.6 MU.BI.IM GÁNA 30

col.iii	1	ga-àm-ma-ši-⌜re$_7$-en-dé-en⌝		⌜i ni-it-ta-al⌝-[ka]-aš-[šum	101
	2	hé-em-ma-ši-su$_8$-bé-eš		⌜li-it-ta-al⌝-ku-ni-šum	102
	3	gen-àm-ma-ši-en-zé-en	38bis	at-la-ka-ni-iš-šum	103
	4	ga-àm-a-ši-re$_7$-en-dè-en		i ni-it-ta-al-ka-šum	104
	5	hé-em-ma-ši-su$_8$-bé-es		li-it-ta-al-ku-ni-iš-šum	105
	6	gen-àm-mu-še-en-zé-en	39	at-la-ka-nim a-na ṣe-ri-ya	106
	7	ga-ám-mu-e-ši-re$_7$-en-dé-en		i ni-it-ta-al-ka-ak-kum	107
	8	hé-em-mu-e-ši-su$_8$-be-eš		li-it-ta-al-ku-ni-kum	108
	9	gen-né-zé-en	40	al - ⌜ka⌝	109
	10	ga-re$_7$-en-dè-en		i ni-il-[lik]	110
	11	hé-su$_8$-bé-eš		li-il-li-[ku]	111
	12	gen-né-ši-zé-en	41	al-ka-⌜šum⌝	112
	13	ga-àm$^{!}$-ši-re$_7$-en-dè-en		i ni-il-lik-⌜šum⌝	113
	14	hé-em-ši-su$_8$-bé-eš		li-il-li-ku-šum	114
	15	gen-ba-zé-en	42	at-la-ka	115
	16	ga-ba-re$_7$-en-dè-en		i ni-it-ta-la-ak	116
	17	ha-ba-su$_8$-bé-eš		li-it-ta-al-ku-šum	117
	18	gen-ba-ši-zé-en	43	at-la-ka-šum	118
	19	ga-ba-ši-re$_7$-en-dè-en		i ni(text: li)-it-ta-la-ak-šum	119
	20	ha-ba-ši-su$_8$-bé-eš		li-it-ta-al-ku-šum	120
	21	àm-su$_8$-bé-eš	49	i-il-la-ku-nim	121
	22	àm-su$_8$-bé-en-dè-en		ni-il-la-kam	122
	23	⌜àm-su$_8$-bé⌝-en-zé-en		ta-al-la-ka-nim	123
	24	⌜àm⌝-[ši]-⌜su$_8$-bé-eš⌝	50	i-⌜il⌝-la-ku-ni-⌜šum⌝	124
	25	am-ši-su$_8$-bé-⌜en-dè-en⌝		⌜ni-il-la-ka-aš-šum⌝	125
	26	àm-ši-su$_8$-bé-en-zé-en		ta-al-la-ka-ni-iš-⌜šum⌝	126
	27	mu-e-ši-su$_8$-bé-eš	54	i-il-la-ku-ni-ik-kum	127
	28	mu-e-ši-su$_8$-bé-en-dè-en		ni(text: i)-il-la-ka-ak-kum	128
	29	àm-ma-su$_8$-bé-eš	51	it-ta-al-la-ku-nim	129
	30	àm-ma-su$_8$-bé-en-dè		ni-it-ta-al-la-ak	130
	31	àm-ma-su$_8$-bé-en-zé-en		ta-at-ta-al-la-ka	131
	32	àm-ma-ši-su$_8$-bé-eš	52	it-ta-⌜al⌝-la-[ku]-ni-iš-šum	132
	33	⌜am⌝-ma-ši-su$_8$-bé-en-dè-en		ni-it-ta-al-la-ka-aš-šum	133
	34	[am]-⌜ma-ši-su$_8$⌝-[bé-en]-⌜zé-en⌝		ta-at-ta-⌜al⌝-la-ka-ni-iš-šum	134
	35	⌜àm⌝-[mu-e-ši-su$_8$-bé-eš]	53	[it]-⌜ta⌝-al-⌜la-ku⌝ -ni-ik-kum	135
	36	⌜àm-mu-e⌝-[ši-su$_8$-bé-en-dè-en]		[ni-it]-⌜ta⌝-al-la-ka-⌜kum⌝	136
	37	ì-su$_8$-⌜bé -eš⌝	45	[i-il-la-ku]	137

	38	ì-su_8-bé-en-dè-en		[ni-il-la-ak]	138
	39	ì-su_8-bé-en-zé-en		ta-⸢al⸣-[la-ka]	139
	40	in-ši-su_8-bé-eš	46	i-il-la-⸢ku⸣-[šum]	140
	41	in-ši-su_8-bé-en-dè-en		ni-il-la-ak-[šum]	141
	42	in-ši-su_8-bé-en-zé-en		ta-al-la-ka-[šum]	142
	43	ba-su_8-bé-eš	55	⸢it⸣-ta-al-⸢la⸣-[ku]	143
	44	ba-su_8-bé-en-dè-en		ni-it-⸢ta-al⸣-[la-ak]	144
	45	ba-su_8-bé-en-zé-en		ta-at-[ta-al-la-ka]	145
col.iv	1	ba-ši-su_8-bé-eš	56	it-ta-al-⸢la⸣-[ku]-⸢šum⸣	146
	2	ba-ši-su_8-bé-en-dè-en		ni-it-ta-⸢al-la⸣-ak-šum	147
	3	ba-ši-su_8-bé-en-zé-en		ta-at-ta-la-ka-šum	148
	4	i-im-re_7-eš	59	il-li-ku-nim	149
	5	i-im-re_7-en-dè-en		ni-il-li-kam	150
	6	i-im-re_7-en-zé-en		ta-al-li-ka-<nim>	151
	7	i-im-ši-re_7-eš	60	il-li-ku-ni-iš-šum	152
	8	i-im-ši-re_7-en-dè-en		ni-il-li-ka-aš-šum	153
	9	i-im-ši-re_7-en-zé-en		ta-al-li-ka-ni-šum	154
	10	mu-e-ši-re_7-eš	64	il-li-ku-ni-ik-kum	155
	11	mu-e-ši-re_7-en-dè-en		ni-il-li-ka-ak-kum	156
	12	im-ma-re_7-eš	61	it-ta-al-ku-nim	157
	13	im-ma-re_7-en-dè-en		ni-it-ta-al-ka-<am>	158
	14	im-ma-re_7-en-zé-en		ta-at-ta-al-ka-nim	159
	15	im-ma-ši-re_7-eš	62	it-ta-al-ku-ni-iš-šum	160
	16	[im]-ma-ši-re_7-en-dè-en		ni-it-ta-al-ka-aš-šum	161
	17	[im]-ma-ši-re_7-en-zé-en		ta-at-ta-al-ka-ni-iš-šum	162
	18	im-mu-e-ši-re_7-eš	63	it-ta-al-ku-ni-ik-kum	163
	19	im-mu-e-ši-re_7-en-dè-en		ni-it-ta-al-ka-ak-kum	164
	20	i - re_7 - eš	57	il - li - ku	165
	21	i - re_7 - en - dè - en		ni - il - lik	166
	22	i - re_7 - en - zé - en		ta - al - li - ka	167
	23	[in]-ši-re_7-eš	58	il-li-⸢ku⸣-šum	168
	24	[in]-⸢ši-re_7-en-dè-en⸣		⸢ni⸣-[il]-⸢lik-šum⸣	169
	25	[in-ši-re_7-en-zé-en]		⸢ta⸣-al-li-ka-šum	170
	26	[ba]-⸢re_7⸣-eš	65	it-ta-al-ku	171
	27	⸢ba⸣-re_7-[en]-⸢dè-en⸣		ni-it-ta-la-ak	172

171 (b) C : it-ta-al-[

172 (b) C : ni-it-ta-⸢al⸣-[

28	ba-re$_7$-[en-zé]-⌜en⌝		ta-at-ta-al-ka	173
29	⌜ba-ši⌝-[re$_7$-eš]	66	it-ta-al-ku-šum	174
30	ba-ši-[re$_7$-en-dè-en]		ni-it-ta-la-ak-šum	175
31	ba-ši-re$_7$-⌜en⌝-[zé-en]		⌜ta⌝-at-ta-al-ka-šum	176
32			⌜ŠID⌝-B[I]1.20. MU.BI.IM	177
33	gen-àm-me	67	al-⌜kam ni-a-ši⌝-im	178
34	ga-mu-e-ne-gen		lu-ul-⌜li-kam ku-nu⌝-ši-⌜im⌝	179
35	hé-mu-e-ne-du		li-⌜il⌝-[li-kam] ⌜ku-nu-ši-im⌝	180
36	hé - me - du		li-⌜il-li⌝-ka ni-a-ši-im	181
37	gen-àm-<ma>-me	68	at-⌜la⌝-ka ni-a-ši-im	182
38	ga-àm-mu-e-ne-gen		lu-⌜ut⌝-ta-al-kam ku-nu-ši-im	183
39	hé-mu-e-ne-du		li-it-ta-al-kam ku-nu-ši-im	184
40	hé-em-me-du		li-it-ta-al-kam ni-a-ši-im	185
41	àm-me-du	69	i-il-la-kam ni-a-ši-im	186
42	àm-me-du-un		⌜ta-al⌝-la-kam ni-a-ši-im	187
43	mu-e-ne-du		⌜i-il⌝-la-kam ku-nu-ši-im	188
44	mu-e-ne-⌜du⌝-[un]		[a-al]-⌜la⌝-kam ku-nu-ši-im	189
45	àm-⌜ma⌝-[me-du]	(70)	[it-ta-al]-⌜la⌝-ka-ni-a-ši-im	190

5.1.2 de$_6$ = *wabālum* etc. (*UET* VII 102)

The restoration in the various broken portions of this text are made by comparison with better preserved sections of the same text in which the structure is parallel, or else by internal deduction.

col.i	1	[			bi-la-ni-a]-ši-im
	2	[ga-			lu-ub-la-ak-ku]-nu-ši-im
	3	[			ta]-⌜ab-la⌝-an-ni-a-ši-im
	4	[		]	⌜lu⌝-ut-ba-la-ak-ku-nu-ši-im
	5	[		]-en	tu-ub-ba-la-an-ni-a-ši-im
	6	[		]-⌜dè⌝-en	ub-ba-la-ak-ku-nu-ši-im
	7	[nu		]-en-dè-en	ú-ul ub-ba-la-ak-ku-nu-ši-im
	8	[		]-en-dè-en	ub-la-ak-ku-nu-ši-im
	9	[nu	]x	- en-dè-en	ú-ul ub-la-ak-ku-nu-ši-im
	10	[ba	]x	- en-dè-en	at-ba-la-ak-ku-nu-ši-im

173 (b) C : ta-at-ta-⌜al⌝-[x]-⌜ka⌝
174 (b) C : ⌜it-ta⌝-al-ku-[x]
175 (a) C : ba-ši-re$_7$-en-⌜dè⌝
175 (b) C : [ni-it]-ta-al-[x]-ak-[x]
176 (b) C : ⌜ta⌝-[
177 C om.
181 (b) C : li-il-li-ka-ni-ši-im
184 (a) C : ⌜hé⌝-e-ne-du
185 (b) C : ⌜li-it⌝-ta-al-kam ku-nu-ši-im
189 (a) C : mu-e-ne-du
190 (a) C : àm-me-du

11	[ ]x	- en-dè-en	ub-ba-la-ak-ku-nu-ši-im
12	[nu]x	-en-dè-en	ú-ul ub-ba-la-al-ku-nu-ši-im
13	[hé]x	-en-dè-⌜en⌝	li-ib-la-ak-ku-nu-ši-im
14	[na-]x	-en- ⌜dè-⌝-[en]	⌜la⌝ ub-la-ak-ku-nu-ši-im
15	[ ]-de$_6$-en-⌜dè⌝-[en]		ub-lam ku-nu-ši-im
16	[nu-]-de$_6$-en-⌜dè⌝-en		ú-ul ub-lam ku-nu-ši-im
17	[ba-]-de$_6$-en-dè-en		it-ba-la-ak-ku-nu-ši-im

18	[ ]	-⌜en-dè⌝-en	bi-la-ni-a-ši-im
19	[ga-	] - ⌜dè⌝-en	i nu-ub-la-ak-ku-<nu->ši-im
20	[	]-⌜en⌝-dè-en	ta-ab-la-<nim> ^{erasure}ni-a-ši-im
21	[	]-⌜dè⌝-en	i ni-it-ba-la-ak-ku-nu-ši-im
22	[		tu]-⌜ub⌝-ba-la-an-ni-a-ši-im
23	[	]	⌜ub⌝-ba-la-ak-ku-nu-ši-im
24	[nu-		ú-ul] ⌜ub⌝-ba-la-ak-ku-nu-ši-im
25	[		ub-la-ak] -ku-nu-ši-im
26	[nu-	]-⌜en⌝	⌜ú-ul⌝ [ub-la-ak-ku]-⌜nu-ši-im⌝
27	[ba-	]-⌜en-dè⌝-en	ni-it-ba-la-⌜ak⌝-[ku-nu-ši-im]
28	[	] -ne	ub-ba-lu-ni-ik-⌜ku⌝-[nu-ši-im]
29	[nu	] -ne	ú-ul ub-ba-lu-ni-ik-ku-nu-ši-⌜im⌝
30	[hé-	]-⌜e?⌝-ne	li-ib-lu-ni-ik-ku-nu-ši-im
31	[na-	]-⌜e?⌝-ne	la ub-ba-lu-ni-ik-ku-nu-ši-im
32	[	]-en-dè	ub-lu-ni-ik-ku-nu-ši-im
33	[nu	]-en-dè	ú-ul ub-lu-ni-ik-ku-nu-ši-im
34	[	]-en-dè-eš	it-ba-lu-<nim> ni-a-ši-im
35	[	]-⌜zé⌝-en	mu - ug - ra
36	[ga-	]-⌜dè⌝-en	i ni-im-gu-ur
37	[	]-⌜zé⌝-en	ta-ma-an-ga-ra
38	[	]-⌜dè⌝-en	ni-ma-an-ga-ar
39	[nu-	]-⌜dè⌝-en	ú-ul ni-ma-an-ga-gar
40	[	]-⌜dè⌝-en	ni-im-gu-ur
41	[nu-	]-⌜dè⌝-en	ú-ul ni-im-gu-ur
42	[	]-⌜dè-⌝-en	ni-im-ta-ga-ar
43	[	]-⌜dè?⌝-en	⌜i⌝-ma-an-ga-ru
44	[nu-	]-⌜dè?⌝-en	[ú]-ul i-ma-an-ga-ru
45	[hé-	]-⌜dè?⌝-en	li-im-gu-ru
46	[na-	]-⌜dè?⌝-en	la i-ma-an-ga-ru
47	[	-še-ge-eš]	⌜im⌝-gu-u$_4$-ru
48	[nu-	-še-ge-eš	ú-ul] ⌜im⌝-gu-u$_4$-ru
49	[	-še-ge-eš	im-ta]-ag-ru

50	[	-zé-en	mu-ug]-⌜ra⌝-šu
51	[ga-	-še-ge-en-dè-en	i ni-im-gu]-ur-šu
52	[	-še-ge-en-zé-en	ta-ma-an-ga-ra]-šu
53	[	-še-ge-en-dè-en	ni-ma-an-ga-ar]-šu
54	[nu-	-še-ge-en-dè-en	ú-ul ni-ma-an-ga-ar-šu]
col.ii 1	mu-un-[?	-še-ge-en-dè-en	ni-im-gu-ur-šu
2	nu-mu-⌜un⌝-[?	-še-ge-en-dè-en	ú-ul ni-im-gu-ur-šu
3	ba-an-na-[	-še-ge-en-dè-en	ni-im-ta-ga-ar-šu]
4	an-na-ab-⌜še⌝- [	ge - ne	i-ma-an-ga-ru-ú-šu]

47,48 (b) should read im-gu-ru-u$_4$ (cf. ii 8-9, 22-3).

5	nu-an-na-ab-še-⌜ge⌝- [ne	ú-ul i-ma-an-ga-ru-ú-šu]
6	hé(text: ga)-en-na-ab-še-ge-ne	⌜li-im⌝-[gu-ru-u_4-šu]
7	na-en-na-ab-še-ge-ne	la i-⌜ma⌝-[an-ga-ru-ú-šu]
8	in-še-ge-eš	im-gu-ru-u_4-[šu]
9	nu-in-še-ge-eš	ú-ul im-gu-ru-u_4 -[šu]
10	ba-an-na-še-ge-eš	im-ta-ag-ru-ú-[šu]

11	še-ga-mu-ub-zé-en	mu-ug-ra-ni-in-⌜ni⌝
12	ga-mu-ri-ib-še-ge-en-dè-en	i ni-im-gu-ur-ka
12a	mu-un-še-ge-en-zé-en	<ta-ma-an-ga-ra-ka>
13	<mu-un-še-ge-en-dè-en>	ni-ma-an-ga-ar-ka
14	nu-mu-un-še-ge-en-dè-en	ú-ul ni-ma-an-ga-ar-ka
15	i-še-ge-en-dè-en	ni-im-gu-ur-ka
16	nu-un-še-ge-en-dè-en	ú-ul ni-im-gu-ur-ka
17	ba-e-še-ge-en-dè-en	ni-im-ta-ga-ar-ka
18	mu-e-še-ge-ne(text: -en-dè-en)	i-ma-an-ga-ru-ú-ka
19	nu-mu-e-še-ge-ne(text: -en-dè-en)	ú-ul i-ma-an-ga-ru-ú-ka
20	hé-ši-ge-ne(text: -en-dè-en)	li-im-gu-<ru->u_4 -ka
21	na-an-še-ge-ne (text: -en-dè-en)	la i-ma-ga-ru-ú-ka
22	mu-e-še-ge-eš	im-gu-ru-u_4 -ka
23	nu-mu-e-še-ge-eš	ú-ul im-gu-ru-u_4 -ka
24	im-mu-<e->še-ge-eš	im-ta-ag-ru-u_4 -ka

25	[gíd]-an-zé-en	mi - ṣi - a
26	[ ]-⌜an?⌝-dè(text: zé)-en	i ni-im-ṣi
27	[ ]-⌜en⌝-zé-en	ta-ma-aṣ-ṣi-⌜a⌝
28	[ ]-⌜dè⌝-en	ni-ma-aṣ-⌜ṣi⌝
29	[nu-	ú-ul ni-ma-aṣ-ṣi]
30	mu-un-gíd-[en-dè-en	ni-im-ṣi]
31	nu-mu-gíd-⌜en?-⌝-[dè-en	ú-ul ni-im-ṣi]
32	ba-an-gíd-en-dè-en	⌜ni⌝-[im-ta-ṣi]
33	mu-un-gíd-dè-eš	im-⌜ṣu⌝-ú
34	nu-mu-un-gíd-dè-eš	ú-ul im-ṣu-u
35	hé-gíd-dè-eš	li-im-ṣu-ú
36	na-an-gíd-dè-eš	la i-ma-aṣ-ṣu-ú
37	mu-un-gíd-dè-eš	im-ṣu-ú
38	nu-mu-un-gíd-dè-eš	ú-ul im-ṣu-ú
39	ba-an-gíd-dè-eš	im-ta-ṣu-ú
40	gíd-àm-zé-en	mi-ṣa-a-nim
41	ga-gíd-[[da]]-en-dè-en	i ni-⌜im⌝-ṣi-a-kum
42	àm-gíd-da-en-zé-en	ta-am-ṣi-a-nim
43	àm-gíd-da-en-dè-en	ni-ma-ṣi-a-kum
44	nu-àm-gíd-da-en-dé-en	ú-ul ni-ma-ṣi-a-⌜kum⌝
45	mu-ši-gíd-[[da]]-en-dè-en	ni-im-ṣi-a-kum
46	nu-mu-ši-gíd-[[da]]-en-dè-en	ú-ul ni-im-ṣi-a-kum
47	ba-ra-gíd-[[da]]-en-dè-en	ni-im-ta-ṣi-a-⌜kum⌝
48	mu-ra-gíd-da-ne [[en]]	i-ma-aṣ-ṣu-ni-ik-kum
49	nu-mu-ra-gíd-da-ne [[en]]	ú-ul i-ma-aṣ-ṣu-ni-ik-kum

12a (b), 13 (a) omitted by haplography. Mr Andrew George kindly checked the tablet and pronounced the copy correct.

33f. (b) errors for *imaṣṣû.*

33-6 (a) -gíd-dè-eš error for -gíd-i-ne.

42 (b) error for *tamaṣṣiānim.*

	50	hu-mu-ra-gíd-i-ne	li-im-ṣu-ni-ik-kum
	51	nam-mu-ra-gíd-i-ne	la i-ma-ṣu-ni-ik-kum
	52	mu-ra-gíd-[[i]]-dè-eš	im-ṣu-ni-ik-kum
	53	nu-mu-ra-gíd-[[i]]-dé-eš	ú-ul im-ṣu-ni-ik-kum
	54	im-ma-ra-gíd-[[i]]-dé-eš	im-ta-ṣu-ni-ik-kum
	55	gíd-mu-zè-en	mi-ṣi-a-šum
	56	ga-mu-gíd-en-⌜dé-en⌝	i ni-im-ṣi-i(text: a)-šum
	57	mu-ni-ib-gíd-en-zé-⌜en⌝	ta-ma-aṣ-ṣi-a-šum
	58	mu-ni-ib-gíd-en-⌜dè-en⌝	ni-ma-aṣ-ṣi-i-šum
	59	nu-mu-ni-ib-gíd-en-[dè-en]	⌜ú⌝-ul ni-ma-aṣ-ṣi-šum
	60	⌜mu-un⌝-na-gíd-[en-dè-en]	⌜ni⌝-im-ṣi-šum
	61	⌜nu⌝-mu-⌜un⌝-na-gíd-[en-dè-en]	⌜u⌝-ul ni-im-ṣi-šum
col.iii	1	[ba-]-⌜gíd⌝-en-⌜dè-en⌝	ni-⌜im-⌝-< ta- > ⌜ṣi⌝-i(text: a)-[šum]
	2	[ ]-⌜ne⌝-[[en]]	i-⌜ma-aṣ⌝-ṣu-ú-[šum]
	2a	<nu- -ne	ú-ul i-ma-aṣ-ṣu-ú-šum>
	3	[hé-]-ne	li-[im]-taṣ-⌜ṣu-ú⌝-[šum]
	4	[na-]-ne	la i-ma-aṣ-⌜ṣu-ú⌝-šum
	5	[ ]-eš	im-ṣu-ú-⌜šum⌝
	6	[nu-]-⌜gíd⌝-[-]-eš	ú-ul im-⌜ṣu-ú⌝-[šum]
	7	[ba- ?]-⌜ni⌝-ib-⌜gíd⌝-[-]-eš	im-ta-ṣu-⌜ú-šum⌝

8	⌜ta$_{12}$⌝-a-ab-[zé]-en	ez-ba
9	ga-ab-ta$_{12}$-en-⌜dè⌝-en	i ni-zi-⌜ib⌝
10	mu-ni-ib-ta$_{12}$-ta$_{12}$-a-[an]-zé-en	te-zi-⌜ba⌝
11	mu-ni-ib-ta$_{12}$-ta$_{12}$-a-[an]-⌜dè⌝-en	ni-in-zi-⌜ib⌝
12	nu-mu-ni-ib-ta$_{12}$ -ta$_{12}$ -a-[an]-dè(text: zé)-en	ú-ul ni-in-zi-⌜ib⌝
13	ì-ta$_{12}$-en-dè-en	ni-zi-ib
14	nu-ì-ta$_{12}$-⌜en-de⌝-en	ú-ul ni-zi-ib
15	ba-ta$_{12}$-⌜en-dè⌝-en	ni-te-zi-ib
16	mu-ni-ib-ta$_{12}$-ta$_{12}$-⌜ne⌝	i-iz-zi-bu
17	nu-mu-ni-ib-ta$_{12}$-ta$_{12}$-⌜ne⌝	ú-ul i-iz-⌜zi⌝-bu
18	hu-mu-ni-ib-ta$_{12}$-ta$_{12}$-⌜ne⌝	li - zi [[x]] - bu
19	nam-mu-ni-ib-ta$_{12}$-ta$_{12}$-[ne]	la i-iz-zi-bu
20	in - ta$_{12}$- [eš]	i-zi-bu
21	nu-un-ta$_{12}$-[eš]	ú-ul i-zi-bu
22	ba-an-ta$_{12}$-[eš]	i-te-ez-bu

23	ta$_{12}$-ma-ab-zé-⌜en⌝	ez-ba-a-nim
24	ga-àm-ab-ta$_{12}$-en-dè-en	i ni-iz-ba-am
25	àm-⌜mi⌝-ib-ta$_{12}$-ta$_{12}$-en-zé-⌜en⌝	te-ez-zi-ba-a-nim
26	⌜am-mi⌝-ib-ta$_{12}$-ta$_{12}$-en-dè-en	ni-iz-zi-ba-a-m
27	[nu-àm]-⌜mi⌝-ib-ta$_{12}$-< ta$_{12}$- >en-dè-en	ú-ul ni-iz-zi-ba-am
28	[ ]-ta$_{12}$-[[⌜dè⌝]]-en-dè-⌜en⌝	ni-iz-ba-am
29	[ ]x-ta$_{12}$-[[dè]]-en-dè-⌜en⌝	ú-ul ni-zi-⌜ba⌝-am
30	[im-ma]x-ta$_{12}$-en-dè-⌜en⌝	ni-te-ez-ba-am
31	àm-mi-ib-ta$_{12}$-ta$_{12}$-⌜ne⌝	i-iz-zi-bu-ú-nim
32	⌜nu⌝-àm-mi-ib-ta$_{12}$-ta$_{12}$-ne	⌜ú-ul i⌝-[iz]-⌜zi-bu-ú-nim⌝
33	hé-em-ta$_{12}$-ta$_{12}$-ne	li-⌜zi⌝-[bu-ú-nim]
34	na-àm-ta$_{12}$-ta$_{12}$-ne	la i-⌜zi⌝-[bu-ú-nim]
35	im-ma-an-ta$_{12}$-eš	i-[[zi]]-⌜zi⌝-[bu-ú-nim]

36	nu-um-ma-an-ta$_{12}$-eš	ú-ul ⸢i⸣- [zi-bu-ú-nim]
37	im-ma-an(text: in)-ta$_{12}$-eš	i-te-ez-[[⸢zi⸣]]-[bu-ú-nim]

38	ta$_{12}$-an-na-ab-zé-en	ez-ba-ni-[šu-
39	ga-àm-ab-ta$_{12}$-en-dè-en	i ni-zi-[ib-šu-
40	mu-un-na-ni-ib-ta$_{12}$-ta$_{12}$-en-zé-en	te-ez-zi-ba-[šu-
41	mu-un-na-ni-ib-ta$_{12}$-ta$_{12}$-an-dè-en	ni-iz-zi-ba-[šu-
42	in-na-ni-ib-ta$_{12}$-ta$_{12}$-an-dè-en	ú-ul ni-iz-⸢zi⸣-[ba-šu-
43	in-na-an-ta$_{12}$-en-dè-⸢en⸣	ni-[[iz]]-zi-ib-šu-[
44	nu-in-na-an-ta$_{12}$-en-⸢dè⸣-[en]	⸢ú⸣-ul ni-[[iz]]-zi- ib-[šu-
45	na-an-ba-ta$_{12}$-en-[dè-en	ni]-⸢te⸣-zi-ib-šu-[
46	mu-un-na-ni-ib-⸢ta$_{12}$⸣-[ta$_{12}$-ne	i-iz]-zi-bu-⸢šu⸣-[
47	nu-mu-un-na-ni-[ib-ta$_{12}$-ta$_{12}$-ne	ú-ul i-iz-zi-bu-šu-]
48	hu-mu-un-na-[ni-ib-ta$_{12}$-ta$_{12}$-ne	li-zi-bu-šu-]
49	nam-mu-na-⸢an⸣-[ni-ib-ta$_{12}$-ta$_{12}$-ne	la i-iz-zi-bu-šu-]
50	in-na-an-[ta$_{12}$-eš	i-zi-bu-šu-]
51	nu-in-na-an-[ta$_{12}$-eš	ú-ul i-zi-bu-šu-]
52	[ba]-an-[na-an-ta$_{12}$-eš	i-te-ez-bu-šu-]

col.iv 1	[	]-li-a-am
2	[	]x-li-a-am
3	[	]-⸢li⸣-a-am
4	[	]-⸢še⸣-li-a-am
5	[	]-⸢te$^?$⸣-li-⸢a⸣-am
6	[	ú - še] -el-lu-⸢ú⸣-nim
7	[nu-	ú - ul]ú-še-el-lu-u$_4$-nim
8	[he-	li -] še-lu-ú-nim
9	[na-	ú - ul li-] še-lu-u$_4$-nim
10	[	ú -] ⸢še-lu-ú⸣-nim
11	[nu-	ú - ul]ú-še-lu-u$_4$-nim
12	[ha-ba-	li -] -⸢iš⸣-te-lu-ú-nim
13	[	u - še-]el-li-a-aš-šu-nu-ši-im
14	[	ú-]ul ú-še-el-li-a-aš-šu-nu-ši
15	[ ]	li-iš-te-li-a-aš-šu-nu-ši-im
16	[-zé]-en	šu-li-a-ni-iš-šum
17	[ ]-⸢è⸣	lu-še-li-⸢a⸣-aš-šu-nu-ši-im
18	[he-]-⸢è⸣	li-še-li-aš-šu-nu-ši-im
19	[na- -è]	⸢ú⸣-ul li-še-li-aš-šu-nu-ši-im
20	[ha-ba-]	li-iš-te-li-aš-šu-nu-ši-im
21	[	]-⸢ik⸣-kum
22	[	]-⸢ik⸣-kum
23	[	] - ⸢kum⸣
24-27	*carent*	
28	[ ]-⸢ne⸣	⸢i-na⸣-aš-šu-u
29	[nu-]-⸢ne⸣	ú-ul i-na-aš-šu-ú
30	[ ]-⸢ne⸣	na - šu - ú
31	[-zé-en]	na-ši-a-tu-nu
32	[ba- -zé-en]	ta-at-ta-ši-a
33	[ba- -zé-en]	ta-at-ta-ši-a
34	[nu-]-⸢zé⸣-en	ú-ul ta-na-aš-ši-a
35	[nu-]-⸢zé⸣-en	ú-la ta-na-aš-ši-a

36 [	]-⸢gùr⸣-ru	ul-la-a-nu-um lu-un-na-a-ši [[a]]
37 [he-	]-ne	li-iš-šu-ú
38 [ba-	]-ne	it-ta-šu-ú
39 [	-zé]-en	i-ši-a-ni-in-ni
40 [	]-ne	i-na-aš-šu-ni-in-ni
41 [	]-ne	na-ši-a-nu
42 [	]-⸢ne⸣	i-na-aš-šu-ú-nim
43 [	]-⸢ne⸣	la i-na-aš-šu-ú-nim
44 [ba-	]-⸢ne⸣	it-ta-šu-ú-nim
45 [he-	]-⸢ne⸣	li-⸢iš⸣-šu-ú-nim
46 [he-	]-⸢ne⸣	li-iš-šu-ni-in-ni
47 [	]	⸢iš⸣-šu-ni-in-ni
48 [		]x-ú-nim
49 [		]-⸢nim⸣

at least four more lines to end of tablet

5.1.3 nag = *šatûm* etc. (*UET* VII 99)

col.I	1 [	]-lu
	2 [	]-lu
	3 [	]⸢ik⸣-ka-lu
	4 [	]-⸢ka⸣-al
	5 [	]-⸢ik⸣-ka-al
	6 [	]-lu-kum
	7 [	]-⸢x⸣-lu-kum
	8 [	]x
	9 [	]-⸢ul⸣
	10 [	] x

col.ii	1	]x[	
	2	in-nag-[eš	iš-tu-ú]
	3	nu-un-nag-eš	⸢ú-la⸣[iš-tu-ú]
	4	ì-nag-dè-en	ni-iš-⸢ti⸣
	5	la-ba-an-nag-dè-en	ú-la ni-iš-ti
	6	⸢al⸣-nag-nag-ne	i-ša-at-tu-⸢ú⸣
	7	nu-⸢nag⸣-nag-ne	ú-la i-ša-at-tu-⸢ú⸣
	8	ì-nag-nag-ne	ta-aš-ti-a
	9	i-nag-dè-en	ni-iš-ti
	10	ba-e-nag	ta-aš-ta-ti
	11	la-ba-e-nag	ú-ul ta-aš-ta-ti
	12	ba-e-nag-zé-en	ta-aš-ta-ti-⸢a⸣
	13	[ba-nag-dè]-⸢en⸣	ni-iš-ta-[ti]

5.2 The text K4808 and its duplicates

The composite text of these fragments has not been published before, although K4808 (then unnumbered) and K4225 were published by Haupt in *Die akkadische Sprache* (Berlin, 1883) as plates IX (= XIII), X (= XIV) and XI (= XV). Excerpts in transliteration from these were published in *MSL* IV, p.202, where K4808 was erroneously numbered K7781. Professor Lambert kindly made available to me his own transliteration of the fragments.

---

5 (a) error for nu-nag-dè-en.

8 (a) error for ì-nag-zé-en.

SIGLA

A = K4808	(obv.?)	lines 1-27
B = K4225	obv.	lines 15-27
	rev.	lines 28-44
C = K7781	parts of	lines 31-36
D = BM78532 (Bu 88-5-12, 440)	obv.	lines 13-21
	rev.	lines 22 -30

A, B and C are neo-Assyrian in script; D is neo-Babylonian. For lines 1-27 the text of A is used as a basis; for lines 28-44 that of B. 'Line 1' is probably not the first line of the text; and K4225 has room for approximately 14 more lines after line 44.

		]	in	[
ag	KU$_4$$^?$]	⌜er⌝- ba	ag ku$_4$ um	⌜e⌝- [pe - šu e - ⌜ re⌝-[bu ri - a - [tum
ma	TUŠ	ti - šá - ab	ma ^{e}e$_4$ tu-uš tuš	ES NÍ [pa - šá - ⌜hu⌝ a - šá - ⌜bu⌝
ar	ŠÈR	nam <-ru> e-tel-lu	ar še-er šèr	na - ma - ⌜ru⌝ e - tel - lu EME.SAL
		šu - up - ši - ih	si-ig sìg ba	pa - šá - hu MÌN i-na : a-na
		lu - re - eš - ka	ra li tum	ana - ku NIGÍN AN ra - a - šú at - ta NIGÍN SIG
bí	IGI	⌜lu - up - pa - lis - ka⌝	bí e igi	EŠ NÌ BA NÍ.KÚŠ SIG- ⌜tum⌝ a - ma - [ru
tum	ÁR	lu - 'u - ud - ka	tum ár	at - ta NIGÍN ⌜AN⌝ na - a - du
si	SUH	lu - us - su - uk - ka :	si suh	ka - a - šu na - sa - qu

14 (e) D : at -tú
17 (d) D : igi$_{i-gi}$
18 (e) D : at-tú NIGÍN AN SIG

ba	ban	am - ru has - su	ba pà an	li-i šá ma-⌜a⌝ a - ma - rú šu - taq - tu - ú
⌜ru⌝]	DÚ	le - é - ’u$_4$ - um	ru ú dù	AN MURU$_4$ SIG le - é - ’u$_4$ - [um mu - du - [u
um	e	ba - an ka - la	um da ag	⌜ri⌝- [ya - a - tum ⌜ka⌝- [la ⌜e⌝- [pe - šu
ba	NÌ	e-pí-iš mi-im-ma šum-šú	ba nì	EŠ [mim-ma [šumšu
la	ZU	mu - da - u	la ^{e}e$_4$ ⌜zu⌝	x[x[
da	DÚ	mu - še - pí - ⌜iš⌝ [[	da dù	
li	UR	taš - mi - ⌜e⌝ [[	li ur?	
i	HI	u - sa - [[	i hi	
iš	[		iš	

5.3 Further grammatical vocabularies from Nippur and elsewhere

Baking, cleaning and re-examination of the sources have resulted in a join and a number of improved readings. These transliterations supersede those in the first edition.

5.3.1 Ni4125

obv. i

1'	traces	
2'	[gen-àm]-ma	at-la-[kam]
3'	[àm-m]a-du-un	a-ta-la-kam
4'	[a-na-à]m ga-ba-ni-ib-⌜gi$_4$⌝	mi-na-am lu-pu-ul
5'	[ ]-en ki ga-ab-dug$_4$	ša x x x lu-qí-bi
6'	[x]-a-nu	ṣú-úh-ra-am
7'	[ ]⌜x⌝-an-gá?-⌜e⌝-en	lu-uṣ-hu-⌜ur⌝-ma
8'	[geštu-zu] gá-al ga- [a]b-tag$_4$	ú-zu-un-ka ⌜pé⌝- ⌜te!?⌝
	(end of col. i)	

---

25 (a) restored from B.
28,29 (e) restored from D.
31,32 (e) from Haupt and Lambert; now missing.

obv. ii

1' ⸢x⸣-ba-[
2' ⸢su$^?$⸣-ur-
3' dah-ma-
4' ba$^?$ mu-ra-n[i
5' inim-ma gi-b[-íb-
6' KA-zu nam-bi$^?$-x [
7' gá-e-me-en inim ga-r[a-ab]-
du[g$_4$
(end of col. ii)

rev. i

1 me-àm nu-UD$^?$ x [
2 níg-sur-ra [
3 a-na-aš$^!$ a-ši-ir ki x [
4 NE-a igi-zu$^!$ u$_6$ bí-i[b-
5 a-na-àm ki še-er bi$^?$ x [
6 inim-bi ha-ra-da-ab-[
7 níg ⸢x x x⸣ šu mu-na-[
8 LAGAB àm ki$^?$ ⸢x⸣-àm [
9 níg dingir-re-e-n[e
10 in-gar-ra$^?$ x [
11 níg-nam x [
12f. traces

5.3.2 Ni4143 (*İSET* p. 135, no. 77)

1' traces
2' [x]-kad$_4$-kad$_4$-dè-e[n
3' ⸢x⸣-kad$_4$-kad$_4$-dè-en-d[è-en
4' ⸢é$^?$⸣ gíd-da-àm
5' ga-àm-gíd
6' ⸢é$^?$⸣ bu-ù-un-zé-en
7' ga-àm-ma-gíd-i-dè-en
8' nu-⸢x-gíd⸣-i-dè-en   ú-la ⸢x⸣[
9' é gú gi$_4$-ib   bi-ta-[am
10' gú ga-ab-gi$_4$ ⸢am-ša/ta⸣[
11' ri-ba-⸢ab$^?$⸣[   ]x-ab-[
12' ⸢ga⸣-ba-[ ]
13' [ga]-ba-ri ŠE [ ]
14' traces

5.3.3 N4217 + N6939 (joined by Civil)

The following revised transliteration of N4217 + N6939 supersedes that given in *MSL SS* 1, p. 91; the number given there as N2417 should be N4217.

obv. i'

1'	[im hé-sì]g	lu-um-ha-[aṣ]
2'	[i]m al$^{!}$-sìg-ge-en	a-ma-ah-ha-aṣ
	(note: nu-sìg-ge-en according to *MSL SS* 1, p. 91)	
3'	im nu-sìg-ge-en	ú-ul a-mah-aṣ
4'	im hé-sìg-ge	lu-mah-aṣ
5'	im nu-sìg-ge	ú-ul i-mah-aṣ
6'	⌜sal$^{?}$⌝-sal-la-ab	ru-uq-qì-iq
7'	[x] ⌜dug$_{4}^{?}$-ga$^{?}$⌝-ab	pi-si-il
8'	[ ]-⌜x-x⌝	ru-uq-qì-iq
9'	[ ]⌜x⌝ GAR-g[in$_{7}^{?}$]	⌜ki$^{?}$ ma$^{?}$⌝ ha-ah-[hi$^{?}$...]
10'	traces	
11'	traces	

obv. ii'

1'	⌜x(-)mu-ni⌝-[ ]
2'	dab$_{5}$-ba-ni-ib [
3'	sar-ra-ab [
4'	⌜ga-sar⌝ [
5'	⌜ba⌝-[ ]

(Obv. i' and ii' should be close to OBGT III lines 84–105, concerned with making tablets and writing.)

rev. i'

1'	nu-[	
2'	na-an-[	
3'	hé-x[	
4'	al-peš-[peš	
5'	nu-peš-[peš	
6'	hé-peš-peš[	(lines 4'–6' parallel to OBGT III 154–6)
7'	al-búr-[búr	
8'	nu-búr-[búr	
9'	hé-búr-b[úr	
10'	na-an-búr-búr[	(lines 7'–10' parallel to OBGT III 160–3)
11'	al-gú-gú [	(for dur-dur?)
12'	al-KIN-KIN [	(read sag$_{11}$-sag$_{11}$)
13'	šu an-[x	
14'	šu-⌜ni al⌝-[	(lines 13'f. parallel to OBGT III 170–2)

rev. ii'

1'	e]n?	[t]a-ra-⌜ap⌝-[
2'	]-en	ú-ra-ap-pa-x[
3'	]-šú	du-um-mu-um
4'	]-šú	ú-ul du-um-mu-um
5'	]-⌜šú⌝	lu du-um-mu-um
6'	]	la du-um-mu-um
7'	]	du-um-mu-ma-ku
8'		⌜ú-ul⌝ du-um-mu-ma-ku
9'	[ ]-⌜x⌝	su-ru-ú (su perfectly clear; lu-ru-ú clear in CBS 9053)
10'	[em]e-dar-tar	ku-uṣ-ṣú-rum
11'	sa-az	su-uk-ku-kum
12'	SAG? si-sá hé-ag-e	li-x-nam li-še-er
13'	SAG? si-sá na-an-ag-e	a ⌜i⌝-še-er
14'	SAG? si-sá nu-ag-e	ú-[u]l i-⟨⟨x⟩⟩-še-er
15'	[-ti]-ti	⌜ú-re⌝-ši-a-an-ni
16'	[ ]	[ ]-⌜x⌝-a-ni

(lines 9'–15' = N6939 lines 1'–7', parallel to OBGT III 221–233)

It now seems clear that both N4143 and N4217 + N6939 contain material fairly closely parallel to OBGT III (A) (see pp. 15ff.). OBGT III (A) is the tablet CBS 9053 (not 9853, as stated in MSL IV p. 68). Conceivably the text of Ni4143 (described by Civil as 'apparently part of the same Ni tablet' as N4217 + N6939) follows the section of OBGT III (A and B) ending in 109, and might therefore even join either ms. at this point. So far the only actual overlap with OBGT III (B) is that of N4217 + N6939 rev. ii' lines 15'(f.) with lines 232–3, which raises the possibility that N4217 + N6939 might join Ni10293 (OBGT III (B)) here.

5.3.4 Ni9688

obv.

1	dub-sar-me-en	ṭú-up-[ša-ru-um a-na-ku]
2	dub-sar-me-en	ṭú-up-[ša-ru-um at-ta]
3	[l]ú-e dub-sar-ra	an-nu-um [ṭú-up-ša-ru-um(-ma)]
4	[lú]-ri dub-sar-ra	ul-lu-um ṭ[ú-up-ša-ru-um(-ma)]
5	[nam]-dub-sar-ra á-sum e-da-sum	ṭú-up-ša-ru-[tam
6	[na]m-dub-sar-ra á-sum e-da-sum	ṭú-up-ša-ru-[
7	nam-dub-sar-ra á sum-mu-⌜da?⌝	ṭú-up-ša-ru-[
8	nam-dub-sar-ra e-da-⌜gál⌝	ṭú-up-ša-r[u-
9	nam-dub-sar-ra mu-da-⌜gál⌝	[ṭ]ú-up-š[a-
10	nam-dub-sar-ra an-da-⌜gál⌝	[ṭ]ú-up-[
11	(broken)	

rev.

1' eme-gi$_7$-ra T[U
2' uri ga-ra-x [
3' si-sá nu-e-zu-z[u$^?$
  inim-bal[
4' si ha-ra-ab-sá-⸢sá-e$^?$⸣

5' níg - ga/bi x

5.3.5 Ni10269

rev. i'

1'	] x x [	
2'	x x ŠU.⸢NIGIN⸣[	
3'	ki-ŠU.NÍG.TUR.LÁ	ši-ip-[
4'	šu sur-ra-ab	x lu x [
5'	šu tab-ba-ab	2
6'	sal-sal-la-ab	ru-[uq-qì-iq] (cf. N4217 obv. i'6')
7'	]-ag-a-ab	[2]
8'	]-ag-a-ab	[3]
9'	] x ab	[4]
10'	]-ab	[5]
11'	]⸢ab⸣	[6]

rev. ii' blank

5.3.6 Another fragment of a grammatical vocabulary parallel to OBGT III (A and B) is 'UET 6/3 618' (published here in transliteration by kind permission of the Trustees of the British Museum), which is clearly fairly close to the passage in N4217+N6939 obv. i' and ii' above, concerned with instructions for the making of tablets:

1	im ha$^?$-za-a[b	
2	im im-šub-ba-t[a	
3	im sìg-a	
4	sal-sal-la-ab	ru-[uq-qì-iq]
5	DÙN-bal gar-ni	ki-[ma ha-ah-hi ?]
6	ša-ka-la-ga-ab	pi-[si-il]
7	dub dím-ma-a[b]	
8	BU-BU mu-a-[	
9	ab/dub$^?$-sag x [	
10	sar-[ra-ab	
11	gub-b[a-ab	

5.4 Further verbal paradigms from Nippur and elsewhere

Here too baking, cleaning and re-examination of the sources have resulted in a join and a number of improved readings.

5.4.1 N3321

obv.

1'	[ ]⌜x⌝-ši-DU [	
2'	[ ]⌜e?⌝-da-⌜DU⌝[ ]	
3'	[ ]⌜x⌝-da-ši-DU [	
4'	[ ] x-da-ši-du-dè-en	
	(three erased lines)	
8'	[-n]e-da-ši-DU	[
9'	[ ]⌜x⌝-ši-DU	x [
10'	[ ]-ne-ši-du-dè-en	a-[
11'	[-d]a-ne-ši-du-dè-en	x [
12'	[-d]a-ne-ši-DU	a-[
13'	[ ]-ne-ši-du-dè-en	a-⌜di?⌝[
14'	[ ] x-ši-du-dè-en	a-⌜di?⌝[
15'	[ ]-ne-ši-gen-na	at?-[
16'	[ ] x-ši-gen-en-na	x [
17'	[ ] x-ši-gen-en-na	[

rev.

1'	(traces)
2'	] x-da-ne-ši-re$_7$-en-zé-e[n]
3'	à]m-me-da-ne-ši-re$_7$-en-zé-e[n
4'	]-NE-da-ne-ši-re$_7$-eš
5'	]-da-ne-ši-re$_7$-en-dè-en
6'	] x-me-da-ne-ši-r[e$_7$-
7'	]-⌜da?⌝-ši-re$_7$-[
	(rest broken)

5.4.2 N3513 has been joined by Civil to N3592, the missing corner, restoring the beginning. Part of the beginning of col. ii is still missing, but can be restored by deduction.

This ingenious paradigm of gen/du [= *alākum*] is so far unique in that it lists Sumerian forms only. I am very grateful to Mr G. Zólyomi for several fruitful suggestions concerning its analysis. It consists of singular forms with 1st and 2nd ps. singular and plural complements. All the forms listed have the affix (-)m- (which in bilingual paradigms is set against Akkadian ventive) and all the forms in the righthand columns (here ii and iv, i.e. columns obv. ii and rev. i according to conventional notation) have the prefix ba-, which appears as -ma- after -m-, and as -mu- after -m- and before -e-. The infixes representing the pronominal complements (technically in the terminative case) are: 1sg. -muši-, 2sg. -eši-, 1pl. -meši-, and -eneši-, evidently intended for 2pl. Thus far, all this corresponds with the procedures noted in section 1.2 above for the bilingual paradigms from Nippur. (-)m- apppears as (-)mu- before -e-; and, interestingly, as im- or am- in initial position before -ma- (< ba-) or before the infixes -meši- or -muši-. The structure of the paradigm shows that, in these forms with (-)m-, the alternation in initial position between mu- and im-/am- is phonological, and this raises wider questions about the correct analysis of forms beginnings with im- or am- (see p. 26 above). The opposition between im- and am-, on the other hand, is a grammatical one, depending on the presence of gen (im-) or du (am-), and it appears that this can be parallelled in the usage of other verbal paradigms. (For certain exceptions in col. iv see below.) The other prefixes occurring (apart from ba-) are nu- and na-. This na- is probably the 'prohibitive' na-, rather than the 'narrative' na-, since it appears in the section 5–8 (with base du) but not in 9–12 (base gen), and prohibitive na- is known to require the secondary verbal base. The choice of reading gen or du is unambiguous only in lines 1–12 and 23–4. Since 14 = 19 (iv 17), i and iii 15 = 20 (ii only approximately; iv 16 = 22), and 16 = 22 (not col. iv), it seems reasonable that all the forms in 13–16 (without na-) are to be read as gen and those in 17–22 (with na-) as du, given the presence of na- in the section 17–22, a deduction reinforced by the presence of am- in iv 13. The arrangement is as follows:

Cols. i and ii: plural complements, cols. iii and iv: singular complements. Since lines 1–2 unambiguously give a 2nd ps. form with a 1st ps. complement followed by a 1st ps. form with a 2nd ps. complement, it seems reasonable to assume that this is the procedure followed throughout the first half, i.e. that forms with 2nd ps. complements are to be taken as 1st ps. forms and vice versa, and that 'impossible' combinations are omitted, as elsewhere in grammatical paradigms. However, while this seems the more likely interpretation, it leads to the conclusion that e.g. iv 6 na-àm-mu-e-ši-du-un is a 1st ps. sg. form with 2nd ps. sg. complement, i.e. a 'prohibitive' na- with a 1st ps. sg. form, unless one is to assume the occurrence of regularly constructed but meaningless forms in the paradigm. (Prohibitive na- is regularly used with 2nd and 3rd ps., and is found with 1st ps. pl., but apparently not with 1st ps. sg.) The second half of the paradigm (13–24) appears to give 3rd ps. sg. forms. Lines 23–24 were evidently omitted by mistake from col. iv. The scribe mistakenly inverted entries 15 and 16 in col. iv, and wrote àm-⌜ma⌝-[mu-ši-du] and na-àm-[ma-mu-ši-du] in iv 13 and 14 for the expected *im-ma-mu-ši-gen and *nu-um-ma-mu-ši-gen. In iv 17-22 he reversed the order of prefixes found in cols. i-iii (na-, nu-, am-/im- instead of am-/mu-, na-, nu-), and wrote im-m[u-e-ši-du] in iv 22 corresponding to àm-mu-e-ne-ši-du in ii 20.

On this basis, 1–12 give alternately 1st and 2nd ps. sg. forms with, respectively, 2nd and 1st ps. pl. and sg. complements (except that 9–10 are both 2 + 1 and 11-12 both 1 + 2). 12–24 give 3rd ps. sg. forms with 1st ps. (13–14), 2nd ps. (15–16), 1st ps. (17–19) and 2nd ps. (20–22) pl. and sg. complements. The first two entries of the paradigm (1–2) and the last two (23–24) are non-indicative forms (2nd ps. imperative, 1st ps. volitive and 3rd ps. optative respectively, with 1st and 2nd ps. complements as appropriate), framing the indicative forms. The prefixes are arranged in groups as follows: (-)m-/na-/nu- (3-8), (-)m-/nu-, (-)m-/nu- (9–12), (-)m-/nu-, (-)m-/nu- (13-16), (-)m-/na-/nu-, (-)m-/na-/nu- (17–22). Thus the paradigm can be seen as a study in positive ((-)m-) and negative (nu-) forms, with non-indicative forms represented by 1–2 (positive) and 5–6 (na-, corresponding negative), and 23–4 (positive) and 18 and 21 (na-, corresponding negative). The verbal bases in the indicative forms (3–22) alternate chiastically as follows: du (3–8), gen (9–12), gen (13–16), du (17–22).

The revised transliteration is:

obv. i

1 ⌜gá⌝-àm-[me-ši]
2 ga-⟨àm⟩-mu-e-ne-ši-[gen] (written -ši-ne-)
3 àm-me-ši-du-⌜ù⌝-[un]
4 mu-e-ne-ši-[du-ù-un]
5 na-àm-me-ši-du⟨-un⟩
6 na-mu-e-ne-[ši-du-un]
7 nu-um-me-ši-[du-un]

8 nu-mu-e-ne-ši-du-[un] (= former line 1')
9 [i]-⸢im⸣-me-ši-gen-en
10 nu-um-me-ši-gen-en
11 mu-e-ne-ši-gen-en
12 nu-mu-e-ne-ši-gen-en
13 i-im-me-ši-gen
14 nu-um-*me-ši-gen
15 mu-⸢e⸣-ne-ši-gen
16 nu-mu-e-ne-ši-gen
17 àm(A)-me-ši-du
18 na-àm-me-ši-du
19 nu-um-me-ši-du
20 mu-e$^{!}$(UN)-ne-ši-du
21 na-mu-e$^{!}$(UN)-ne-ši-du
22 nu-mu-e$^{!}$(UN)-ne-ši-du
23 hé-em-me-ši-du
24 [hé]-mu-e-ne-ši-du

ii

1 [gá-nam-ma-me-ši]
2 [ga-àm-mu-e-ne-ši-gen]
3 [àm-ma-me-ši-du-ù-un]
4 [àm-mu-e-ne-ši-du-un]
5 [na-àm-ma-me-ši-du-un]
6 [na-àm-mu-e-ne-ši-du-un]
7 [nu-um-ma-me-ši-du-un]
8 [nu-um-mu-e-ne-ši-du-un]
9 im-m[a-me-ši-gen-en]
10 nu-um-ma-[me-ši-gen-en]
11 im-mu-⸢e⸣-n[e-ši-gen-en]
12 ⸢nu⸣-um-mu-⸢e⸣-[ne-ši-gen-en]
13 ⸢im⸣-ma-me-š[i-gen]
14 nu-um-ma-me-[ši-gen]
15 im-mu-e-[ne-ši-gen]
16 ⸢nu⸣-um-[mu-e-ne-ši-gen]
17 àm-ma-[me-ši-du]
18 na-àm-ma-me-ši-du
19 nu-um-[ma-me-ši-du]
20 àm-mu-e-ne-ši-du
21 na-àm-⸢mu-e-ne⸣-ši-du
22 nu-um-mu-e-ne-ši-du
23 hé-em-ma-⸢me⸣-ši-du
24 ⸢hé$^{?}$⸣-em-mu-e-ne-ši-du

iii (conventionally rev. ii; 'rev. i' in first edition)

1 ⸢gá-àm⸣-mu-ši
2 ga-mu-e-ši-gen
3 àm-mu-ši-du-ù-un
4 mu-e-ši-du-un
5 [na]-àm-mu-ši-du-un

6 [na-mu-e]-ši-du-un
7 [nu-um-mu]-ši-du-un
8 [nu-mu-e]-ši-du-un
9 ⸢i-im⸣-[mu]-ši-gen-en
10 nu-um-mu-ši-gen-en
11 mu-e-ši-gen-en
12 ⸢nu⸣-mu-⸢e⸣-ši-gen-en
13 i-im-mu-ši-gen
14 nu-um-mu-ši-gen
15 mu-e-ši-gen
16 nu-mu-e-ši-gen
17 àm-mu-ši-du
18 na-àm-mu-ši-du
19 nu-um-⸢mu⸣-ši-du
20 ⸢mu⸣-e-ši-du
21 na-⸢mu⸣-e-ši-du
22 nu-mu-e-ši-du
23 hé-em-mu-ši-[du]
24 hé-⟨em⟩-mu-e-ši-⸢du⸣

iv (conventionally rev. i; 'rev. ii' in first edition)
1 gá-⸢nam⸣-ma-mu-ši
2 ga-àm-mu-e-ši-gen
3 àm-ma-mu-ši-du-ù-un
4 àm-mu-e-⟨ši⟩-du-un
5 na-àm-ma-mu-ši-du-un
6 na-àm-mu-e-ši-du-un
7 nu-um-ma-mu-ši-du-un
8 nu-um-mu-e-ši-du-un
9 im-ma-mu-ši-gen-en
10 nu-um-ma-mu-ši-gen-en
11 im-mu-e-ši-[gen-en]
12 nu-um-mu-⸢e⸣-[ši-gen-en]
13 àm-⸢ma⸣-[mu-ši-du]
14 na-àm-[ma-mu-ši-du]
15 nu-um-[mu-e-ši-gen]
16 im-mu-[e-ši-gen]
17 na-à[m-ma-mu-ši-du]
18 nu-um-m[a-mu-ši-du]
19 àm-m[a-mu-ši-du]
20 na-à[m-mu-e-ši-du]
21 nu-um-m[u-e-ši-du]
22 im-m[u-e-ši-du]
23 ⟨hé-em-ma-mu-ši-du⟩
24 ⟨hé-em-mu-e-ši-du⟩

Civil's collations showed that 'in most lines in this tablet where i-im- was transliterated previously, hé-em- instead is now absolutely clear', i.e. in entries 23–4. However, the structure of the paradigm shows that i-im- must be correct in i and iii 9 and 13.

N5475 is obviously a dialogue fragment and should be omitted.

5.4.3 The following fragment of an Old Babylonian grammatical paradigm of [ku_4] = *erēbum*, with only the Akkadian entries preserved, was discovered in 1986 during the 9th season of excavations at Isin (excavation no. IB1697; IM 121968). It will be published by Dr M. Krebernik, most probably in the next volume of Professor B. Hrouda's *Isin – Išān Baḫriyāt*, and I am very grateful to these gentlemen for permission to cite the transliteration here in advance of their publication:

obv.?

1']-⸢ri⸣-ba-x [x x x]
2']-⸢úr?⸣-ba-a-ni-im
3']-⸢úr?⸣-ba-a-ni-iš-šu
4'] tu-še-⸢er?⸣-ba-ni-im
5'] ⸢šu⸣-ri-ba-šu
6'] ⸢nu?⸣-še-ri-⸢ba?-aš?⸣-šu
7']-ru-ba-aš-šu
8']-te-er-ba-aš-šu
9'] x-er-ru-ub-x [x x]
10'] x [ ]

rev.

1']⸢te⸣-x [
2']-te-er-ba-x-[x]
3']-ba-šu-nu-[ši-im?]
4']-⸢er⸣-ba-šu-nu-⸢ši⸣[-im?]
5']-ru-ub-šu-nu-[ši-im?]
6']-ru-ba-am
7']-⸢ru⸣-ba-šu-nu-ši[-im?]
8'] x x -am
9'] x-šu
10']-šu-nu-ši
11'] x [(x)]

5.4.4 A fragment of an Old Babylonian verbal paradigm, BM 17127, was published by M. J. Geller in *BSOAS* 49/2, pp. 564–5. It is a list of forms of dug_4/e [= *qabûm*] with various dimensional infixes, not sufficiently well preserved to detect any systematic patterning. It is difficult to understand the presence of the sign dé in obv. 6' and it seems more likely that the sign should be read as a defective ne, i.e. that the entry is hu-mu-un-⸢ne⸣-en-⸢zé-en⸣[...], yielding a form with the same rest of the paradigm.

5.4.5 The following fragment from Nineveh, K.21419, was kindly drawn to my attention by I. L. Finkel and is published here in transliteration by kind permission of the Trustees of the British Museum. It is possible that it belongs to the Akkadian sub-column of column one of a bilingual paradigm, since the traces of a column-division line appear to be preserved at the righthand side of it. Cf. K.8410 (=NBGT 6).

1']-ri-ib
2']⌜qar⌝-ra-bu
3']⌜tu?⌝-qar-rab
4'] x -bu

5.4.6 ROM 910x209.473 (=D.1006)

Dr G.J.P. McEwan was kind enough to bring to my attention this Old Babylonian verbal paradigm of unrecorded provenience, acquired at some time before the founding of the Royal Ontario Museum in 1911 and since then housed in the Museum. I am much indebted to him for copying the tablet and to Dr. L.D. Levine for permission to publish it. A transliteration, accompanied by the copy (at end of book), is given below. Apart from what is perhaps the catch-line to an associated paradigm, on the left edge (uš-ta-ba-al-x, ? Št present of *wabālum*), the forms in this paradigm are all of the verb ku_4 = *erēbum* 'to enter'. Phonetic spelling is used throughout, thus -ku-re- for-ku_4-re- and-ku-ku-te for-ku_4-ku_4-dè; note also kur-re in line 29. The types and alternations of verbal forms listed will be familiar from the paradigms from Nippur and Ur, although there is no particularly systematic structure here beyond the grouping of related forms in twos or threes.

The irregular behaviour of the Sumerian verb ku_4 has yet to be satisfactorily accounted for. The present paradigm does not provide us with an exhaustive or sufficiently rigorous selection of forms to make a complete analysis; but it should be noted that here the verbal base varies between standard ku_4 (set against Akkadian preterite) and secondary -n-ku_4-ku_4-d- (set against Akkadian present; but note ha-ku-ku, ha-ba-ku-ku). That is, (a) in the secondary construction the affix -ed- is regularly used, as with the verb te 'to approach' (-te-ge_x-d-), and (b) while one might expect the person who enters to be construed as an inert (English intransitive subject), apparently a need is often (and in the secondary construction always) felt for a 3rd person infix -n- of uncertain reference, with consequent marking of the enterer as a suffixed *agent*, e.g. mu-un-ku-ku-te- (for -ku_4-ku_4-de(-en)) = e-ru-ba-am (for *errubam*) 'I (shall) enter here'.

It is uncertain how genuine forms like ba-an-ku-ku-te-eš (ba-an-ku_4-ku_4-dè-eš) (25) are. In particular ba-ra-an-ku = *uštērib* and ba-ra-ku-re-eš = *ustēribu* (for *ušterbu*) (33f.) are unique both in that the infix -ra- is used for the expected -ni- (corresponding to Akkadian Š theme) and that the 'Št' preterite of *erēbum* is not elsewhere attested.

The identifiable forms listed here (Akkadian) are G pres. 1sg. ventive (32), Št pret. 3sg. and pl. (33-4), Gt and G 3sg. optative (35-6), G pres. 1sg. ventive + 2sg.? (37), Gt pret. 3sg., 2sg. and 3pl., all ventive (38-40), Gt pret. 3sg. (41) and G pret. 3pl. negative (42).

obv. 1-4 destroyed
5]-ba-am
6]-ku?
7]x
8]x x
9]x x x x x x
10]x -am
11]x e-ru-ba-am
12]e-ru-ub
13]i-ru-ub
14]x ru-ub
15]i-te-ru-ub
16]-ku-te e-te-ru-ub
17]x ru- bu-ni

	18		]x[ ]x
	19-20	destroyed	
edge	21	ba-an-ku- x[	
	22	erasure [	
	23	ba-an-ku-re-e[š	
rev.	24	ba-an-ku-re [	
	25	ba-an-ku-te-eš[	
	26	mu-un-ku (erasure)	i-[ru-ba-am
	27	mu-mu-un-ku x[	
	28	nu-mu-un-ku-re-⸢eš⸣	[*ūla īrubūni*
	29	kur-re-⸢ma?-a?⸣-ni e-[	
	30	nu-mu-un-ku-ku-te[	
	31	mu-un-ku-ku-te e- x[	
	32	mu-un-ku-ku-te	e-ru-ba-am
	33	ba-ra-an-ku	uš-te-ri-ib
	34	ba-ra-an-ku-re-eš	uš-te-ri-bu
	35	ha-ba-ku-ku	li-⸢te⸣-ru-ub
	36	⸢ha-ku-ku	li-ru⸣-ub
	37	mu-ra-an-ku-ku-te	e-ru-ba-kam
	38	im-ma-an-ku	i-te-er-ba-am
	39	im-ma-an-ku-re-en	te-te-er-ba-am
	40	im-ma-ku-re-eš	i-te-er-bu-ni
	41	im-ma-ku x	i-te-ru-ub x
	42	[nu-mu]-un-ku-re-eš	ú-la i-ru-[bu
	43	[ ] x x [	
left edge	44	]x x ku$_7$	uš-ta-ba-al x

5.5 Collations of grammatical texts published in *MSL IV*

One or two collated readings are offered here for some of the grammatical texts published in *MSL* IV; certain others are noted at appropriate points in the text above, and can be traced through the index of texts and passages cited, appendix 5.6 below.

OBGT XV	32	The sign printed as ma looks more like ba, which is what is expected. Of the k[i] only the flourish of the tail remains.
NBGT I	314	Read iš-tu bīt(É)
NBGT II	39f.	C has ma not ma-a
	74 (not 75)	A has ⸢mu⸣ a-⸢na ya-ši⸣ (not ya-'-š[im])
	83	A has ga-mar-t[u]
	111	A has šu-a-ti (with blank before the break)
	198	A now has only it-ti[
	200	A now has only a-na ka-[
	207	A has e-ne-e-a ku-nu-⸢ti?⸣
	219	It is not clear that B is blank in the righthand col. here, since the tablet is joined across this line.
	224	B has in righthand col. šu (not broken, no trace of u)
	244	in righthand col. traces of šim in C only
	248	no trace now of ditto sign in A or C; traces of -⸢a-šim⸣ in C only

Text	Column	Line	Note
		256	In A the sign bí is written on the far right of the lefthand col.
		257	C has ana šu-a-t[i] in righthand col.
		274	In A the signs : ti are written small and beneath the -a- of šu-a-šum
		277	A has (in righthand col., second line) a-na šu-a-šu u ga-mar-tum (not šu-a-šum)
NBGT V	col. ii (? col. v)	6	The damaged sign is probably not LAGAB but something more complex
		12	This line is to be deleted
	col. iii (? col. vi)	11	The tablet has it-tu
NBGT VI		2	The sign after gub is probably bu; after dè there is an erased en before the second, correct en
		3	In the righthand col. part of KI.MIN is preserved
		4	Read [h]u-e-ne-gub-bé-en
		5	Read [b]í-gub-dè-en
		7	Read [l]i-bí-in-gub-dè-en
		15	⸢gub⸣ is preserved, below the gub in the line above
NBGT IX		35	The sign looks more like LU, which is expected.
		55f.	In both lines only the first two horizontals of the sign transliterated as BI are preserved (in B only; A_2 is broken)
		118	The tablet has TIL-tum : ya-ši (correct in *CT* 11 42)
		125	The last sign is ⸢ta⸣
		216	The damaged sign could equally well be šum
		264	The damaged sign begins with ŠE — so perhaps e.g. ša NÌ.SUD
		274	The damaged sign is not RI but looks like NIGÍN
		275	The traces in the righthand col. are too wide for i alone; perhaps i following an erasure.

Text A of NBGT IX also carries a standard Ashurbanipal colophon in col. vi.

5.6 Index of Texts and Passages Cited

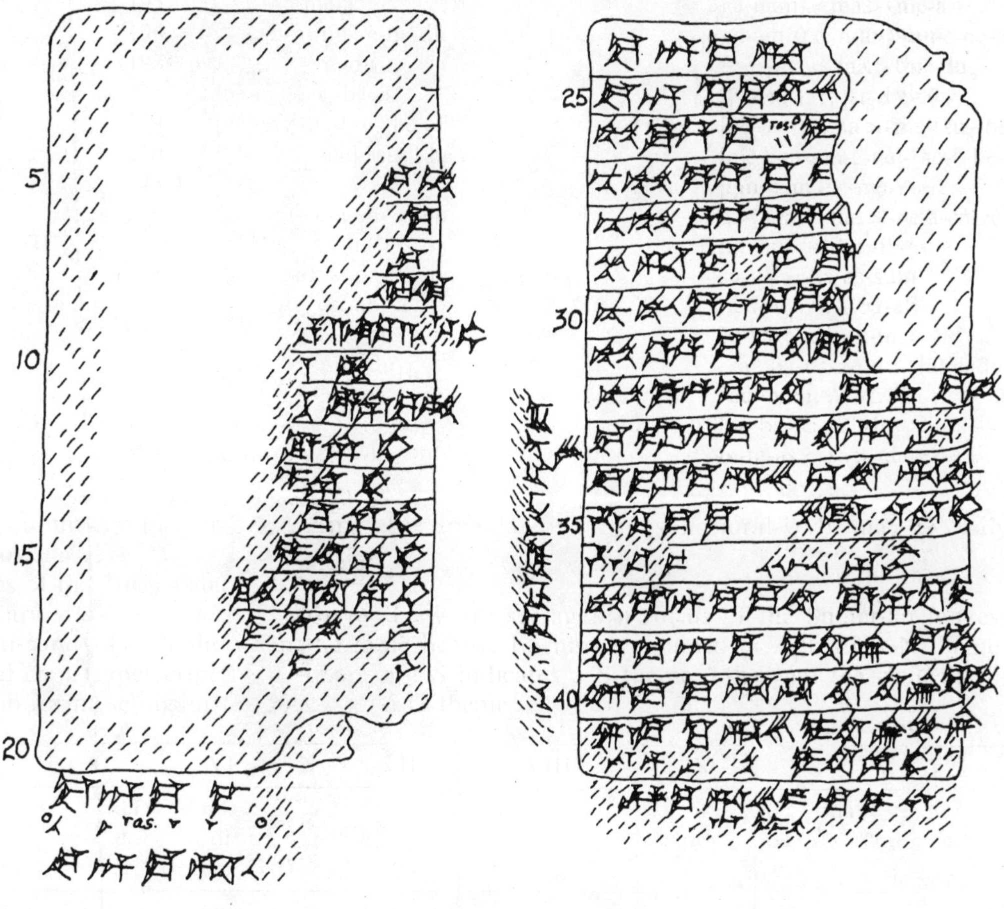

ROM 910x209.473 (=D.1006)

The dimensions are 5.4 x 10.2 cm; scale 1:1.

Finito di stampare
nel mese di Luglio 2004

presso la tipografia
"Giovanni Olivieri" di E. Montefoschi
00187 Roma • Via dell'Archetto, 10, 11, 12
Tel. 06 6792327 • E-mail: tip.olivieri@libero.it